Ardmore Memory and Story

The history, traditions and stories of
an Irish village.

Siobhán Lincoln

This edition edited by Marie Fahey, Miriam Walsh, Willie Whelan

for Waterford County Museum

Cover Design by Martin Whelan

Cover Photo by Patrick Kenealy

2021 photos by Eddie Dee

Historic photos from the Waterford County Museum Image Archive & from the original publication.

'Tigaluinn' photo courtesy of the Horgan family

1 An engraving by W. H. Brooke of the Cathedral & Round Tower, Ardmore, c1824.

Foreword

by Fergal Keane

The past slips away from us quietly. We are too consumed with the drama of the present to notice the departure of old ways and traditions. In an age of economic growth without parallel in the history of the state, we are all urged to speed into a bright new future. The places we came from, the landscape of our past recedes and is in danger of being lost.

And so when a remarkable book appears like that now offered by Siobhán Lincoln it is important that we pay it proper attention. It is said that every village in Ireland has a historian: I can't vouch for that but know that Ardmore is blessed to have a woman like Siobhán who is so passionate in the cause of saving memory for the coming generations.

My own family relationship with Ardmore goes back to my great-grandfather who served as an RIC sergeant in the village. His son Paddy, my grandfather, was born in the house which would later become Quains and later still the White Horses Restaurant. In the post war years he built a small cottage near Goat Island where my mother's family would spend every summer. I grew up listening to tales of the 'Island' and of Terry's farm. My childhood Summers were spent here in the village with my grandmother, May Hassett, who rented Mockler's house at the top of the street.

For me there is in every life a place that is sacred. For me Ardmore will always be that place. So much of my past is bound up with the place, that I could no more imagine life without a link to Ardmore than I could life without the hands that write these words. That was why I bought a property in the village myself in the early 1990s and why I return relentlessly. There is much that one can learn about the village from walking its hinterland and talking to older residents. One of the cherished memories of my childhood is of sitting on the edge of conversations at the Fitz's fire just down the street from Mocklers.

But my knowledge of the Ardmore of the distant past is, to put it mildly, severely limited. I had read with great joy the copies of the *Ardmore Journal* put together by James Quain but I have always longed for a full book which could bring to life the traditions and happenings of a vanished era.

Thankfully there is now such a book. I had the privilege of reading Siobhán's material before it went to print and was delighted with the blend of history, tradition and humour which infused the pages. There is always the danger when dealing with historical material that the writer will be unable to bring that other time to life. But Siobhán Lincoln succeeds wonderfully well. Her background as a teacher has, I am sure, been of huge importance in developing the skills of clear communication on display here.

In my work as a journalist I am forced to read a great many books and reports of unremitting dullness. It is to Siobhán Lincoln's credit that I never once found my attention wandering while reading the book. Everybody in the village knows Siobhán but to the wider audience I can only describe her as a formidable character, a woman of learning and wit. I know of few other grandmothers who would happily set off for China with her teenage granddaughters and meet every challenge along the route with relish.

When I met her in Hong Kong with her delightful entourage it was 'Granny' who blazed the trail in the tropical heat. That energy and curiosity about the world are clearly evident in this book. I am sure it will be a huge success: it certainly deserves to be.

The village of Ardmore cannot be immune to the economic boom which is sweeping the country: but if there is one message which shines from these pages. it is the necessity to protect the older values of community. The culture of money and acquisition are no friends to those values. I urge you please to read this book and reflect on its message.

Preface

Ardmore: *Memory and Story* has been many long years in the making. I was born in 1919 and, apart from some temporary absences at school and college, I have lived here in Ardmore all my life. I have therefore some experience of the different aspects of life in our parish throughout most of the twentieth century.

The advent of a new century and a new millennium has, of course, been the immediate occasion for putting this book together. But the material has been gathering ever since I put on the white pinafore of Ardmore school girls in the 20s and learnt from Mothers Ita and Teresita how to read and write.

I kept on reading and writing. I read anything that would satisfy my curiosity about Ardmore, headstones included. I kept on writing and, indeed, earlier versions of some sections of this book appeared first in the *Ardmore Journal* which James Quain edited from 1984 to 1993. *Ardmore: Memory and Story* is greatly indebted to the ten volumes of the *Ardmore Journal*. These pages are dotted with references to and quotations from the *Journal*.

Ardmore: Memory and Story is in a real sense a community project. Those who have helped me with memories, stories and photos are just too numerous to mention. Nevertheless, | must make a few exceptions: Jimmie Rooney's name occurs in these pages more frequently than anyone else's; Eileen Fitzgerald is largely responsible for the section on 'Twinning' and Paddy Foley for that on the 'GAA'; Tom Gartland is wholly responsible for the section on 'Farming'; Fergal Keane, the BBC special correspondent and distinguished journalist whom Ardmore is privileged to have as a member of its dispersed community, has contributed a Foreword which is embarrassing in its brilliance and he has kindly agreed to launch the book in Pattern Week.

I want to say a hundred thousand thanks, however, not only to these few in particular but to the community of Ardmore as a whole for its encouragement and support. Our parish priest, Canon O'Connor, has given expression to this encouragement and support by getting the *Benemerenti* medal for me from the Vatican for my efforts to keep the memory of St Declan alive. This honour was a great surprise. | was quite taken aback and confused but deeply grateful all the same.

Ardmore: Memory and Story is a family and a community project. My grand-daughter, Sarah Lincoln, who is beginning her studies at the National College of Art and Design in Dublin, designed the cover and drew the map of Ardmore. Her sister, Katie, who has just completed a course on Film Studies at the Dunlaoire Institute of Art, Design and Technology, helped me to order the various materials which I had gathered down the years and put them into chapters. In addition, and above all, both Katie and Sarah have helped by the interest they have taken which has cheered me up considerably from time to time, And it is Katie and Sarah's mother and father, Mary and Richard, who run Ardmore Pottery, who are publishing the book.

My sister and two Jesuit brothers have also been a great support: Eileen Colbert helped with her prodigious memory, Michael Hurley helped with his considerable experience as a writer and did the final editing of the text; James Hurley, who is based in Hong Kong, helped with encouragement from afar - as did my son, Colm, who is based in London.

It remains to thank the staffs of the Dungarvan Library, the Lismore Library, and the National Archives in Dublin who have been most courteous in giving me access to materials: Tricia Brabazon, who undertook the trying task of typing the manuscript; Brendan Murray, S.J., Editor of the *Sacred Heart Messenger*, who, despite other pressing commitments, gave generously of his time and expertise to design and typeset the book; Cosmon Design who printed it so expeditiously to meet the deadline of Pattern Week; the Youghal Credit Union who helped financially; and Tom Keith and the National Millennium Committee who contributed £900 towards the cost of the project.

To them all my heartfelt thanks.

Siobhán Lincoln

The Village

Growing Up in Ardmore

What a privilege it was, to grow up in Ardmore, with the sea and the cliffs all round and the Round Tower and so many other ancient monuments emphasising the glory of our past. We probably did not appreciate all this fully at the time, but we did indulge our sense of adventure and have wonderful memories, for example, of going up the glen in the evenings, through the field on the Rocky now occupied by two new houses, over the fence into the glen, climbing the stone wall at the corner of the New Line by steps inbuilt into it (now out of use, of course) and emerging at Flynns now Gartlands.

There might have been a session on the swing there, or more likely, with the Flynns we'd have pushed on further, say to the 'Cúlam' a cliff in front of the castle, where there is a goilín (a little inlet) which widens out into a grassy bank half-way down the cliff and is invisible from above. That was a favourite rendezvous, as indeed the surrounding cliffs were, where we went in search of seagull's eggs in May. We were always convinced the seagulls were familiar with the calendar and knew the 1st of May and laid the first of three eggs on that day. We extracted one egg, blew it and brought it home for a collection. Often (should I say?), it was with great danger to life and limb; I do remember once a school mate (was it Noreen Downey) hanging on to my foot as I reached over and down the cliff and the three or four of us saying an act of contrition. We probably would have forgotten all about the incident but that Deug Flynn, then the village postman, was an

1

observer in the vicinity and relayed the story, so there was a court-martial at home.

2 Ardmore round Tower and the west gable of Ardmore Cathedral, 2021.

Another quite different May time occupation was gathering wild flowers for the May Altar at which the family Rosary was said during the month.

3 Ardmore Round Tower & Cathedral, c1900. The Cathedral to the left of the photograph was originally built as a small church in the 9th or 10th century, with a second phase c.12th century and the final phase in 1203. The tower was built c.12th century.

The Tea Flag around the cliffs was another popular rendezvous. We scrambled down to the flat surface, found our way around the corner to the smooth sandstone rock, where countless people have inscribed their names over the years (some of the inscriptions date back to 1818 and before). We did likewise, but of course, ours did not survive. We also climbed over the edge of the Tea Flag and were able to get right down to sea level at the base of the cliff. We investigated fully all round, discovering what we called a cave, really a large archway under part of the rock.

On other occasions, we went (or often I went alone) right around the cliff path to McKennas, i.e. Ardo House and back by the road, most mundane after the cliff. The path went right down to the edge of Gleann Phiarais, down down, over the river and up again at the other side. There were times when we went down some of the cliffs too. McKennas always had a strange eerie fascination with the ruins of the old house and splendid farmyard and the soughing of the wind in the pines on the avenue. Naturally, we were well acquainted with the angel guarding the vault containing the remains of Sir Joseph and Lady McKenna and could say by heart the inscriptions on the angel's plinth.

There were high stone walls around the orchard with only a small door (always closed) giving access, so that was most provocative. One day, we went around to the back, climbed up on a tree which grew beside an approach wall, went along said wall on to the orchard wall, but the bull was in residence below, so we left well enough alone and retreated. (It is interesting to note that our accomplices on this venture were the Creans of Riverchapel, Gorey who came to Ardmore every year. Their uncle, Tom Crean from Annascaul, Co. Kerry, was one of those who went on Scott's South Pole expedition in 1901 and in 1914-17 went with Shackleton. This expedition involved an epic 800 miles rescue mission, one of the most famous Polar survival stories).

I'd love to have walked on the storm wall in front of the Catholic Church but never dared to do it. It was too public a place and the story would have been relayed home with dire consequences. When an east wind gale blew and the waves were dashing over the storm wall at high tide, running in and out dodging the waves was a favourite occupation. You waited till the big wave came and then you just ran.

4 Back: Mary Flavin, Jack Conway, Ellen Conway, Johnny Conway, Maggie Shine, visitor. M: Seamus Shine, Joan shine, Peg Shine, Mary Anne Conway (SL godmother), author, Rita Conway. F: Breeda Conway, Eileen Colbert (SL sister), Michael Hurley (SL brother).

Coming home from school by climbing the sycamore tree at the back of the church and traversing the wall into our back yard (Tigaluinn) was often preferred to walking around the road. We played 'cobby', laying out a house among the rocks at the left-hand side of the Boat Cove entrance; each little section of rock was an apartment in the house.

One of our chores was going up to Quains of the cliff, for milk twice daily. The milk tin had to be thoroughly washed and scalded and on no account should the morning's and the evening's milk be mixed. That says something about the long-lasting milk we have now (better not stop and think on why it is so long lasting). On a darkish winter evening, one always found the road a trifle scary between the Straoilleán and Port na mBád. There was a very high bank there and of course there were absolutely no streetlights. There are as yet no streetlights on this dark section.

At home inside in the house, it was always important to have the lamps filled with oil and the wicks trimmed. I can still see my father reading the paper at the light of the kitchen lamp. One could play shadow games, holding one's fingers up and forming them into shapes, which cast shadows of various little animals on the walls.

At that stage, there was Rosary and Benediction every Sunday evening, also every evening in May and October. As we ran down the road on moonlight nights, we played games of standing on one another's shadows on the ground. It was always magical seeing the moon shining on the sea and imagining oneself skipping on to that wonderful moonlight road, which would bring one to the end of the world or wherever.

Powers' (of the strand) threshing was another favourite rendezvous of the village children. We looked forward to it eagerly each year but how they tolerated us in such a busy location, I just don't know.

We learned to swim in the Boat Cove (self-taught of course) then graduated to the pier, where we boasted of diving from so many steps of the ladder, then of diving from the pier itself and the best feat of all, was running along the parapet at the back of the pier and jumping in. We found out about Poll a Doimhne (The Deep Pool) later; this was just at Ardmore Head and from the top, looks almost impossible of access, but there is a way down around the back of the platform of rock a short distance down from the cliff path. We had wonderful swims there. It must have got its name from its depth; at the very lowest of tides, I never saw the bottom. But there was a most tragic accident there; on a fine summer evening in the 60s. A holidaying family from Belfast came and the two lads came to the Head to fish, having been familiar with it since the previous year. One boy slipped down the blow-hole on the platform of rock and evidently injured himself on the way down and was probably knocked unconscious. It was more than a week afterwards before divers recovered the body.

There are caves above sea level at the Head. I never ventured in, having a horror of perhaps encountering rats. For the same reason I never explored the caves up the glen near the graveyard; I know my sons did so in later years. These were used during the troubled times.

I did explore the Putty Hole, some distance out from St. Declan's Well and accessible at low tide, by means of a path which at one time led down from the Well precincts. The first time we went in, we had no light and encountered a wall of rock, which seemed to be the end. The next day, we came better equipped with a candle and a ball of twine, and saw that the wall of rock was only five or six feet high and we could climb up and reach a higher level, from where three passages led. There was actually a stick embedded at the edge of one, ready to tie a ball of twine on it. This was really exciting and we kept going, heads bent, until we saw light coming through at the cliff edge. I pushed my sister out first (we were on our face and hands) and then got myself out, and found we were half way down a cliff in the next 'goilin'. We scrambled down and found our way back to the 'main entrance' to retrieve our ball of twine and candle. We were quite muddied by this time and tried to wash off some in the rock pools, so as not to attract too much attention on our homeward journey.

I'm afraid we knew the back gardens of practically all the big houses along the Rocky and up Dawsons' Road. On the site of Green Shutters was an old stable with a coach of ancient vintage (suggesting Cinderella's Coach to us.) We climbed up the shafts and on to the loft, where so many swallows had nests. Then there were the high trees of the college (now all gone) to be climbed.

The Coastguard Station was another interesting place. We explored it outside and inside, up the spiral stone steps to the top where we could cling on to the wall and go around all the ledge which still remained of the non-existent floor. Somehow or other, our guardian angels prevented us falling down the deep well of the pump outside, which only in 1999 was filled in. Indeed, we seemed to keep these guardian angels rather busy, during our childhood days and should be deeply grateful to them.

I must say that before going out after school in the evenings, my mother usually said "I hope now you're not going in any dangerous places", and I said "no", not really meaning to tell an untruth but knowing very well that my mother's interpretation of the word "dangerous" and mine most probably did not coincide.

Roads And Houses

The Odell family acquired Duffcarrick (as well as Ballinmertina and Curragh) in 1837. It would be reasonable to assume that it was after that, the village was laid out in its present form.

A Grand Jury map of 1818 does not show the Rocky Road or the road leading up from the middle of the village street towards what can be called the for convenience sake Tigaluinn Cross, and onwards to Cliff House. It does show 'telegraph' at Ram Head.

The Ordnance map of 1841 shows the village street and all the roads now in existence except the New Line and the road further

8

south parallel to it. These were probably famine roads. Rock house, Glebe House, Ardmore House (later Coláiste Deuglán) were the only big houses, so there must have been a big building programme in the second half of the 19th century.

A post office is indicated in what has become known as Sleepy Lane. That, Coffee Lane and Chapel Row were all one-storey houses. Jimmie Rooney tells of the people living in the houses in Coffee Lane; nine Rooneys and parents at the end of the road (now Brison), four Gradys (i.e Fitzgeralds) in a one-roomed house with no back door, which is now the top room in Bryson; twelve Broodies in what is now Dunnes' workshop; fourteen Briens in the house above that; then Andys and the Guiry family in Tigaluinn. We remember Norry Brien, Matty's mother who lived in Coffee Lane. She was a tall stately women who wore very wide skirts (to the ground of course) and I can still visualise her coming around the corner like a ship in full sail. She worked at Dawsons and also spent whole days in her plot in Dysert (the present soccer field), bringing up panniers of seaweed on her back and also cold boiled potatoes to sustain her until the evening. As regards Jimmie's remarks 're' the Broodies in what is now Dunnes' workshop, I myself have no recollection of them but I do remember distinctly in the 30s and 40s, the house being occupied by Tom and Mrs Monsell, Paddy their son, Tom Foley (Mrs Monsells brother), and Bridg Donnell (no relation). Tom Foley and Paddy Monsell slept in the bedroom to the right; the back of the kitchen was curtained off for Tom and Mrs Monsell and Bridg Donnell occupied the room to the left above the kitchen. Mrs Monsell liked to lean on the half door and greet all and sundry going up and down the road.

Up to the 40's Chapel Row had people in all its four houses; each one had a different coloured wash and they presented a delightful picture viewed from the strand. The school was partly in front of them and on fine evenings, the gable end was used as a ball alley and it was quite a gathering place for young people.

Johnny and Mrs Mulcahy's house was recessed between the church wall and the boathouse. Mrs Mulcahy resented the ball going into her yard; this frequently happened at play-hour at school so there were several rows on that score. Below the boathouse, there were quite extensive ruins now incorporated in the roadway, and this place was known as Mr O's i.e. O'Shaughnessy. He had a butchers shop there.

The c. 1910 photograph of the end of the village street, shows Mrs Wolsey's house, now also incorporated in the roadway. Moloneys remained an L shaped house for some years, the section which made the L was really another house. The gap at its east end was the entrance to the forge, an unusual 2-storey building (behind Moloneys and not now visible) which was of course, one of the social centres in the village. The banding stone (for banding a wheel) is still in evidence on the ground but the familiar sound of the anvil is no more.

Opposite Harty's house, formerly The Hotel were the derelict buildings known as Harris' stables. These are evident in some photographs of the 1967/68 Pattern sports. They have now been replaced by new brightly painted houses.

The Barracks was located in Ivy Lodge, at the corner of Sleepy Lane, at the south side of the street and later on, in the lovely Georgian house which preceded White Horses restaurant. Another photograph shows the deplorable ruins of the Barracks, and these remained until the late 1930's, when Jim Quain bought them and built the modern shop which was replaced a few years ago by the restaurant.

It has been tantalisingly suggested that the space between O'Reillys (Tigh Beag) and Murphys' thatched house might have been the entrance to Ardmore Castle. If so the castle would have been much higher up on the hill, to the south. That remains a mystery.

Mrs Odell's painting shows a picturesque village street with no traffic problems. Two of the houses are still thatched.

Aird a Mhinistir, Parson's Hill, has not changed too much. Looking down, Sunnyside (thatched) is still in evidence in the photograph, with the plot at the side where my father put Ardmore's first petrol pumps in 1931. The view uphill shows the cottage at the Cross, now gone. The entrance to Monea Lodge (now occupied by the McCarthy family) is at the bottom of the hill on the west side. On the 1841 map, a dispensary is shown here. In our young days, we referred to the house as the old convent. The well-known Mrs Barry having bought it for the Cappoquin nuns, and finding it a bit small for the purpose purchased the house now known as Stella Maris. George Dwyer was an occupant for some time. Later on Miss Kathy Fitzgerald had a guest house there.

Recessed at the other side of the road with a nice garden, is the Grey House, property of John and Agnes Fitzgerald. At one stage, this functioned as a Protestant school and in our young days, Rev. Mr Warren, the Rector, was the owner. Jack Fogarty, an old lady still lived there and my first visit to Waterford was when she moved with her belongings to a residence for elderly Protestant ladies there. I was thrilled to be ensconced in the middle of the luggage in the back of my father's lorry.

The Rocky is gradually getting built up, as is the New Line. There are about 12 private residences in the Crescent off Bóthar na

Trínse. Farrengarret has become a suburb of Ardmore with more than 40 very well-presented houses and many more to come.

School Days in Ardmore

There were of course free primary schools all over the country throughout this century. In our parish, we had Grange and Ardmore National Schools. The attendance was inclined to fluctuate; children were often kept at home to help with farm work and bad weather had an influence here too, as all (children) walked to school.

The School Attendance Act of 1926 brought a great improvement; according to law, all children now had to attend school between the ages of 6 and 14. Special forms indicating absentees had to be filled in by the teacher each week and sent to the local Garda station. We have distinct recollections of a guard cycling over the strand with one of the 'missing links' behind on the carrier. This happened on more than one occasion. Parents were prosecuted in court for non-attendance of their offspring at school.

Until 1966, very, very, few attended second-level schools. The very small minority who could afford it sent their children to boarding school. Most of the others who went to this stage, cycled in to Youghal to the Christian Brothers or to the Presentation or Loreto Convents, so their secondary education was hard earned. A very few utilised the mail car for getting in and out and a few others took lodgings in town. So for the majority, school ended at 14. Life was grim.

Garret Ducey (formerly of Crossford) remembered what were termed 'servants' classes'. These children would have left school early without being confirmed; they would have had to go to work to a local farmer probably for about 5/- a week and now before the bishop's arrival, would have had to attend these classes for religious instruction. He remembered how a local young lad on the morning of his confirmation had to get up at 5a.m. and go to milk the cows at Sand Road and walk up then to Grange Church.

The Ardmore schoolhouse we remember was a very nice stone building on the seafront with no grounds. The lease to the site would have been granted by the Odell family and before the regrettable demolition of the building in 1956, Mary Odell (who died in 1976) the last representative of the Odell family went to the Department of Education to protest. Her protest was ineffectual, and she would not have had the wherewithal to initiate legal proceedings.

The eastern gable-end of the school was used as a ball-alley by the local lads and it was there that Jimmy McGrath of Dysert (ex-garda now living in Kanturk) got his initial training before becoming national handball champion. The area was a great venue on summer evenings, with crowds of young people around watching the play.

There were two large rooms in the school, one being the boys' school where R. Lincoln (from 1929) and Mrs Keevers (Johns' mother) presided and the girls' school where the teachers were two nuns from Cappoquin Mercy Convent and a Miss Murphy paid by them and staying at the Convent (Stella Maris). The two nuns and Miss Murphy of course all taught in the one room, but there were also classes in 'The Shed'.

At the western side, was 'The Shed' a corrugated iron building which had been erected by Lady Sandeman about 1911 at the rear of the Boathouse for teas, when flower shows were an annual event in the Boathouse. When the flower show was changed to St. Declan's Hall, the tea-room was either purchased by the Church or donated to the school nearby, according to Jack Crowley one of the five sons of Patrick Crowley, former Principal of Ardmore Boys' School. Jack was a teacher himself and taught in Cork and was deeply interested in Ardmore local history. He died about ten years ago.

There were frequent classes in 'The Shed'. The floor was of rough concrete, the pebbles through it being quite visible. Behind a draught screen, the fuel for the school fire was stored (when the shed was demolished at a later stage, the boathouse opposite, then the property of Eileen Hurley was used for storing the school fuel, with incidentally never a word of recognition from "the powers that be"). A beshawled nun sat in front of the class. The place must have been very cold but somehow, I have no recollection of that.

When I first went to school in 1923, I wore, as most of the other girls did, a white lace-edged pinafore tied behind the back. They must have looked very nice. It's a pity they went out of fashion. At that period there was a gallery at the bottom of the school, but this was later removed and new dual desks installed. At the other end, the three old long desks remained. At that end too was the coal fire (a small range). Betty Flynn (later Mrs O' Reilly) when she occasionally got the job of lighting it availed of the opportunity to push forward a little, the hands of the clock on the mantel-piece above.

Furnishing and school conditions have changed immeasurably over the years. Heating in Winter came from one fireplace and naturally that did not reach far. The cleaning was generally performed by the pupils themselves. Sanitary arrangements were of the most primitive kind. The outside toilets of Ardmore were allegedly flush ones and the water came from a large tank in the Church yard above, but this quite often had to be supplemented by water from the river at the entrance to the Strand, and transported from there in buckets by the pupils themselves.

The present school in Ardmore is the fourth in the village. Two in the region of the present beach were carried away by the tide. Fr. Wall built one of those in 1857; Fr Enda Ducey's (O. Cist.) mother (nee Keane) went to school in it.

The third national school in Ardmore was built in 1875 by Fr. John Shanahan, on a site on the seafront given by the Odells. There was no playground but that did not present a problem as the road surrounds of the school were used freely by the children, the traffic then being negligible. The only problem was when the ball went into Mrs Mulcahy's yard and she re-acted strenuously when the boys went to retrieve it. She and her husband Johnnie lived beside the Boathouse and the yard was in front of the house. The school was a pleasing building regrettably demolished in 1956.

Mr Patrick Crowley was appointed Principal of Ardmore School until his retirement in 1929 and Richard Lincoln was appointed. Mr R Keating (whose relatives, the Mooneys still live in Ardmore) left in 1920. Mrs Caroline Keevers (then nee Burke) came in 1916 and remained until 31st December 1955, when she retired, having decided not to go to the new school.

Mrs Barry (nee Dwyer) had come on the educational scene in Ardmore in the 1900s. She was also very involved in the Temperance movement and was a close friend of the famous Fr. Mathew, apostle of temperance. Mrs Barry had sisters in the Cappoquin Mercy Convent and went to Bishop Hackett and offered to provide the nuns with a house, 'if they went to teach in Ardmore Girls' School. She bought Monea Lodge (now belonging to the McCarthys) for them and five nuns came in April 1900. We are told she paid a pension to the existing teachers so the change-over was effected without incident. Miss Davis, former teacher, occasionally visited the school later.

In 1923 she bought a larger house from Lady Clodagh Anson, the present Stella Maris, and had the nuns transferred there. Sr. Gertrude (who was the aunt of Monsignor Walsh, Mrs G McCarthy, and Mr Tom Walsh, Cloghrue) was the first local superior.

The coming of the nuns brought a new regime in the school. The senior girls did cookery, using a small stove at the top of the school, and they went to the convent to do laundry. The nuns taught music and took charge of the choir in the church. Long before the advent of the Co. Library, the nuns had one in school and books were borrowed at 1d a week.

About the mid-twenties, Srs. Ita and Teresita came to Ardmore and were responsible for many innovations.

The children in the school were well organised as a work force. Turns were taken in sweeping the school on Friday evenings. Sand had to be first got from the nearby strand and scattered on it. Eileen Colbert remembers doing it every five weeks with Kitty Keane, Crossford, who lived in the house now occupied by Cissie Burke, so she had a long walk home alone when the chore was completed. All the children walked to school then. The sweeping operation was overseen by Miss Murphy, as was the dusting at 4pm, two others taking turns for that. The clean dusters would have been folded under the side desk and brought up to be laundered at the convent. The standards of cleanliness were meticulous, and woe betide the one who marked the new desks in any way. Another chore was sweeping the porch after the midday break.

There was a major cleaning, before school holidays. The windows had to be cleaned and Eileen Colbert has memories of being terrified standing on the front windowsills; she never had a head for heights. The desks were polished and the covers of the inkwells 'brassoed'. The inkwells themselves were washed, being brought down to the river. I well remember two of them floating off down the river. We were also sent up to dust the church on occasion and also to collect sticks for the fire from the churchyard.

Litter as a problem, I don't remember, but then children partook of real food at lunch hour, as distinct from their present-day contemporaries, the most of whom eat junk food for lunch and its attendant plastic packaging naturally causes major litter problems.

5 Lizzie Foley's Grocery Shop, Lower Main Street, Ardmore with back l - r: Mary Collins, Clonmel; Lizzie Foley. Front: Declan Collins, Clonmel; & Ed Keating, New York; 1954.

Sweets were bought by the lucky ones at Lizzy Foley's (R.I.P.) in the shop adjoining the Beachcombers. Lizzy took a small sheet of paper and wound it into a cone called a 'tomhaisín' (a little measure) and dropped the sweets into it. Her brother Sonny

(R.I.P.) used the pages of old copybooks, there being some barter system between him and the copybook owners. My mother (Joe Foley who lived in what is now Paddy Macs' Bar) was mortified on one occasion, when Sonny for a joke placed a blotted page of her copy book on the shop window. That was another peril with which we contended, in the days of N pens and ink, the peril of blotting your copybook, it just wasn't done.

Of course, nobody raised an eyebrow at corporal punishment. It was accepted as the norm. For failure at lessons etc., one was kept in after school. That meant being brought up to the convent and doing 'one's time' there at the 'garage' which held a boat. I remember investigating Will Mockler's scythe there and trying it on some potatoes, a fact of course which was noted afterwards and due punishment meted out.

Organisation of the School

Everything was very neat and tidy, the copy books in particular. One wrote one's essay at home; it was corrected and only the corrected version found its way to the school copy book. Mother Teresita in particular had extremely high standards in English. Eileen Colbert can still reel off whole passages from Macbeth, and we were well ground in the mysteries of the 20 rules of syntax and such things as metaphors and similes and onomatopoeia.

We were very resentful of the fact, that on election days, the girls had to go to school, while the boys next door had a free day, the school being used as a polling booth. We also had to go to school on bank holidays.

Examinations

The annual Diocesan Christian Doctrine examination was dreaded. We had to have the answers to the questions in the *Green*

Catechism (junior material) and then the *Red Catechism*, also *Schuster's Bible History* and the *Manual* which last was a succinct résumé of Doctrine including such things as the Matter and Form of all the Sacraments, Fast Days and Days of Abstinence, and the Ember Days. Eileen Colbert remembers writing out the Ember Days 14 times; apparently she had failed to identify them initially,

We were brought to school on Saturdays before the Diocesan examinations and specially before Confirmation which happened every two years. Such was the dread engendered, that one girl, on the eve of St. Brigid's Day, instead of putting out the usual Brat Bride (a piece of cloth which after that held a cure for various ailments) put out instead her Bible and Catechism. We're not sure whether or not St. Brigid co-operated. We were tried out with series of questions sent from other schools already visited by the Diocesan inspector. We were allotted our places in the class which stood around him. I suppose giving a judicious mix of 'the sheep and the goats.' To make our examiner more comfortable, an armchair was taken down from the convent for the duration.

The coming of Miss Earle, the needlework inspector was a day dreaded by me, as I wasn't over proficient in that subject. We had sampler books, with samples of our work displayed in it, gathers, patches, gussets etc. I'm sure Ann Flynn (R.I.P.) sister of Kitty Gartland did a few of mine, as she was a wonderfully neat 'needle-woman'. Likewise, both Biddy and Mary Power were requisitioned to do some of the knitting for the "duds" in that sphere.

Treats and Play Hour

On at least one, if not two occasions we had a most wonderful treat, a Christmas tree with Santa Claus distributing presents from it. This was really a memorable event.

As regards play-hour, motor traffic was non-existent so it was quite safe to play on the roadway.

Rounders was a game played by the bigger girls and there must have been some Irish left in the area, as I remember the two leaders calling sides and beginning with "Cuirim ort" and the other said "Ligim leat". 'Colours' and 'Hide and Go Seek' were other games played and vigilant as the nuns were, they didn't know that some had games at jumping across the stream and also of daring one another to walk as far as possible on the narrow ledge behind the storm wall.

A concert in the hall once a year was a major event and our nun teachers really excelled in preparing us for them, and went to endless trouble rehearsing us in songs, dancing and little plays. The costumes all had to be perfect, in fact every detail had to be perfect.

The nuns introduced the custom of the First Communicants coming to the convent for breakfast afterwards, a treat to which all eagerly looked forward.

In 1934, because of falling attendances, the nuns left Ardmore and returned to Cappoquin, but still retained the house, which has since become the property of the Mercy Sisters in general in Ireland. Now the school became a mixed one of just two teachers. Mrs Keevers presiding over the juniors in what had been the girl's school and Richard Lincoln over the seniors in the other room. He it was, who introduced teaching through Irish. There are still people in Ardmore who do arithmetical calculations in Irish, sé faoi ceathair, fiche ceathair, (six fours – twenty four) etc.,

In October 1956, a new school was opened out the Youghal Road, this being the fourth primary school in Ardmore. There are now four teachers in this school; the Principal Victor Mullins, Olive

Keane, Bernadette O'Brien and Maeve Curran. The school has a telephone and the pupils do not have to get involved in the cleaning. It is centrally heated as is Grange School, unlike the previous ones, which just had a coal-fire at the top of the room, that being lighted and looked after by the pupils and teachers.

Most of the children are driven to school. Their predecessors walked, even those who were at a distance of 3 miles.

Until 1966, very, very, few children went to second-level schools. Then came Donogh O'Malley as Minister for Education and he quite suddenly launched free secondary education. Now there are buses picking up children all over the country side and bringing them to the secondary schools in town. Everyone takes it for granted now, but it was an absolute revolution in its time. It depends on the individual child, whether he/she can secure a niche in the numerous third level courses which are available.

Halla Deuglán

6 St. Declans Hall as it was. On the truck a group of officials and friends on their way to the opening of the new GAA Grounds in 1994.

Halla Deuglán was built in 1912 at a cost of £153, twelve local farmers being guarantors for £12 of this. Fr. Galvin who came as Parish Priest in the 1920s decided to apportion the rest as part of parochial expenses.

Otherwise, it was the result of a corporate, voluntary effort under the leadership of the then C.C. Fr. O'Shea. Local people brought the sand and gravel. The building of it was put out to tender; there was one Irish one from Smith & Pearsons, Dublin but the lowest one was from J. McManus, Hammersmith, London. They sent the materials to Ireland: galvanized sheeting, doors, windows, and timber all cut and ready. These had to be collected from the railway station at Youghal, by horse and cart. The material was galvanise lined with timber and felt in between. Local tradesmen, backed by voluntary help, worked on the assembly.

7 St. Declan's Hall, Mounting Nets; Denis Lenihan, Jim Moloney and his brother Niall. Reading newspaper, John Revins.

The hall was opened on a fine June Sunday; it was packed to capacity for a performance by a Lismore group of a play *The Shamrock and the Rose*. Johnny Fitzgerald (former occupant of Paddy Carlton's house) had brought the scenery from Villierstown Ferry by horse and cart.

A big wooden sign spanned the hall 'For Happy Homes for Ireland, for God'.

The hall served as a club and the first caretaker was Jim Eddy (an old coastguard who lived on site of Jimmie O'Connor's house) who kept a roaring fire in the central stove. People came at a charge of 2d to play billiards, cards, throw rings or read the newspapers provided. A small billiard table had been provided by Captain Turner of the Anchorage, one of the houses overlooking the pier. There were woodwork and cookery classes too. Cinema performances – with lighting by carbide - took place during the War period 1914-1918. Later on, there were frequent concerts and dramatic performances, and later on again, it was used very much as a dance hall. Jim Rooney speaks of very fashionable dances, inaugurated by the West Waterford Hunt, being held here. He speaks of the ladies with sleeveless long dresses but, with long gloves covering the arms completely. We remember the 4d hops and 1/- ones on a Sunday night, during the late thirties and early forties. All the many organisations and groups in the area used it as a venue for meetings and for fund-raising.

However, it didn't suit the changing modern needs of the local community, and the fabric had given long years of wear and was showing its weaknesses. There was a number of public meetings, and it was finally decided that a new hall would be built on the site and that it should continue to be an integral part of the local community.

8 Halla Deuglán 2021.

The actual building was done under the ANCO Youth Training Scheme, so the labour was free. Co. Council assisted with drawings and plans and the local community provided the funds.

It is a great tribute to the hard-working local committee who met weekly to monitor the situation. Naturally, there were many headaches and differences of opinion along the way, and it was a proud day for all concerned, when it was officially opened by his Excellency, President Hillery in July 1987.

All organisations are represented on the Hall committee which holds monthly meetings.

St. Declan's Church

9 St. Declan's Church and part of the National School in the early 1890s. Note the embrasures in the façade of the church, the white pinafores of the girls and the front section which looks like an unfinished storm wall.

Rev. Fr. P. McGrath was responsible for the erection of the churches of Ardmore, Grange and Old Parish, while he was parish priest 1836-1846. Old Parish was later cut off from Ardmore and joined with Ring. The building of the three churches was an extraordinary achievement for the pastor and people of the area in pre-famine times. As a matter of fact, it seems to have been an almost impossible achievement for a poverty-stricken people. Not surprisingly, they remained without furniture for some years.

The following is taken from the *Ardmore Journal*: Local tradition tells of a thatched chapel or Mass House up the cliff near the pier. Some evidence for this is provided by two holy water fonts found at Cliff Cottage and also by the story of the Mass path. People from Ardo and Whiting Bay used to come to church along an old mass path which started up near the Rectory. The path went in front of Curran's Cottage (now Joe Callaghan's), crossed the stream and went along through the fields in an easterly direction behind Melrose, Maycroft and Lacken following the boundary line between Duffcarrick and Dysert. The remains of this track can still be seen behind Melrose.

'According to Paddy Mockler the end of it was the (idir) 'Dhá Thig' the path which descends steeply from Dawson's Road to the Cliff between Stone Steps and Rosary Cottage. According to Jack Crowley a link with these times is provided through a reminiscence of Tom Cullen of Ardo. Tom Cullen, (father of J. Cullen who wrote 'Lovely Ardo' and of D. Cullen of Coláiste Deuglán), was born in the 1830s and was over ninety when he died. Tom recalled following his parents to Mass, as a child along this route to the cliff. By the time he was old enough to go to mass the present Church had been built.'

An article in the *Monthly Illustrated Journal* of July 1883 describes a visit to Ardmore Church:-

"A turn to our right, a few moments along an even roadway with more whitewash to contrast with the blue expanse of waters before us, and we were in the little Catholic Church. A wonderfully humble sanctuary, with unpretentious wooden altars, tiny statues, flagged with large squares of dull stone, railings and pews stained a dark brown, a dim religious light prevailing everything. The one spot of colour some devotional pictures above the high altar, and the smell of the sea breeze borne on the fresh breeze through the open windows. It seemed to me a perfect sailor's chapel, so neat, so spotless, so guileless of any attempt to hide its honest simplicity."

There are still some interesting plaques in the church, two of them placed there by our present Parish Priest, Canon O'Connor. One commemorates the visit of Cardinal Ó Fiaich in 1987, for the 150th anniversary of the church; another commemorates Fr. Prendergast P.P. who distributed food here during the famine and who is buried in front of the High Altar.

A plaque near the fourth Station of the Cross commemorates Fr. Patrick Costin who died in March 1875 aged eighty six years and sixty years of his sacred ministry. A little framed photograph of him used to hang on the wall beside the plaque. A brass plaque over the holy water font at the church door is in memory of 'his deceased parents' and presented by Mr Patrick O'Brien of Boston in 1914. The well-known Mrs Barry née Dwyer, who dominated the Cliff for so many years, donated the Stations of the Cross.

Willie Dwyer of Cork, donated the high altar in thanksgiving for the recovery of his son, Declan from an accident. The late Paddy Mockler, Sacristan at the church all his life (in succession to William, his father who had been Sacristan since 1927) remembers the original wooden altar being replaced, and seeing as a school child, the cases containing the sections of the new altar being unpacked. Misses Amy and Snow Dwyer, Star Cottage, donated the altar rails. The side sections of them still remain.

After the death of Fr. Wall in 1875, the people erected by subscription, a side-altar of marble dedicated to the Sacred Heart of Jesus. A plaque was inserted beside the memorial altar is inscribed, "Pray for the soul of Rev. Patrick Wall P.P. to whose memory this altar was erected by the parishioners of Ardmore and Grange" (cf. *Parochial History of Waterford and Lismore* by Canon Power). The plaque is no longer in evidence.

We still have some note-worthy relics of the past in our churches. In Grange church there is a chalice dating from 1818 presented by 'the house-keepers of the parish'. It is extraordinary to remember that this was made years before the church was built. In the *Ardmore Journal* of 1990, there is a very interesting article on *Patrick Troy, Wainright, Móin Bhaile Shiobhaín*. The author, Michael Mulcahy, describes the set of six funerary candelabra made by Patrick Troy for Grange Church and there are two illustrations, side view and front view, of the exquisite tabernacle he also made for Grange church.

In Ardmore Church there is a chalice 'presented by Mary Foley in memory of her father, James Foley Ardmore 1926'. Ciss Quain remembers Fr. Galvin P.P. announcing this to the congregation. Mary Foley was in the U.S.A. and in order to identify her father, James Foley, said he was known in Ardmore as 'Jim the Boy'. There is another most interesting chalice in the Mass kit which goes out to the 'Stations'. It says "Dom^s Thos Power de Ardmore fieri me fecit A.D. 1751". It is again extraordinary to think that this preceded the building of the present church by so many years and was probably in use in the old thatched Church on the cliff, which is shown on a map of 1818. (A font from this church is still in existence. See *Ardmore Journal* 1987).

Down through the years various families donated pews in the side aisles and these were known as 'belonging to' such and such a family, right down to the 40s and 50s. Every year, there was a collection for the church pews, families of the original donors being exempt from this. Fr. O'Byrne, when Parish Priest, discontinued this collection. In fact, the side aisles, especially the ones at the Sacred Heart side were practically taken over in summertime by the influx of visiting nuns in the 50s and 60s. Before this, the Cappoquin nuns were in occupation of the top pew at the right-hand side and had a heavy red curtain around it. At one stage, Fr. Draper when curate, asked the nuns not to come to last mass on Sundays in order to leave room for the ordinary congregation. In our youth, we remember that the men invariably occupied the left-hand side of the middle aisle and the women were on the right.

As a result of the Second Vatican Council the liturgy is now in the vernacular and the priest faces the congregation. We also have altar girls, Eucharistic ministers and readers. All this took time, but we have become quite used to it now. The Second Vatican Council which began in 1964 led to great changes in churches throughout the country.

In Ardmore, the first change involved making a large wooden platform for the altar and bringing it some feet further down towards the congregation. The second lot of changes occurred in the seventies in Fr. Meehan's time. Fr. Aidan, O. Cist. from Melleray was very much involved. In the late 70s the altar (re-cycled from the former high altar) was made free-standing and the tabernacle inserted in the wall behind. The niches up high which had held statues were filled in and some of the statues dispensed with. Various plaques have disappeared too. During the alterations, St. Declan lost his silver heart-shaped brooch which had been presented by a Mrs Appleby, in return for a cure for her alcoholic husband.

The sanctuary lamps were removed and sold to two parishioners but owing to the diligence of Mrs Eileen O'Brien of Grallagh, one of them has been traced and returned. It had been bought by and forgotten by the late Eddie Colbert who had no difficulty in relinquishing it in to her custody when she enquired about it. She performed a wonderful job of restoration on it and with the help of her brother, Tom Curran, Ballylangadan, made it ready for installation again in Ardmore Church. The flagged floor of the church was taken up and a new one laid down. Regrettably, the original mullioned windows of plain glass were dispensed with, both in Ardmore and in Grange.

During all this upheaval, the late Mrs. Mockler did trojan work each weekend, preparing the church for Sunday mass. There was just one Sunday, when we were guests of St. Paul's (Church of Ireland.)

In the old regime, part of the duties of Paddy Mockler, the sacristan was standing at the church gate with a wooden box, collecting coppers from the people going in. This of course, has been replaced by the offertory collection, and coppers are not expected in this. Up to the 50s, the result of the annual collections for the priests of the parish were read out from the altar and the congregation listened with avid attention, as each section of the parish was taken in turn, for eg, Main St., the following gave £1 each - Jack Brown, John White etc., The following gave 10/- each Joseph Smith, John Moriarty and so on, down to the smallest donations. Nowadays things are done much more discreetly, baskets are passed around at the Offertory.

In the churchyard, at the west side, there are three headstones of priests who have been buried in the church:-

> Fr. Prendergast of the Famine period.
> Fr. Shanahan who was responsible for the building of the school.

30

Fr. Patrick Wall, who died on Good Friday 1875.

It is remarkable that two priests of the parish died not alone in the same year – 1875 - but in the same month i.e., Fr. Patrick Wall and Fr. Patrick Costin (plaque near the fourth station already referred to). Fr. Galvin P.P. and Fr. Wall P.P. are both buried at the west side. Fr. Meehan died 1978 and Fr. Cahill 1975 are buried at the eastern side.

The Terry family has a burial plot and headstone at the back of the church, near the sacristy and Mick Terry of Whiting Bay was buried there in 1998.

10 The interior of St. Declan's Roman Catholic Church, c1940.

An interment took place about 1928/30 at the eastern side quite near the graves of Frs. Meehan and Cahill. There were bushes and trees in the area at the time. The horse-drawn hearse, with the horse caparisoned in black, arrived shortly after 3pm, so we inquisitive school children trooped up to investigate, but nobody now remembers who was buried there. Also at the eastern side a new grotto has been erected, dedicated to Our Lady Star of the Sea and commemorating those from the parish who were lost at sea. Bishop Lee consecrated it in December 1997.

I was upset that the sycamore and willow trees, which framed the church, were cut down, they helped to soften the stark utilitarian aspect of the building. Many generations of my forbears have worshipped here, so I have a special regard and affection for my local church.

St. Pauls Church

The church of St. Paul is a pleasant building with Gothic Revival windows of simple pointed arches filled with leaded panes and a large decorated 3-light east window with fine stone tracery. It was built in 1838, which is at the same period as the Catholic churches in the parish were being built. Up to this time, part of the old Cathedral in the graveyard was still roofed and services were being held there.

The campaign for repair of the old church or the erection of a new one on another site was in motion since 1829 (according to the Vestry meeting of July 1829). Difficulties existed as regards changing the site and at a Vestry meeting of 2nd January 1836, it was unanimously resolved that a petition from the parishioners be drawn up and signed, praying his Excellency, the Lord Lieutenant of Ireland 'to suffer the site of the present church of Ardmore be changed to the ploughland of Dysert in said parish'. This was forwarded to the Privy Council.

At the April Vestry Meeting in 1836, there was a charge of 10/- for a fender and fire-irons for the church, so it was still in use. It's fascinating to think of a fender and fire-iron in use there.

The Lord Lieutenant and Privy Council had looked on the petition with favour and the Vestry Meeting of 16th April 1838, was held 'in the Glebe House of Ardmore, the church being dilapidated and the new church not yet finished'. The Easter Vestry of 1839 held on 1st April was in the parish church of Ardmore.

What a tragedy, that a church had been built on a new site, if only the old one had continued in use, it would probably have been adequately repaired in the meantime, and how wonderful it would have been to have had Christian service continuing there down through the years, instead of its being open to the elements as now.

The Tudor baptismal font was brought down to St. Paul's. There is an inscribed chalice dated 1726, which had disappeared from the church and was restored by Robert Day F.S.A. who purchased it at Sotheby's in London, where it was for sale. Service is conducted weekly during the summer; and during the Christmas period, there is a wonderful ecumenical carol service. We have attended a baptism there, some wedding ceremonies and funeral ceremonies and we were the guests of St. Paul's for mass one Sunday in the 70's, when St. Declan's Church was in a state of upheaval during the re-organisations there with Vatican II regulations.

In April 1973, Rev. Rector McManaway, Rector of Youghal was instituted as Rector of Ardmore Parish. St. Paul's was added to the Youghal Union of Parishes, having been transferred from the Diocese of Lismore to the Diocese of Cork, Cloyne and Ross.

Big Houses in Ardmore

I have had access to the *Griffith Valuation* sheets of 1850s and also updates of these, from the Valuation Office, Irish Life Centre, Dublin.

I have looked in particular at the six big houses, all in the townland of Duffcarrick and listed one after another.

1. Mercy Convent, now known as Stella Maris.
2. Lacken (or Byron Lodge).
3. Maycroft.
4. Dhucarraig (Carrick-on-Suir Presentation Sisters).
5. Melrose.
6. Atlantic Lodge.

Stella Maris

The first house, now known as Stella Maris, from 1855 to 1860 was occupied by Nelson Foley with Edward Odell as lessor.

In the 1861 - 1883 period Odells were in occupation

In the 1884 - 1893 period Col. Henry Cotton was in occupation (Catherine Fitzgerald and H. Odell's names were inserted and crossed out).

In 1894 - 1908 Patrick Walsh was in occupation

In 1909 - 1920 Miss Mary J. Walsh was in occupation and the house is now referred to as Ardmore House

1920 Lady Clodagh Anson; then the Sisters of Mercy

The story of Maycroft and Lacken given by Mrs Dowson is a quite adequate account of both houses.

Lacken

Lacken, in the early years of the last century was lived in by two sisters, Mrs Sealy and Mrs Dawson. Mrs Dawson was a very good gardener; Mrs Sealy had a room furnished as a dispensary and local people often came to her for cures for minor injuries and ailments.

Mrs Dawson had three sons, Lionel, Gus, and Reggie. Reggie was a professional entertainer in London; he performed in St. Declan's Hall in 1915. Lionel was in India. Gus was secretary to Newcastle Sanatorium. We think it was he who married a Miss Gates from Kildorrery. The Gates established the first co-operative society in Cork, in Kildorrery and the family is mentioned in Elizabeth Bowen's books. They stayed a lot in Rock House during the summer. Mrs Gates would not allow any meals to be cooked on Sundays; they all had to be cold. Ciss Quain remembers a Lucy Gates and a Jim Gates who disguised his age in order to join the army for the 1914-18 war.

Lacken is now owned by Mrs Mary Byron-Casey who runs a very successful guesthouse there.

Maycroft

Maycroft, next door to Lacken, is a large semi-detached house, now the property of the Ahearne family, Cork. It was occupied and owned for the greater part of this century by the Pollock family from London. Mrs Pollock was nee Barry, a family from around Clogheen. There were three boys and two girls, and they came to Ardmore each summer and while in residence, a flag flew from one of the trees.

David Pollock had a back ailment and died at the age of twenty-five: Patrick was drowned with a friend in a boating accident in England: Dick who had hounds and a horse in the premises below Tigaluinn, now owned by the Rooneys, died in India where he was serving in the army. Catherine and Rosemary's husbands had colonial posts. During the war years, Mr & Mrs Pollock senior lived in Ardmore with their grandchildren (children of

Catherine's), John and Susan under the charge of a young girl, Eva Roland who later married in Kinsale and became Mrs Jacob. Later on, Mrs Dowson (Rosemary) and her husband home from Kenya lived in Maycroft for some years with her two grand-children, one of whom, Charles, went to school in Ardmore in the sixties.

They had wonderful memories of Ardmore and Mrs Dowson had some hair-raising stories of their youthful exploits; one concerned an underground passage in the graveyard into which they stumbled by mistake; one was an account of being let down by rope over the steep cliff at Faill na Sleannaire in order to explore an aperture half-way down. Mrs Dowson has left this account of Maycroft.

"The history of the house necessitates a reference to the vicissitudes of two families who possessed in succession, the neighbouring mansion and property of Ardogenna, built in the 18th and 17th centuries, a house capable of maintaining a strong defence, and was then the seat of the ancient Irish family of Coghlan. Towards the end of the 18th century, the Coghlans leased the property to the Lawlor family.

Towards the middle of the 19th century, this latter family was represented by two females only and the family was deeply in debt to the National Bank of Ireland, which institution notified the sisters that it intended to foreclose and take possessions of the property on a certain date. The sisters purchased two plots of land in the village of Ardmore, and with the assistance of the country people, pillaged Ardogenna, with the result that the two houses in Ardmore - Maycroft and Lacken - incorporated much material removed from the older house (the roof slates, windows, doors, some fire-places etc.).

The date of the building of Maycroft and the adjoining house, Lacken, is commonly given as 1846, but there is no means of proving this to be the actual case.

The ladies Lawlor both married and soon sold their houses, that of Maycroft being purchased by Staff-Commander R.N., William Bagge Triphook, who being ordered abroad by the Admiralty settled his affairs but died before his departure abroad in 1867 aged 55. He married Ann Bagge who died in 1905. His son Major Triphook, Durham Light Infantry succeeded and died in 1887. This gentleman erected the present greenhouse, and he made the tennis court.

Anne Triphook continued to live in Maycroft but sold it in 1904 to Katherine Cecil Thurston, once well-known as a successful novelist. She died in 1911 and left the property to her life-long friend, Nancy Inez Pollock. Major Triphook and his mother are buried in adjoining graves in the old churchyard."

The Triphook headstone in the local cemetery testifies to the varied military career of Simon Bagge Triphook (died 1887). He was involved in the Maori campaign in New Zealand; at the Curragh Camp and at Jhelum in the first Afghan war.

For further information on the Thurstones, see *Ardmore Journal* 1984.

Dhucarraig

The house, Dhucarraig in its own grounds between Maycroft and Melrose, has been the property of the Presentation nuns, Carrick-on-Suir, since the early 1920's. Apart from the Cappoquin Mercy Order, which by this time was well established in Ardmore, there were no other nuns in the village at the time. Even as children we felt that the nuns were shy and ill at ease and just not used to being outside the convent walls. The property had been owned by the Aldworth family from Newmarket, Co. Cork and we always referred to it as 'Aldworths'.

Aldworth Court at Newmarket had close connections with John Philpot Curran, his daughter, Sarah, the betrothed of Robert Emmet is buried in Newmarket. The Aldworth family had been given a grant and charter by James I, confirmed by Charles II. One of the Aldworth family is reputed to have become the first and only lady Freemason. The family left it in the 1920s and it came into the ownership of the Sisters of St. Joseph of the Sacred Heart for some years.

I am indebted to an account in *The Cork Examiner* for this information.

A copy of the *Evening Echo* of October 1999 describes St. Finbarres Cathedral and says, "A brass tablet on the floor near the pulpit indicates the tomb of Elizabeth Aldworth (1695-1775) the only women to be initiated into Free Masonry".

From the update of the *Griffith Valuations* sent by the Valuation Office in Dublin one sees that Captain Thomas Thornton (and later on, his representatives) was occupier of the house from the 1850s through to 1893.

Then came John C. Aldworth, 1909 - 1919, the death of whose mother-in-law Henrietta Cecil Collins is recorded in the Register of Deaths in Dungarvan in 1914. The family must have used the house quite extensively.

A German governess was resident with them at one period, and in July 1914 she was drowned while swimming on Ardmore Beach. She was Gertrude Schmalzle, aged 20 and she was buried in the local graveyard. The inscription on the headstone is now illegible.

Relatives have come to Ardmore, enquiring on a few occasions, the last occasion being in September 1999.

The Presentation Sisters, Carrick-on-Suir acquired the house in the 1920s and they are still the owners.

Melrose

11 Melrose House

An interesting point about Melrose is that the valuation of the building is more than twice of any of its neighbours, so it must have been bigger and more impressive always.

In the 1855 - 1860 period Rev. Thomas J. Thurtle was occupier (lessor E. Odell).

In the 1861 - 1876 period Richard Chearnley and representatives.

In the 1877 - 1883 period Mrs Bagge.

In the 1884 - 1920 period Catherine Fitzgerald.

Then came the Barrons, The Collises, and Martin Hurley, my father. I lived there for ten years after my marriage in 1945; then my sister, Eileen Colbert, had a guest house there until the beginning of the 1990s. It is now owned by a German family, the Schumans.

Atlantic Lodge

12 George Beresford Poer with his wife Florence (née Gator), on a horse and trap at Atlantic Lodge, Ardmore, c1900.

Atlantic Lodge on the Rocky Road next door to Melrose was occupied up to 1863 by Leopold Keane, Rev. John Wallace being lessor. Lodgers are noted as occupiers in the 1864-1876 period. Then came Albertine Zehender. In the 1884 - 1893 period Samuel B. Poer was occupier with Captain H.J. Wallace as lessor. It is with the Poer family that we associate the house.

The Mockler family had a special connection with them. In the last of the pre-1920 years, William Mockler (died 1985), a tall, powerfully built man was appointed guardian to George Poer, also a tall well-built man who evidently suffered from a mental condition. They went on very long walks, over to Old Parish, to the Lickey with fishing rods and a wicker pannier to carry home the fish, which were never caught, and out on Carraig a Phúintín at low tide from which Will Mockler had to more or less forcibly remove him, as he would have remained oblivious to the incoming tide.

During the World War II years, a Poer family member who lived in India used to send regular packages of tea to the Mocklers, what a boon in the ½oz tea days. Later on, they came on annual visits to the Mockler family and brought them to visit them in Monkstown.

There are four Beresfond Poer headstones in Ardmore graveyard, the last internment being in 1985, so evidently, they had warm recollections of their time in Ardmore.

The house was bought as the curate's house in the early 20s and later was sold to the present owners, Monica (nee Casey with Ardmore Irish American connections) and her husband Anton Willam, an Austrian.

The Hotel

The house in the village formerly known as The Hotel is the long two-storey building on the south side of the street, now the residence of Billy and Ber Harty. The Cup and Saucer restaurant, property of Mr & Mrs Matt Power, was formerly part of it.

It has been said that a family of Fitzgeralds were the original owners. In the *Primary Valuation of Tenements* for the village of

Ardmore about 1851, there is a Timothy Fitzgerald who apparently kept 'lodgers'. He had a house and garden, net annual value £3/10/0. Would this have been the person who initiated the hotel?

In 1864, the *Register of Deaths* records the death of a young man, Michael Fitzgerald, aged 25, hotel keeper. Then in 1865, the same register records the death of John Fitzgerald 82, hotel keeper. The story goes that the Fitzgeralds were evicted from the hotel and the blind old lady being evicted, had herself led around the house and poked her stick through every window and cursed the lot. Jimmie Rooney thinks the expense of enlarging the building precipitated their ill fortune, I wonder too, was the death of the young man in 1864 a relevant factor.

Deug Fitzgerald, his wife Mary and son Paddy, lived up to the 40s in a one-room apartment, which is now the part of 'Brisen' adjoining Dunnes furniture factory. It is generally thought they were of the same family who built and were evicted from the hotel in the village. They had a covered car bed and Paddy slept in the settle bed. There was no back door, and they were constantly up and down to the ruins of the boat-house, property of the British Marine, and now occupied by the Fire Brigade building and the public toilets. They had two pigs there and a donkey and had the customary plot in Dysert where they grew four acres of wheat and slashed it for food. In the '40s the people of the village built a one-roomed house for Paddy in Mary Ellen Burke's (of Chapel Row) back garden and that's where he spent the rest of his days.

Paddy was a member of the Rocket Life-Saving Service and became number one man more by default than anything else. On one occasion, Mr. Morgan on visitation had the members of the service lined up at Goat Island, and asked a question about a certain combination of lights on a vessel and what kind of steam ship it indicated, Paddy didn't know and in his embarrassment conveyed the prompt from behind, "a steam-roller, sir."

The next occupants of the hotel were Ahearns, from around Aglish, it is thought. The hotel was apparently flourishing for some years and army officers from Cobh were met at Youghal Railway Station and conveyed to Ardmore by the hotel jarvey car (Tommie Quinn, the driver) and there they spent the weekend and we had the beginning of tourism in Ardmore. Groups came by wagonette from Youghal also. Mick Ahearne was musical and played the melodeon and there was dancing on a platform in the garden. So, Ardmore was a popular venue in the 1880s and 1890s. The large flat piece of ground between Green Shutters and Quarry House was known as the Croquet Ground and was owned by the hotel people too and apparently used frequently by the guests.

An article in the *Monthly Illustrated Journal* of July 1883 gives an account of a trip to Ardmore "The twilight was fast disappearing over the Bay as we returned to the Hotel. While waiting for our trap, we were shown upstairs into the prettiest parlour imaginable. One side of it was almost all let into a long window, that looked out on a garden, which was one mass of soft verdure. Trees and shrubs and flowers all were covered with a southern luxuriance of foliage, a large fuchsia transformed the window frame into a bower, its dull crimson bells with their purple centres showing dimly through the profusion of brilliant green. Somehow as we rested on the low loungers, I thought that verdant garden the most refreshing sight we had seen that day."

The Ahearnes had no family of their own and in the 1890s, two Prendergast sisters (their father John Prendergast a marine captain) Hannah Margaret and Dote were ensconced in the hotel with their aunt, Mrs Ahearne, and lived in comfort there. She left the hotel to one of the sisters. In 1896, James Willoughby, a mechanic from Youghal married Hannah Margaret. The Willoughbys and Dote continued to live in the Hotel, but in 1901, Mrs. Willoughby died in childbirth.

Apparently, the hotel was sold and bought by William Harris, a native of Bruree, Co. Limerick and a veteran of the Boer war. It was not then run as a hotel, but as a licensed premises.

The Harrisses were four in family, Ciss the only surviving girl; Willie became an engineer, married a Dungarvan girl and died soon after; Jack became a Christian Brother and Joe became a priest. Ciss was a good-looking girl with many suitors all repulsed by her father. His wife had died in the severe flu epidemic of the 1920s.

Fr. Joe had meant to be a diocesan priest but changed his mind and became a Jesuit, a decision of which his father did not approve at all, especially when he was sent to China. "I'd convert more of them at the point of a bayonet, than he would by his prayers." is the remark attributed to him.

Fr. Joe (known as Fr. Richard, in the Order) was in Canton, later in Hong Kong, where he was a member of the community during the Japanese occupation. After the war he became rector of the Regional Seminary for southern China situated in Hong Kong. Subsequently he became superior of Irish Jesuit Mission in Hong Kong. He was later in retirement in Sydney and was visited (summer 1997) by Mrs Nicholson, aunt of Dr. Joe Meehan. She reported him hale and hearty with a lively, active mind. He died in 1998.

In 1984, when my niece Helen and I were in Canton, we were trying to cross the street one evening in front of a relentless avalanche of bicycles and a little Chinese man came to our aid. He had excellent English and we got chatting at the side of the river.

He brought us to see a Catholic church and priest; the church was then emerging from a penal situation. Our newfound friend acted as interpreter, and you can imagine our astonishment when the priest enquired for Fr. O'Meara and Fr. Harris. Fr. O'Meara was uncle of Mary, James Quain's wife and Fr. Harris was our own Joe, from down the road at home. The Chinese priest had been a pupil of theirs' at the seminary in Hong Kong. In a teeming Chinese city, thousands of miles from home, it was amazing to be asked about two people whom we knew so well.

13 Frank Nugent proprietor of the Cliff Hotel, Ardmore, pours a glass of Guinness, c1955.

The next owners of the property were the late Frank Nugent, Cliff Hotel and the late Jack O'Brien in the village. Frank Nugent transferred the seven day bar licence to Cliff House; Mrs O'Brien had a small shop there for a while. Then came the Carltons who had a supermarket there; it is now the private residence of Ber and Billy Harty.

Religious Orders

As stated elsewhere (the account of Ardmore School), Mrs Barry had brought the nuns to Ardmore, in April 1900. They were installed in Monea Lodge on Tower Hill (now home of the McCarthy family) and in 1923, she bought the house now known as Stella Maris, for the Cappoquin nuns (her sister was one of them). It is now the property of the Irish Mercy Sisters in general, and various orders take turns in renting it during the summer, for instance, the Cahir Mercy nuns and the Clonakilty Mercy nuns.

The Presentation nuns, Carrick-On-Suir were the next order to buy a house of their own, Duffcarrick. We remember, as small children in the early 30s the nuns being quite apprehensive about crossing the road. The house is still their property.

In the 1950s and '60s, Ardmore became very popular with religious orders, mostly nuns. There were Christian Brothers too; I remember a group of brothers from Waterford staying in Melrose; also an English group. They must still have been in black, as some English person staying in Tigaluinn got permission to park a car there and asked "would all the parsons mind".

The Dungarvan Mercy nuns bought the new extension of Coláiste Deuglán but sold it after a few years. It is now the Round Tower Hotel, at first the property of Michael Ronayne and now of Aidan Quirke.

The Bon Secour order bought Quarry House, formerly owned by Sir John Keane of Cappoquin; the nuns are still the owners. The Thurles Ursuline nuns bought the former Garda Barracks (before this, the residence of the Cottons). The Thurles Presentation Order bought Ard Carraig on the Cliff, a house originally built to store material during the building of the pier in 1908.

Other orders who frequently came to Ardmore in the past and rented houses are the Ferrybank nuns, the Clonmel Presentation sisters, the Mountmellick nuns, the Kildare Presentation nuns, the Callan Mercy nuns and the Brigidines from Mountrath.

The nuns went swimming at the far end of Ardmore Strand, also in Curragh Strand, so that at one stage, it was referred to as the nuns' strand. They wore home-made voluminous bathing costumes, which were a great source of curiosity and amusement to irreverent teenagers, who were also genuinely interested in the many layers of underwear worn by the sisters.

A problem frequently encountered by Miky Moloney post master at this period, was correspondence addressed to say "Sr. Evangelist, Presentation Convent, Ardmore" the writer not realising there were probably five or six Presentation Convent communities in Ardmore.

The number of sisters is now much diminished, but they still come in quite appreciable numbers, a gentle pleasant presence among our holiday makers.

The Sea

Fishing In Ardmore

Salmon Fishing

The earliest we know of fishing in Ardmore is in 1616, when the Earl of Cork, - according to *Life and Letters of the Great Earl of Cork* by Dorothea Townshend, published 1904 - "was putting up salting and fish houses and a fish press at Ardmore, where he and the Hulls were setting up a fish curing establishment". Sir William Hull was Vice-Admiral of Munster, living in Leam Con Castle near Crookhaven and the fisheries there were worked by Sir William in partnership with Boyle. In the same year 1616, the Earl made a memorandum "Delivered to Captain William Hull £20 as earnest money to buy casks for fumados upon an agreement to have half of his fish to be taken the next season at Crookhaven in which he and I are to be partners and Captain Hull is to adventure £100 with me in my next seasons fishing at Ardmore." The connection with Sir William Hull dates from his marriage to the widow of Boyle, Bishop of Cork, brother of the Earl.

Another fish anecdote relates to Mr Lancaster, one of the fellows of Youghal College who came in 1616 to beg the Earl for preferment. He was given his travelling expenses and in 1619, the Earl agreed to give him "as Parson and Vicar of Ardmore", a free gift of half the fish, which formerly had been a due of the dissolved St. Molana's Abbey, to which Ardmore had belonged.

In the beginning of the 20th century, there was no tradition of drift-net fishing for salmon in Ardmore. The only family who engaged in fishing were the Gearys (who lived where Tigaliunn is now) who had a licence for salmon fishing and fished with what was called a bag net, leaving it in position all night and collecting the fish in the morning, and transporting them by horse and cart to the Ferry Point and there to Youghal. The catch in the bag net could amount from 100 to 200 fish.

14 Ardmore fishermen, c1920.

When Fred Keane, Star Cottage, one of the Keane family of Cappoquin, came to live in Ardmore around 1910 he acquired a boat and employed Patsy McCarthy and Maurice Flynn to fish for salmon; they were paid a weekly wage plus a 1/- a fish. The fish were brought up to the coach house of Rock House and from there, transported to the Ferry Point and Youghal in a special spring-dray called a jingle. Later on he had to get men from Ring to fish for him. They stayed in 'Stone Steps' i.e. the house overlooking the Boat Cove, now owned by Finbarr and Mrs Crowley of Cork. They walked home to Ring every Friday evening, over by Fuges, Ballyquin, and along a cliff path; they returned on Sunday evenings.

Others followed the example of Fred Keane. Jamesy Quain and Seán Faítch (O'Brien); Nick Rooney about 1910 (he eventually acquired three boats); Johnny Mansfield; Paddy Fitzgerald (generally called Grady); and Jim Pender. They tended to fish only in summer and to go to sea in two oared boats on suitable days. Nick Rooney was the first to start fishing in February. He and Eamon Mulcahy caught a salmon of 48½lbs weight, probably the heaviest ever caught in the bay. Seán Faítch (O'Brien) acquired his own four oared boat as did Paddy Brien, also Tom Harty of Curragh. Deug Rooney and Tom Rooney came home from America to go fishing, but they returned to the US after some time.

Some of the other Ardmore fishermen were Willie Flynn of Dysert, Jimmie Carey. 'Dr' Walsh of Whiting Bay, John and Tom Smith, Whiting Bay, and from Curragh, Jack Corbett, four Hurtin fishermen, Simon Fletcher, Deug Brien and Danny Donovan. Johnny Mansfield had a boat, so had Tom Foley and Ned Foley.

Jimmie Rooney remembers eighty-four fishermen during his years of fishing. There were nine boats when he began his fishing career in 1925, at the age of 16 and gave up he thinks about 1972. Paddy Power and Paddy Flynn fished with him for about thirty-three years. He remembers on one occasion catching six salmon averaging 20lbs weight each; one of them weighed 38½lbs. On another occasion on a Fool's Day, they caught thirty fish.

In the 1930s he had three boats made for him at Murrays in Youghal. Each one, plus a pair of oars cost £14. 200 yards of net was the length allowed in those days and the salmon licence cost £3. There was no fishing from 8 am Saturday morning until 6 am on Monday morning. The laws were enforced by the Lismore Board of Conservators. One chose one's berth at the beginning of the week. That was an important decision and often caused friction. The position of one's berth was achieved by being first out on Monday morning and it was retained until Friday evening. The distance between each berth was 200 yards.

Some of the fish went to Cappoquin, Billy Baldwin being the vendor; more to Waterford where a better price prevailed. Later, they were taken by O'Connor of Cappoquin, the fish being brought every evening up to Tigaluinn, our home, where my father Martin Hurley weighed them in the back kitchen, and a small docket issued, and then, on a Saturday, they were paid. We have visions of our father with the Ready Reckoner each weekend. Each man in the boat got a share, with an extra one for the boat owner, who would of course have the obligation of paying for the licence and nets. A register of the salmon had to be kept, noting all that were bought or sold and to whom, and this was examined by the fishery inspector, from time to time.

So salmon fishing continued in Ardmore throughout the late twenties, thirties and forties. The season began on 1st February and there was special Mass, and the priest went to the Boat Cove to bless the boats and nets. The licence cost £3 and fishing continued till the end of July, but the men really regarded May as the last month.

The preparation went on for quite some time in advance, the nets having to be oiled before January and then mounted. Seeing the men mounting the nets at various locations in the village, was part of the memories of childhood. Corks had to be bought and these were brought to the forge to be holed in the fire there. During the fishing season, the nets were hauled in each evening and draped across the special poles at the pier.

In 1947 there was a memorable invasion of sharks during the month of May. Everywhere one looked there seemed to be eight or nine fins together, and of course they played havoc with the nets. Between 1926 and 1954, the seasons were very bad, but the salmon fishing continued to a certain extent. John Keevers joined the ranks in 1946.

1935 was the year the *Muirchú* (our only Irish naval boat at that period, a veteran of 1916, when she was British owned and shelled the G.P.O.) came to the bay. Nobody suspected her of having an interest in the salmon boats, but she had. Discrepancies were noted and in 1936 she came again to the bay and the law cases were held in the local courthouse. However, the occasion was remembered with hilarity.

There was a big resurgence in salmon fishing in the late seventies and eighties. There was more of an emphasis then on the peel or young salmon which appeared in May. In one day, John Cronin had a record catch of 210 fish. Boats tended to get 40-60 fish each day. About 12 boats were fishing, John Keevers, Farrisseys, Paddy Foley, John Cronin, Jimmie O'Connor, Martin Troy, Dick Linehan, Vinnie Rourke, Mick Fitzgerald, Revins, Paddy Morrissey, Jim Flynn, and Jim Moloney (who had bought with him from London, a young Australian teacher who spent the season salmon fishing in Ardmore). It was about this time, that we were intrigued at the idea of some of the fishermen landing at Cliff House on the early mornings and treating themselves to breakfast at the hotel, and often a special lunch later in the day. Tourists along the cliff walk were greatly interested at seeing a salmon being taken from the rock angle. All in all, it was a halcyon period, now come to an end.

The whole concept of salmon fishing was now entirely different. The boats were bigger and powered with engines. The length of nets was much greater and there was a great deal of controversy about monofilm nets, which have now become legal.

52

In 1977 it was being argued that the numbers of salmon were decreasing and in the interests of conservation these was a decision by the Department to reduce the depth of nets from 60 meshes to 30. The length was confined to 800 yards and the cost of a salmon licence increased from £3 to £50. Monofilm nets were outlawed. The opening of the season was postponed to 15th March and ended on the 20th June and fishing was not allowed on Mondays nor, of course, on Saturdays and Sundays. Naturally, these laws gave rise to great upset and dissension, specially from those under the Lismore Board of Conservators.

15 Salmon Fishermen protesting outside Leinster House, Dublin, in 1977, led by Jim Moloney. Fourth from right is Liam Lincoln, the authors eldest son who drowned in 1982.

In March 1979, 50 fishermen from Youghal, Ardmore and Ballycotton took part in a picket outside Leinster House, but the minister, Brian Lenihan stood firm. The same year, an application was taken to the High Court, by Jim Moloney and Dick Lenihan to have the law declared invalid, but it ended in failure. In April 1979, the fishermen decided to defy the rules and went fishing in

Ardmore on a Monday. No action was taken by the Gardaí or bailiffs present. The men from Youghal did likewise the following week.

The *Fisherman's Lament* appeared in the *Dungarvan Leader* in June 1979.

I'm just a fisherman, no business, no land;
With my wee boat and nets, the Blackwater I fished.
Sure life was just grand.
I made a nice living, I was always content,
Until Brian struck the blow, and laid us all low
With his bye-laws and ban.

One fish at a time, St. Peter,
Is all I'm asking of you;
Give me the grace not to fly in God's face
For what those blackguards all do
At times, I feel mad, St. Peter
No future for me but the dole,
Oh for God's sake help me today
My mind to control.

Do you remember when you fished here on earth,
St. Peter you know if you're looking below
It's worse now than then;
Four days out of seven
From mid-March to July,
But we know to our cost
What the poor man has lost,
A Sad man am I.

Salmon fishing continued to a very limited extent, the season being from 1st June to 31st July, the salmon license costs £150 and a craft of nets £1500.

In 1998 the Blackwater Salmon Development Group with the Southern Regional Fisheries Board acting as facilitators, entered into discussions with the Ardmore fishermen, regarding a proposed 'set aside' of the fishery, on a voluntary basis with a monetary compensation for the fishermen. Salmon fishing was being conducted as usual, in 1998 and 1999.

Other Types of Fishing

16 *Fishing for sprats off the Ardmore coast, c1920. L. to r. Sean 'Phaich' O'Brien, Curragh and possibly Jamsie Quain, Ardmore.*

At the end of the last century, two seines were being fished in Ardmore. These were enormous nets which surrounded the mackerel and were pulled in and closed. They were so big that twelve men were necessary for the operation. They were then emptied by cognet into the boat and brought to Youghal, where mackerel were being cured at the time and exported to America. The girls dealing with the fish were from Scotland, so the firm was probably Scottish. This curing station finished in the 1920s, Jimmie Rooney thinks.

Jim Wolsey from Ballycotton was working on a seine; he married Mag and they lived at the bottom of the village, to the north of the Boathouse, an area now part of the roadway. About £100 per crew each week was the pay given to the men. Oars and sails were used in the boats. Jamsey Quain and Seán Fáitch worked on a seine. If the signs were favourable, Jamsey spread a white sail on the wall above the boat cove and this was the signal to the Curragh men to come at once.

Spratts were quite often caught in seines and were brought around the countryside by horse and cart and sold; this was called jolting or rather joulting. People went very long distances with them, often travelling all night. Seán Rua's (Fitzgerald who lived in what is now P. Carltons house in the street) saying has often been quoted. "At the dawning of the day, I fell into Carrick", the word 'fell' being a good description of the last few miles downhill to Carrick-on-'Suir. Apparently when Seán returned from the Carrick expedition the locals gathered into his kitchen to hear the account of his adventures. Incidentally the jennet had to be escorted out of the kitchen to the back garden there being no other means of access at that time.

Jimmie Rooney had an exciting story of the four local men who lost their trammel nets in a storm and proceeded to search for them along the coast. One of the four was Mrs Hackett, and she went instead of her husband who wasn't strong enough to go with the others. They persisted in their search (by foot) away beyond Youghal, even beyond Cork harbour and located them in Kinsale.

They were in touch with the coast guards along the coast and they gave them information to help them in their search and it was with their co-operation that the nets were finally located. Having found them they shouldered the nets and set off for home again on foot as before. When they arrived in Youghal, the men wanted to rest there for the night, but Mrs Hackett insisted on continuing on across the ferry and home so the three men went with her.

Long line fishing was conducted from boats the size of the *Dauntless*, six oars and also sail. They went out rather far to 'grounds' they knew.

The late Tom Veale's father, a teacher in Ardmore owned the *Dauntless* at one stage. It went through numerous hands. My father Martin Hurley owned her at one time, had her repaired in Youghal and Jimmie Rooney and Paddy Neill sailed her home from the quay there. I remember it well as both my sister Eileen and I embarked on it also and sailed around to Ardmore with Jimmy and Paddy. Jimmie gasps at the thought since, as he wasn't proficient at manipulating sails, but we did arrive in Ardmore safe and sound. The poor *Dauntless* didn't go to sea again and after one storm was deposited halfway up Powers' bog.

Herring fishing was carried on in Ardmore too and wasn't supposed to take place between dawn and dusk. The nets were put out at dusk and hauled in at dawn. The coastguards used report any herring nets present during the day. Herrings were 'jolted' too.

An interesting anecdote referring to this practice concerns my mother, sometime in the thirties. It was Pattern time and my mother after her day's work was anxious to do the rounds at St. Declan's Well and brought the late Statia Mansfield with her. Statia was about 16 at the time and was helping her in the house.

It was about 10.30pm on a calm, moonlight night and as they were going up the road, they heard the sound of carts coming towards them. Statia became anxious at this, but my mother said that they'd meet them soon. They didn't and the carts seemed to be coming the other way, and this continued to happen on the return journey too. Statia was getting quite agitated and so was my mother, but she didn't want to pretend this to Statia. A few days later, Mrs Shanahan, an old lady from Monatrea was in and my mother recounted the experience to her. Mrs Shanahan had no difficulty at all in explaining it and couldn't understand why they didn't realise it was the 'old people' (i.e. dead people) coming to do their rounds at the well. Then one day, my mother happened to meet Bridie Troy of the Cliff (she lived where Kings are now) and she asked Bridie if she heard any carts going up and down, the other night. Bridie said yes, there was a haul of herrings and these were being brought up and down to a waiting lorry. The lower or Cliff Road is of course very near the upper one on which Statia and my mother were walking and the sound carried very well on the calm still night, so there was the end of a good ghost story.

Herrings seemed to fade out of the picture for some years, but became lucrative again in the seventies and eighties £14 a box was being paid; this rose to £21 per box and sometimes, as many as 100 boxes of fish per boat were being taken.

Lobsters were being caught, early in the century. Jimmie Rooney remembers the men from Hare Island in West Cork coming fishing lobsters for Fred Keane and seeing them baking bread in pot ovens over some kind of stove in the boat. The only shelter they had was the sails. Just a few months ago some people in Hare Island telephoned me looking for information on their forebears of the beginning days of the last century who came so far to fish lobsters and lived in such primitive conditions.

Lobsters are still being fished in Ardmore. In the thirties my father used buy them, keep them in a large lobster box moored off the pier and then have them packed in sawdust in fish boxes in the boat cove and sent off to Billingsgate. 8/- a dozen was the price paid to the men. As much as five dozen lobster were often taken from the pots.

17 Little boy fishing for shrimp with a net along the Ardmore coastline, c 1920.

The winkles (periwinkles) were also being harvested over the years and my father used bring them in his lorry to Youghal Railway station and send them to Billingsgate. At first (probably in the late twenties) he used a pony and cart to go to Monatrea and even to Knockadoon. Later on, he used a lorry, 6p a gallon was the price paid; now its £26 a cwt. One may still see some winkle pickers operating on the rocks.

The fishing industry has drastically declined in Ardmore in recent years. There are still some fishing boats owned by Tony Gallagher, Hugh Reilly, John Keevers and the Revins brothers have two or three. They use bottom nets for plaice, sole or pollock and there is some shrimp fishing with anchored shrimp pots.

Certainly times have changed in all facets of the fishing industry in Ardmore, an industry where possibilities had been noted and taken advantage of, by the Earl of Cork as far back as 1616.

The Regatta

The Regatta in the thirties was a big event in Ardmore and usually held on a Sunday afternoon in mid-August depending on tides. Jim Quain, Tom Walsh, and Thomas Foley were the most important in the organising committee, and the Dwyers principally Frank Dwyer took charge of and paid for the fireworks that night.

Johnny McGrath (New Line) had the important job of firing the starting gun; but anybody who remembers the Regatta remembers above all, William Mockler announcing the events in a loud clear measured voice over the megaphone, delivery that could well be emulated by many present-day announcers. His son Paddy was secretary of the Regatta for a few years and remembers people queueing up outside his door to enter for various races.

There was always keen rivalry in the four oared salmon boat race. Crews came from Youghal, Monatrea, Clashmore, and Aglish for this. Jimmie Rooney remembers Buttimer's boat from Youghal being disqualified because it was a pleasure boat; he also remembers that the Clashmore and Aglish crews used boats owned by Rooney's, Jack Barron, Tom Kehoe and two Cotter brothers, he thinks were crew of the Clashmore boat. Jimmie Rooney himself is remembered as being an oarsman of outstanding calibre.

There was also a sailing race. This started and finished at the pier and consisted of a triangular course with one buoy over near the Black Rock and one buoy near the Head. The sails were mostly home-made, Ned Foley and Pat Troy being adept at this. It was in one of those sailing races that the incident recorded in the *Cork Chronicle* took place. Pollock's boat, the *Infanta*, got into difficulties. Tom Walsh, Jim Quain and Jack Byrne were in the other boat and Jack Byrne rescued Jimmie Troy, and the hapless crew was taken aboard. Pollock's boat, the *Infanta* sank and was retrieved some weeks later.

Incidentally, Pollock's two boats, the *Nancy* and the *Infanta* were stored for the winter in the garage besides Tigaluinn (now converted into a dwelling house) and their preparation for launching was of major importance every year. It began months earlier, when Patsy Sullivan came to paint them and began his work by cleaning all the crevices with a small quill. When the paint was applied, one daren't produce a ball on the road outside, or indulge in any activity remotely likely to produce a speck of dust. When launching day came, there was no shortage of helpers, as each on got 5/-, no mean amount in those days.

But I digress. In the regatta competition, an item eagerly looked forward to, was the grease pole competition (described by Mrs Dowson and L. O'Connor). Jack Brien, Main Street was the acknowledged champion here. Larry O'Connor and Georgie Martin provided great entertainment on one occasion distinguishing themselves at a hard-fought pillow fight, sitting astride a pole suspended between two boats, and fighting each other with straw filled 'pillows'.

We youngsters were very interested in the swimming races. Michael Hurley (now S.J.) was a winner on one occasion and we cheered ourselves hoarse in the cove, as the 'Corkies' (the Cork visitors) were invariably winners in all those races, and we always figured in the 'also-ran', or rather 'also-swam'.

The duck hunt we enjoyed; a bunch of us were let loose in the water from a boat between the pier and the cove at the same time as a duck was released, but no matter how near one got, the duck always outwitted its pursuers.

Crowds of spectators lined the pier and the cliff to observe the races and there was a great air of excitement and festivity culminating in the fireworks display at night. Our vantage-point was generally down at the Straoilleán, and from there we watched Catherine Wheels etc., taking brief and colourful shape in the night sky. Tom Walsh remembers the wherewithal for this magic, being bought by Frank Dwyer for £12 which later increased to £14. He also remembers one of the fireworks burning a hole in James Dwyer's Harris Tweed sports jacket. We weren't aware of calamities like this and look back nostalgically to what seemed always sun-filled, glorious Regatta days, a kaleidoscope of bunting and boats and gulls and swimmers and just people.

Cliffs And Birds of Ardmore

Below is a list of cliff names extending from Whiting Bay (Beál Abha) eastwards towards Ardmore. They were given to me some years ago by the late Larry O'Connor, who usually spent all the summer months in his bungalow above Goat Island.

> Beál Abha,
>
> Na Spicí,
>
> Carrig a' Lady
>
> Góilín an Ghoire (lard had been washed in from a boat),
>
> Góilín an tSagairt (a priest used bathe there),

Gaill an Eidhnéain (a derrick for taking up seaweed was near this Góilín an Eidhnéain, at the far end of the Goat Island cove),

An Chlais,

Faill an Tóirpín (sea monster i.e. unusual fish),

Carraig an tSasanaigh,

Carraig an Phortáin,

Croch an Oidhre,

Faill an Phréacháin,

Faill na gCaorach,

Faill an Iarainn (steel boat wrecked),

Faill an tSasanaigh,

The Mealbhógs (promontory)

Faill na Bó,

Poll Gaoithe,

Falla Bán,

Coisceím ,

Faill an Mhadra,

Faill Ghlas,

Faill Fhada (down to the second Mealbhóg),

Faillín Dearg,

An Leach Reídh,

Glean Phiarais or (Fíor Uisce),

An Goilín Dearg,

Faill na gCat,

Faill na Rón,

na Gaírdíní.

Máire the Whipa used go down the Goilín Dearg to collect seaweed and bring it up on her back. There is a very narrow path, beginning at the outer or seaside of the goilín - this leads inwards for some distance before turning down towards sea level. She performed this scary chore as usual one day, went home and had a baby and came back to the Goilín Dearg again the next day. This is a perfectly true and well-known episode. She lived in a one-roomed house above Mansfields at the top of the Village Street; the house has long since ceased to exist. Máire died in the mid-twenties.

Below is a list of rocks and cliffs given by Eddy Mansfield of Ardmore, who had a long association with them, from his boyhood. The list begins at St. Declan's Stone.

Goilín na Mairt (a cleft in the rocks), north of St. Declan's Stone. Goilín (pronounced guy-leen, means a small rocky inlet)

Goilín na Muca Mara (another cleft in the rocks), to the east of this.

Goilín Mór, to the left-hand side of the present slip of the Boat Cove.

Carraig an Chabha, a rock on right-hand side of cove, blown up by the council, a few years ago.

Carraigín Áine, extending from end of the slip.

An Caladh: the pier.

The Umar, beyond the pier.

Goilín na mBioránach: spratts.

Faill na Daraí: oak.

Bun an Teampaill: below St. Declan's Well.

An Chlais.

Goilín na Rinne.

Pointe Mhaicreíl.

Poll a' Duine (Doimhne): a very deep pool at the Head.

Carraig Jim Jom: sunken rock.

Faill na Slinneacha, also called Faill na Sleannaire.

An Charraig Liath.

Poll a' Ghliogair: both near the Sampson wreck.

Teach a' Pharliment: cave.

An Lic Neáin: Lic Lónaín.

Ceann an Rámaire: Rams Head.

An Cúlam Beag.

An Cúlam Mór: in front of the castle.

Faill na Rónta.

An Poll Buí.

An Droichidín: beyond Fr. O'Donnell's Well.

Leac an Tae: Tea Flag.

Faill Atoíneacháis, at the side of the Tea Flag.

An Faiche Mór.

Faill na Bó.

Faill na gCat.

Ram Head is celebrated in the following verses:

Tá an Rámaire ag bagairt is faobhar ina ghlór
Is an Charraig Liath á fhreagairt lena bhéal ró-mhór
Ó faire fút a mháirnéalaigh I mbéal an chuain
Is bailigh leat chun calaidh isteach, is fan sa chlúid.

Ram Head is threatening with an edge on his voice.
The Carraig Liath is answering with his too big mouth.
O watch out, O sailor, at the mouth of the bay
And return to the harbour and stay in the shelter.

The following is a list of birds seen around the Cliffs, from Cliff House to beyond the Tea Flag, on Sunday 3rd May 1987 on an outing with the Dungarvan Branch of Bird-Watching Society: Herring Gull, Kittiwake, Fulmar, Peregrine, Kestrel, Chough, Rook, Jackdaw, Dunnock, Meadow Pipit, Stone Chat, Cormorant, Shag, Skylark, House Martin, Swallow, Gannet, Rock Dove, Razor Bill, Sandwich Tern, Raven, Great Black-Backed Gull, Robin.

Ardmore Sea Anglers Club

In the 1991 issue of *The Ardmore Journal*, there are two articles on the Ardmore Sea Anglers Club. One is by Peter Greene, Sea Angling Officer of the Central Fisheries Board; the other is based on records in the *Dungarvan Leader* with the assistance of Rose Coughlan and Mary Moloney. Both accounts are most interesting.

In 1981, the club celebrated its 21st anniversary and is still going strong. John Cronin and Gerard Mansfield are two members who have achieved international fame. Do consult The Ardmore Journal, available in the library in Dungarvan, if you are not fortunate enough to own a copy.

The present members of the Ardmore Sea Anglers Club are:-

Life President: John Keevers
Hon. Chairman: John Cronin
Hon. Secretary: Mary Moloney
Hon. Treasurer: Gerard Mansfield
Ass. Hon. Treasurer: John Cronin

The village and environs are well signposted, indicating the various angling areas and the types of fish generally available in them.

The Boat House

The Boat House, Ardmore, formerly the Ardmore Life-Boat Station was built in 1878, replacing a former Life-Boat House of 1857. It is a typical, 19th century Life-Boat House, the narrow side windows and small buttresses giving it a typical ecclesiastical appearance.... With the casement type windows and back door open, a through draught was available for drying oilskins and gear.... An oil-lamp was hung on a post outside the door to indicate the lifeboat was at sea and help guide it safely home.

18 The Boat House was built in 1878 and was formerly the Ardmore Life-Boat Station, photo taken in 2021.

It was a very quiet station and the only services recorded were to the Brigantine *Diana* in December 1860 and to the barque *Sextus* in January 1865.

Seven of the crew of the *Diana* were saved and awards were made to the crew later. Rev. Mr. Wale, Roman Catholic clergyman was also presented with the thanks of the institution for the important and valuable services he had rendered on that occasion.

The *Sextus* of Malta was totally wrecked at Curragh on 29th January 1865. Ten of the crew were rescued. Formal thanks inscribed on vellum were conveyed to Dr Crawford Poole, Hon. Secretary of the Ardmore Life-Boat Station and to Mr Thomas Coveney, chief officer of the Coastguards; and £3/10/0 to seven other men in 'acknowledgement of their prompt and laudable conduct in wading into the surf and otherwise assisting to rescue' the ten who were saved.

According to *The Life-boat* of the 1st August 1895, the committee of Management at a meeting on Thursday, 14th February 1895, decided that the Ardmore Life-boat Station be closed.... The coast is sufficiently guarded by the neighbouring boats of Youghal and Ballycotton.... The boat-house was handed over to the receiver of the Odell estate, Mr John Arnott of Villierstown.

The foregoing excerpts were taken from the very interesting article *The Ardmore Life-boat Station* by James Quain in *The Ardmore Journal* of 1990.

It was evidently bought by the Sandemans of Rock House.

The following account is taken from an account by the late Jack Crowley whose father had been principal teacher in Ardmore National School until 1929.

"The Boat House was owned by Lady Sandeman of Rock House. She was the wife of Sir Robert Sandeman, then the British governor of Quetta in N.W. India. I well remember two boats in it. The *Dauntless* a large whale-boat, the other was a salmon boat of very wide beam. The *Dauntless* fished for herrings in autumn and early winter and was skippered by Jim Wolsey, a native of Ballycotton who had settled in Ardmore (his wife had charge of the church in the early part of the century). Other members were Maurice Flynn (who lived next door to the Church) and William (Andy) Fitzgerald. Lots of nets were hanging in the building.

On Pattern Sunday, which was then one of the big days in West Waterford, it was customary to hold a concert in the Boat House and needless to say it was a boisterous and noisy affair. I remember being taken to one, by a cousin about 1910. It went on for hours due to disturbance and interruptions and one could not hear a bit of the performance. Neither could we get out as the place was packed tight.

About 1910, a flower show became an annual event and for some years, it was held in the Boat House. On the second occasion it was held, Lady Sandeman had erected a tea-room built of corrugated iron and about 20ft by 20ft, at the rear of the Boat House. When the flower show was changed to St. Declan's Hall, this tea-room was either purchased by the Church or donated to the school nearby. I remember how a big number of local men was mustered by the then curate, Fr. O'Shea. They carried the shed on long spars or planks to the gable of the Girls school."

The Boat House was bought by Martin Hurley when the Sandeman property was sold in the '30s. He used it to store coal and also his lorry. The Quain family bought it in the '70s from Eileen Hurley (now Colbert) and Mrs Quain re-organised it as a dwelling house and lives there now.

The Coastguard Service

The Coastguard Service, as such, dates from January 1822. Much of the information which follows has been obtained for me by Mrs Eileen Weston from the Parliamentary Papers relating to Sir James Dombrain at Kew Archives.

What happened in 1822 was that a number of earlier anti-smuggling agencies were reformed and renamed as the Coastguard. These earlier agencies were:

(a) The Preventive Waterguard (formed in England in 1809, apparently as a sea going force though functioning as a land-based force). The Preventive Waterguard had spread to Ireland and Scotland c 1819, commanded by Sir James Dombrain.

(b) The Riding Officers, (renamed the Mounted Guard, recruited from the Police and Cavalry regiments.)

(c) The Revenue Cruisers.

70

The Coastguard ranks were

1. Boatman.
2. Commissioned Boatman.
3. Chief Boatman.
4. Chief Boatman-in-charge.
5. Chief Officer.

In 1856, the Royal Navy took over control of the Coastguard Service. During the Crimean War 1854/56, large numbers of Coastguards had been called into the Royal Navy, but presumably their places (as Coastguards) were kept open for them.

Smuggling was carried on extensively around the Irish coast, tobacco being the principal commodity involved. Sir James Dombrain in giving evidence to a Select Committee on Tobacco Trade in June 1844, says "smuggling was of tobacco principally and by means of large armed cutters and luggers. A great number of vessels were from America, but principally from Holland and from Flushing". The coastguard has always had many duties, originally largely against smugglers, but gradually, rescue and other functions became important.

For family history purposes, the Coastguard Force is unique in that the families lived with the men in either Martello Towers or coastguard cottages. They were never recruited from the district in which they served in order to reduce undue fraternisation with the community whom they effectively policed.

The first Ardmore Coastguard Station was established in 1836, and there was a Whiting Bay detachment from Ardmore. It is interesting to note that a Grand Jury map of 1818 shows a 'telegraph station' on the cliffs near Ram Head, but no coastguard station existed at this time.

There are houses still occupied at the Goilin in Whiting Bay, which are still referred to as the coastguard station. These began as 'Whitingbay Watchroom'. An official account from the National Archives, Bishop St., Dublin provides the following description: 'Room in a boatman's house, occupied as a watch-room. Held at will from William Jackson, Boatman at an annual rent of £1 from 10th October 1844, the room used exclusively as a watch-room, B.O. 15th October 1844. No. 470'

There are a few pathetic headstones at the western gable of Ardmore Cathedral, which bear witness to the presence of coastguards in Whiting Bay.

Eliza Tiddy, wife of William Tiddy,
Who departed this life, May 3rd, 1847,
Aged 37.
Also to their daughter, Henrietta,
Aged 9 months.

To the memory of Jenny Wills,
Wife of Sampson Wills,
Coastguard Whitingbay,
Who departed this life May 14, 1838,
in childbirth.
Aged 25 years and 5 months.

Erected by Samuel Pile,
Chief Boatman of Coastguards,
To the memory of his daughter,
Elizabeth B. Pile.
Died March 17th 1849,
Aged 18 months,
Also to Ellen T. Pile,

Died May 22nd 1849,
Aged 16 years.
And his infant son, born and died
on 22nd November 1849.

Erected by Lt. Hungerford R.N.
and the Waterguards
in memory of the crew of the sloop,
Lord Collingwood of Penzance.
Lost in Whiting Bay,
December 15th, 1820.

What poignant memories of people who were far from home, in a strange land, surrounded as they would have been, at that time by people who spoke a different language and were of a different faith.

Judging by the dates of the inscriptions, especially that of Jenny Wills, coastguards were in residence in Whiting Bay before the 15th October 1844 arrangement, already quoted.

The first Ardmore Coastguard station was at Ardmore strand on land now washed away by the sea. An official account from the National Archives, Bishops Street, read as follows:

'Description of Premises: Two rooms as a watch-room over a watch tower.

Terms under which held: Held at will from James Terry at an annual rent of £4.12.4 payable quarterly at the period established by the customs - Terry to keep the rooms in repair.

Not Underlet: not insured; no rates paid; not inhabited.

General observations: B.O. 12th May 1836 No. 26
Rent to be paid to Mr. Edward Odell, Terry's lease having expired.

B.O.. 9th February 1853 No. 24.
W.R.H. Roberts appointed Mr Odell's agent.

Later on evidently, there were Coastguard cottages. In his account of the discovery of the crannóg at Ardmore in 1879, Mr R. J. Ussher writes:

'Between the road and the escarpment stood a large school-house and on the landward side of the road was a range of Coastguard houses. Within my memory, the sea has devoured the land here so rapidly that first the schoolhouse, then the road and then the Coastguard cottages have been successively washed away.'

According to the *Griffith Valuation* of the 1850s Rock House was occupied by Richard Ussher. At some period later than this, it is said to have been occupied by Coastguard families.

19 Coastguard Station, Ardmore.

The contract for the fine building which became the next coastguard station on the cliff above St. Declan's Well, was given

74

to W. B. Purser, Hermitage, Dungarvan for the sum of £1938.16.4, the work to be completed on the 1st of July 1869. (Incidentally, W.B. Purser was father of the well-known Irish artist, Sarah Purser.) It was completed and handed over in 1870 (National Archives, Bishops St., Dublin).

From then on, the Coastguard Station and its occupants were an accepted part of the life of the village. They took part in coast watching and lifesaving and were involved in the episode of the *Teaser* ship-wreck; also the well-known story of following the phantom ship to sea.

The Coastguard Station people seemed to be on good terms with the local population. Kathleen O'Brien remembers herself and her elder sister, Rita going to children's parties at Bates (Officer in Charge.) She also remembers Jackie Reynolds, a Coastguard's son who was in her brother, Jimmies' class at school. Catherine Lyons says her grand-mother, Mary Brien (born 19020) talked also of children's parties at the Coastguard Station.

During "The Troubles" in the early 1920s, the personnel at the coastguard station were augmented by twenty five marines. They landed at the pier having come directly from England and practically all their provisions were brought to them by sea. Jimmie Rooney remembers the bags of coal having handles.

Kathleen remembers the marines coming in to the house (a pub); some of them used go upstairs and play the piano and sing; one of them had a stringed instrument. Mr Smalley, Peter Merrit, Lofty Quinn, Captain Thornton are names she remembers. One of them used bring her up to Blackwoods and buy her sweets. Johnny Hallahan ran this shop for Blackwoods of Youghal, so it was generally referred to as Johnny Blackwoods.

The Marines can't have occupied the station too long; there was no armed confrontation at any rate. It was empty when, to prevent the 'Staters' taking possession, the 'Irregulars' took over and 'set fire to it'. Ciss Quain remembers the oil (or petrol) being carried up in buckets.

According to an article on 'The Rocket' by James Quain in the *Ardmore Journal* of 1992. With the establishment of the Irish Free State in 1922, the British Coastguard Service ceased. "Tom Casement, sea-faring brother of Sir Roger, the executed patriot, tried in vain to form a new Irish Coastguard. His efforts did however result in the setting up of the Coast Life-Saving Service. About fifty coast life-saving stations were initially set up around the Irish coast. Ardmore Head was number 23; to the east lay number 22, Helvick Head, and to the west number 24, Youghal."

In 1980, the name was changed from Coast Life-Saving Service to Coast and Cliff Rescue Service with Jimmy O'Mahony as Area Officer.

A few of the Coastguards from the pre 1922 period put down roots in Ardmore. Jim Eddy had joined the navy from Cornwall, in the days of sail. He married in Ardmore and lived in Coffee Lane in a house on the site of Jimmie O'Connors. He had a long beard and seemed to be always gardening. He had two sons and one daughter. One of his sons Jack took part in a memorable escape from Spike Island in 1921.

Eugene Redmond was son of a Coastguard who went to school in Ardmore, as did so many other children of Coastguards. He entered the Irish Civil Service, became secretary of Department of Finance, and had his profile and signature on the Irish pound note. He was a constant visitor to Ardmore all his life and his daughter Maura still pays an annual visit. My sister Eileen Colbert remembers a former Coastguard (Mr. Griffin) coming to stay in Melrose - probably in the 1970s and Pierie Foley's mother coming to meet him. He was very touched by her visit.

Irish Marine Emergency Service

The Coastguard Service has been greatly modernised in every way. Its name has been changed from 'Coast Life-Saving Service' to 'Coast Cliff and Rescue Service' and is now the 'Irish Marine Emergency Service'. At present they have their own motorised wagon with arc lights and generator. There are two sets of uniforms, one for working in and one for ceremonial occasions. Each member has a pager, which is activated in case of emergency - as happened on Sunday 10th October 1999, when a rock-climbing accident happened at Ardmore Head. A Waterford based helicopter is on call. Cliff climbing is part of the training, and the first-aid certificates have to be renewed every year. Gun training is still done at Goat Island, but it is not at all as exciting as it was in our youthful days, when the horse-drawn rocket cart with all the paraphernalia used, set out from Ardmore Coastguard station to Goat Island.

At Goat Island, the men stood in a double row, as Mr Morgan (who was instructor or superintendent, I forget his exact title) quizzed them on their forthcoming duties and other duties in the case of an emergency. The questions were always delivered in a staccato like manner. Some of the answers were remembered with amusement, as for instance when Paddy Fitzgerald was asked what light should be displayed in certain circumstances, poor Paddy faltered and in his embarrassment delivered the prompt from the back row, "a black light sir". Then Padraic Smith was asked what was the first thing he would do on seeing a body on the shore and Padraic answered, "go through his pockets sir".

Eventually, the order came, "Action, Stations" and all rushed to their various posts.

The lighting of the rocket fuse was the next dramatic action and we watched as the rope spun through the air towards the island. Having arrived safely there, it was attached securely to the pole and somebody went into the breeches buoy and was hauled across to the mainland, where the next phase involved the administration of artificial respiration. Goat Island was an admirable situation for this practise, as the island was envisaged as the ship in distress, and there were always a few volunteers for the trip across in the breeches buoy. Rocket practise days at Goat Island was one of the red letter days of the summer, but time marches on.

The current members of the I.M.E.S. are:

Mike Power, Paddy Foley (Deputy Area Officer), Tony Gallagher, Jimmie Mahoney (Area Officer), Michael Mulcahy, John Whelan, William Mulcahy, Cyril Cody, Biddy Power (only lady member), Glynn Moloney, Billy Mahoney and Dennis McGrath.

The name has now been changed again to *Irish Coastguards Ardmore Unit.*

Shipwrecks

Down through the years, many a good ship met her doom along the coastline from Ardmore. The following list of 19th century ship wrecks in the neighbourhood is taken from a volume entitled, *Shipwrecks of the Irish Coast 1105-1993* by Edward J. Bourke.

> 1823 *Hope* (a Youghal ship)
> 1850 *Grace* (of Newcastle)
> 1860 *Echo*

Peig Thrampton (year unknown)
1865 *Certes* (of Malta)
1865 *Sextus* (of Malta)
1875 *Scotland*
1881 *Elizabeth* (of Whitehaven) in Whiting Bay
1895 *Jeune Austerlitz* of Cardiff
1998 *Dunvegan*

According to the *Ardmore Journal* 1988, seventeen ships were lost off Ardmore 1914-1918, fourteen of them in 1917. In most of these cases, the attack occurred ten miles or more out at sea and the survivors were picked up and brought elsewhere, so the incidents passed unnoticed in Ardmore. The *Folia* and the *Bandon*, however, were quite close inshore when torpedoed.

The wreck of the *Teaser* on Curragh strand in March 1911 has been well documented. This abbreviated account is based on an article by Donal Walsh in *Decies*, September 1982. The *Teaser* was bound for Killorglin, Co. Kerry with a cargo of coal and left Milford Haven on 16th March. She had a crew of three and all three were lost.

A very strong south-easterly gale had blown up and the boat was blown on to the rocks at Curragh. John O'Brien sighted her at 5a.m. on 18th March, got as close as possible and saw three men on board but could not communicate with them on account of the noise of the storm. He reported to the Ardmore Coastguards and a message was sent by telegraph to the Helvick Life-boat. Three coastguards, Thomas Bate, Richard Barry and Alexander Neal arrived in the meantime with the rocket apparatus. All three men on board the boat had taken to the rigging. Five rockets were fired; some missed but the men on board failed to operate the others which did reach the boat. Coastguards Barry and Neal tried to swim to the ship along the rocket line, but failed in the attempt.

Fr. O'Shea C.C. Ardmore then came into the story. At his instigation a boat was brought from Ardmore by horse and cart and he called for volunteers to go out to the *Teaser*. Coastguardsmen Barry and Neal, Constable Lawton, William Harris of The Hotel, Patrick Power and Con O'Brien, farmers and John O'Brien fisherman answered the call and were able to get alongside the *Teaser* by hauling themselves along the rocket line and rowing at the same time. Wm. Harris, Constable Lawton and the two coastguards boarded her. The men on board were still alive but only barely. Unfortunately, one of them was dropped into the sea while being taking down, but Barry and Neal dived in and rescued him. Fr. O'Shea administered the last rites. None of the three members of the crew survived. The bodies were laid out in Michael Harty's barn and according to an account by Johnny Larkin, Curragh, two were buried in Ardmore and the Captain's body brought home to Wales.

20 Ardmore Lifeboat crew and volunteers who rescued 24 of the crew of the Marechal de Noailles.

The incident got great publicity and on 13th April 1911, the Committee of Management of the R.N.L.I. meeting in London, awarded the Gold Medal of the Institution to Fr. O'Shea and appropriate awards to all the other participants. The Carnegie Hero Fund Trust awarded all of them as well, and then on 2nd May 1911, Fr. O'Shea and his party were decorated by King George at Buckingham Palace.

21 The Marechal De Noailles ashore at Mine Head, January 1913.

On 12th December 1912, the *Marechal de Noailles* of Nantes left Glasgow for New Caledonia, a French Penal Island in the South Pacific. She carried a cargo of coal, coke, limestone and railway materials. There was a crew of twenty besides the Captain and First and Second Mates. The beginning of the voyage was eventful with seven days being spent at Greenock waiting for an improvement in the weather; a further seventeen days off Aran Island, Scotland; then venturing down the Irish Sea, but about sixty-five miles north of Tuskar having to retrace the voyage, this time to Belfast Lough. At last, they really got going and were a few miles from Ballycotton, when the wind strengthened. They turned about; the captain fired distress signals; eventually the ship was blown ashore three hundred yards west of Mine Head.

Helvick Lifeboat responded to the distress signals but could not approach her. The keeper of Mine Head lighthouse, Mr Murphy telephoned the Ardmore Coastguards, and the rocket crew assembled. Coastguards Barry and Neal, J. O'Brien, J. Mansfield, J. McGrath, P. Foley, J. O'Grady, M. Curran, J. Quain, P. Troy, M. Flynn, Con Byron, Sergeant Flaherty, Constable Walsh and Fr. O'Shea. As the roads were too bad for the rocket wagon to travel, the crew carried the apparatus fourteen miles on foot to the wreck and arrived about 2am. The apparatus was assembled; the first rocket passed over the vessel, but the crew did not know how to deal with it.

Meanwhile, one sailor had been washed overboard and J. Quain encountered him at the bottom of the cliff and explained the workings of the rocket apparatus, by sign language. With the aid of a megaphone, he instructed the rest of the crew still on the ship how to work the Breeches Buoy, and all the men came ashore.

Four had been injured during the night by flying spars and were unconscious and anointed by Fr. O'Shea. All were eventually taken to Dungarvan. Some months later, Fr. O'Shea had a most appreciative letter from Captain Huet Morlaix.

No doubt, it was an unforgettable experience for the Ardmore men, tramping for hours in the dead of night with their apparatus which looked as if it wasn't going to have the desired effect; then the joyful break-through the language barrier and being surrounded by a group of men "quacking like ducks" as one of them put it. So it is not surprising that the name *Marechal de*

Noailles is remembered years afterwards in Ardmore. (The most of this account is taken from the article by Donal Walsh in *Decies*, September 1982.)

Rescued Crew of the Marechal de Noailles Wrecked at Mine Head

Morgan Youghal

22 The crew members of the Marechal De Noailles being brought to Dungarvan in a cart following their rescue, January 1913.

Interesting, disturbing facts which emerge from the story of the *Teaser* and *Marechal de Noailles* are that the crews were ignorant of the life-saving equipment and how to use it; and also that people in general were ignorant of the principles of life-saving and resuscitation. A bystander at Curragh said that at least one of *Teaser's* crew was still alive while being brought ashore but clearly nobody knew how to deal with the situation.

The third ship to be wrecked here this past century was the *Nellie Fleming* from Youghal which went aground on Curragh strand in December 1913, having mistaken their location in the mist. The Ardmore coastguards and Youghal and Helvick Lifeboats were in attendance, but the crew hoped to get her off. Finally, when the water gained on the boat, the crew abandoned ship and returned to Youghal by the lifeboat. Next morning, the owner came and concluded that the boat was going to be a total wreck and handed her over to Lloyd's Agent, Mr Farrell of Youghal.

A group of locals bought the cargo of coal from him and formed a coal company to resell the coal. Jack Crowley with three other lads recalls being sent by his father, the local school master to bring home ¼ ton coal for the school, by donkey and cart. They weren't upset being at the end of the queue which comprised farmers from Grange and Old Parish coming for the cheap coal. He referred jokingly afterwards to the "Curragh Coal Co-op" as being the first Co-op in Co. Waterford. (This account is condensed from an article by James Quain in the *Ardmore Journal*.)

The *Folia* (6704 gross tonnage) was sunk off Ram Head in March 1917. Seven of the crew were killed in the explosion; the others took to the lifeboats and eventually made their way to Ardmore and reached it as last Mass had finished, so there was a large crowd around. The R.I.C. took a rollcall outside the Hotel on Main Street. Many people provided food and clothing and arrangements were made to transport them to Dungarvan, where they were taken that evening in a fleet of cars.

In the *Ardmore Journal* 1988, James Quain in his account of the incident includes an interesting letter from a member of Dr Foley's household, Glendysert. "All the people took some of the crew to each house. We had five, three English, one American (the doctor) and one Dane. Some were without boots, all without socks, some without coats and so on. After looking after creature comforts (they were of course without food since the night before, with the exception of the biscuits, with which each boat is provisioned) they were anxious for music, so we put on the gramophone for them. I believe they danced and sang up at the convent. Sr. Aloysius played for them."

The letter-writer also says of the attack on the boat, "When they had taken to the boats, the captain of the submarine who was very courteous, came up to them and told them they were all right and to row into Ardmore, 4½ miles away."

The article by James Quain goes on to say, 'Some months passed before the salvage began to float in. Wooden barrels of oil were picked up by the Receiver of Wrecks and later sold. Sides of ham, loose or in boxes, 1 cubic yard in size came into Ardmore and elsewhere along the coast. Large slabs of tallow about 3 feet by 2 inches thick floated ashore in boxes or single slabs. These were seized by the locals and used for making candles as paraffin oil for lamps was very scarce.'

As the *Folia* is such a large vessel, 430ft in length and is located only four miles off Ram Head, it has been dived on many times, although it lies in about 120ft of water. According to Lloyds, the ship was carrying a general cargo, but a large number of brass items have been recovered.

The following month on 12th April 1917, the *Bandon* sailed from Liverpool for Cork under the command of Captain R.F. Kelly. On the evening of Friday 13th, when the ship was off Mine Head, she was struck by a torpedo on the port side and immediately began to sink, with a loss of twenty-eight lives. The four survivors including the captain were in the water for over two hours. Following a message from Mine Head lighthouse, they were rescued by motor launch and taken to Dungarvan. The explosion was heard clearly on shore, and when the smoke had cleared away, the Bandon had disappeared.

The late Johnny Larkin of Curragh wrote his own account.

'On the 13th of April 1917, she was sunk two and half miles south of Mine Head and about four miles from the Curragh shore. I saw her go down in less than half a minute. She was sunk by a submarine, according to the British, but I think the crew did not know what sank her. She went so quick some said she was sunk by a mine, or two mines tied to a chain.'

The S.S. *Ary* is the next ship that has to be mentioned in this section on shipwrecks. The spring of 1947 will long be remembered in Ardmore for its severity. Snow rarely falls here, but that year, the place was absolutely snowed in, with men having to go out and dig trenches in order to let the bread van in to the village. It was during this period that the S.S. *Ary*, a ship of 500 tons displacement left Port Talbot, with a cargo of coal for the Railway Company at Waterford. The captain was an Estonian, Capt. Edward Kolk and the fourteen other crew members were of various nationalities. The weather worsened and the cargo of coal began to shift and in spite of all efforts, the list got worse, and the crew had to abandon ship somewhere off the Tuskar Rock. They had no oars, no food or drink in the two lifeboats.

When Jan Dorucki, the sole survivor woke from sleep he found himself surrounded by dead men, who had all died from exposure and being frightened, he pushed them all overboard. For two days more, the lifeboat drifted on and eventually came ashore on the Old Parish Cliffs. Jan was in a dreadful condition, but somehow he managed to climb the cliff and dragged himself to Hourigans' farm-yard, where the dog found him at dawn. He was brought in and wrapped in a blanket and eventually brought to Dungarvan Hospital. A point to remember is that people did not have telephones or motorcars at this period.

Cait Cunningham who was on duty at the hospital when he arrived gave a heart-rending account of it to Kevin Gallagher who has had it published in his column in the *Dungarvan Observer*. He remained in a critical condition for days and eventually had to have both his legs amputated. During his stay the language barrier proved a great obstacle, but Nurse Cunningham says, a Polish officer arrived from England and so did Jan's father; and a Polish phrase book and dictionary they brought were a wonderful help. He returned to Poland after twelve months.

Meanwhile, the bodies of Jan's companions were being washed in along the coast from Ardmore to Knockadoon. Willie Whelan of Ballyquin found a body on the beach; he brought it to Ardmore, where it was identified as being that of a Spaniard and was buried in Ardmore graveyard. During the course of that weekend, the other eleven bodies were brought to Ardmore. According to the inquest, they all died of exposure. I remember seeing the coffins stacked up outside the Fire Station. Later on, they were buried in one grave in a corner of the graveyard. The funerals began at 2p.m. and each coffin was brought up in turn in the hearse provided by Kiely's of Dungarvan. Rev Fr. O'Byrne P.P. and Rev. Warren, Rector of St. Paul's said the graveside prayers.

Fifty years later on November 1st, 1997, Canon O'Connor of Ardmore and Rev Desmond Warren (nephew of the Rector of fifty years before) presided at prayers at a newly refurbished grave and headstone erected by the people of Ardmore. Donald Lindenburn, whose father George was in the S.S. *Ary* came from Swansea; he had his father's naval record book. He had seen war duty on the Atlantic and the Pacific, so it was tragic and ironic that he should perish on the short trip across the Channel to Ireland. He placed a family wreath on the grave and so did Jim Spooner from the British Merchant Navy. The service concluded with the lone piper's lament by Mr Michael McCarthy.

Later on in the afternoon, John and Billy Revins took the Welsh visitors out on Ardmore Bay, where another wreath was set afloat to the memory of the fourteen members of the *Ary* crew. These last paragraphs have all been condensed from Kevin Gallagher's account in the *Dungarvan Observer*.

The *Fée des Ondes* a French boat was wrecked in Ardmore in October 1963. It was blown in to Carraig a Phúintín and all efforts of Youghal Lifeboat to get her off failed. It was with difficulty, the skipper was persuaded to leave, even though the boat had been holed by the rock and began to take in water.

The *Cork Examiner* of October 28th, 1963, says 'Two Frenchmen were rescued by life-boat, and seven crew, one of fifteen years old on his first voyage, by rubber raft in a sea drama, off the beach at Ardmore, Co. Waterford yesterday morning. They were the crew of the 300-ton trawler *Fée des Ondes* out of Lorient, which went aground in poor visibility just before dawn and which was subsequently severely damaged by rocks and pounding waves.'

Youghal lifeboat had been launched and life-saving rocket man, Jim Quain, was alerted, raised the alarm and fired the maroon which brought out the full crew. The crew came ashore by rubber dinghy but the Captain P. Maletta and his mate E. Dantec refused to abandon ship for a considerable time. They were all taken to the village and Mrs Quain provided hot food and clothing. An abiding memory of hers, is, besides the salt water seeping down the stairs, was the incident of the crew sitting around her dining room table where a cask of Beaujolais from the vessel containing about twelve bottles or so was ensconced. They asked her for glasses and imbibed the lot without as much as asking her would she like a glass, never mind a bottle. Lloyds later offered to recompense them for their hospitality, but they declined to accept.

The boat being accessible at low water, it was visited by all and sundry during the following days. The jocose poem by Dan Gallagher gives a pretty good but perhaps exaggerated account of what happened.

If you want the position of 'Receiver of Wreck'
All you require is a bit of neck.
A hacksaw, a crowbar a pony and cart
A low spring tide and you're ready to start.
But, hold on a minute, do you know where to go?
To the strand at Ardmore, when the tide is low.
'Tis there you will find her, a fine boat was she,
'Ere being driven ashore by the wind and the sea.
The sailors and looters worked there, side by side
With one eye on the wreck and one eye on the tide.
They came day and night, they came by the score
From Piltown and Youghal, Old Parish, Clashmore.

They came armed with crowbars, with hammers and saws
With tractors and trailers, flouting all civil laws.
Now the early prospectors got the best of the spoil
they got nets by the dozen and ropes by the mile,
Whiskey, gin, rum and brandy and lovely French wine,
They spent the night drinking and all felt sublime.

Some bottles without labels, distilled water contained
But they like the others, to the bottom were drained.
There were bottles of lotion for salt water rash.
One man drank a bottle and wiped his moustache.
There were oil coats and trousers and boots there to snatch
With pillows and mattresses and blankets to match.

Sure the night shift itself was a sight to behold

With torches on deck and down in the hold.
Some more daring than others, climbed up on the mast
Cutting off rope and pulleys that were firmly made fast.
But the ladder on the foremast was the envy of all
('Tis still lying there, for the mast down did fall).

Both the mast and the ladder would be useful, you see,
To rig up the aerial when we get the T.V.
The farmers were there, day in and day out.
Looting pulleys and chains; they'd be useful no doubt.
The women were there, looking after their men,
With flasks of hot soup, and tea now and then.
And when they were ready and home did retire
They had bags full of wood and corks for the fire.
For in lighting the fire, the black corks they say
Put up a fine blaze in a marvellous way.
There was an odd little bit of jealousy too
When the others got better than me or than you.

A wreck-laden horse-cart, one day on the strand.
Had the French Flag trailing on the sand.
If De Gaulle had seen it degraded that way,
A declaration of war would be here any day.
The poor men with bags didn't get much at all,
With their lack of equipment and payload so small.

To compete with the others he hadn't a chance,
With their tractors and trailers, they led him a dance.
Some need not fear winter, though storm winds may blow
And the ground be covered with frost and with snow,
For the wood piles all mounting round many a home
Not to talk of scrap iron for dealers who roam.

There'll be many bright fires, between you and me
While the family sit round them watching T.V.
Yes, she was a fine boat when she entered the bay
But she's now like the turkey on St. Stephen's Day.
And now that she's gone, to the Lord we must pray
To send us another, without too much delay.

In the late 80s two further tragedies occurred. At the end of a storm in January 1984, the *Anne Sophie* from Lorient landed under the Cliff near Mine Head. Ballycotton lifeboat stood by and the eight crewmen were lifted off by an R.A.F. helicopter, working in gusts of 90mph at night, under the cliff face.

The Maltese-owned 180-foot crane barge *Sampson* was driven ashore at Ram Head, during a south-easterly gale on 12th December 1987, while being towed from Liverpool to Malta. The tow parted and could not be connected, owing to the gale. The crew of two were rescued by an R.A.F. helicopter from Brawdy. The tug *Zam Tug 2* arrived from Cork the next day and remained on stand-by for several hours, before giving up the idea of re-floating the crane ship.

There were initial fears that diesel oil from the badly holed vessel would have polluted the neighbouring beaches, but such a disaster was averted by the prevailing winds. Jim Rooney (formerly of Strand Bar) got to the crane by using a rope and in order to claim salvage, stayed on board in horrendous conditions for forty days. Food and changes of clothing were lowered to him regularly during the period. The incident occasioned great publicity: Jim gave several newspaper interviews and was much photographed, but it is highly doubtful if he benefited at all from salvage money.

A large propeller from the *Sampson* was mounted outside the Commodore Hotel in Cobh in 1991. We still have the wreck at Ram Head.

Phantom Boats

In the *Ardmore Journal* of 1991, James Quain has a very interesting article on 'Phantoms of the Sea'. He tells first of the phantom boat seen by his grand-father Jamesy Quain about 1900. It was winter and he was tilling land out the cliffs when he saw what seemed like a ship's lifeboat out to sea with about a dozen men rowing and another steering and he saw them change seats a few times. He called one of the Coastguards and they both went back to the cliff. The boat was drawing near and almost below them; the crew looked cold, wet, and hungry but strangely did not respond when the two onlookers waved and called. Suddenly, to their amazement, the boat altered course and set out to sea again. It seemed unbelievable, that an exhausted crew could head out from sheltered waters into the open sea.

Jamesy and the Coastguard hurried to the pier and got a crew together, including Pat Troy and Maurice Flynn. They got the sail up and soon began to catch up on the boat heading towards Mine Head. They got within almost 200 yards of it but could not get any nearer; they shouted but got no response. Maurice Flynn said "Turn back, Quain, or we'll all be lost. We're following dead men", so they reluctantly did so. The coastguard telephoned Mine Head lighthouse and alerted the rescue services along the coast, but the boat was never seen again.

Jimmie Rooney had the story both from Maurice and Jamesy. They said they were only just off the corner of the head on the return journey, when a sea broke on top of Seán Spán, "a big wave that would drown a liner, Seán Spán is a sunken rock off Ardmore

Head, where a Spanish ship was wrecked one time. We often got nets caught there at low spring tide." Some days later, they heard a large vessel had been lost out at sea, about a week previously.

Jimmie Rooney, Paddy Downey, Mikey Lynch and Jack Farrissey all give graphic accounts of the phantom boat seen in February 1936. Jimmie and his crew were putting out nets at the Head on a Sunday night when "we saw this vessel bearing down on us from the south-east and thought it was the bailiffs launch coming out from Youghal" and they began pulling in the nets. We waited at Goílín na Rínne but there was no sign of the ship coming round the Head, so after a while, we began to put out the nets again and put Paddy Flynn ashore and we rowed round the Head" but none of us saw anything.

23 23 Brothers John, Thomas, and Patrick Moylan worked as fishermen and lived in this thatched cottage at Caliso Bay, Ardmore, c1945.

Other fishermen had similar experience that same night. Paddy Downey with Tom Harty and Johnnie Brian from Curragh were out at Faill na Daraí putting out the nets, when they saw what they too thought was the *Muirchú*. Mikey Lynch and Jack Farrissey were at the Clais under the well, putting out the nets also that Sunday night, when they saw the big boat coming from the Head towards them. They too thought it was the *Muirchú* and hastily made for the pier, where they met Paddy Downey soaked to the skin, 'with his new blue suit destroyed by the salt water'.

Within a week, a big storm came and the *Nellie Fleming* was lost.

Willie Roche from Monatrea tells of the phantom ship that came into Caliso Bay during the Great War. It was near the old Moylan family home down near the beach and came so close that those watching on shore thought she'd go aground. They could see the naval men in uniform going about the deck. The ship came along by Cabin Point and at Carthy's Cove disappeared off out. A few days later, the news came that Mike Moylan on HMS *Carturian* was dead. He is buried in Ardmore graveyard just outside the cathedral at the S.E. corner.

Another maritime ghost story concerns Martin Troys' grandfather from Curragh, Seán Treo. A neighbour, John Corbett's grandfather who was digging potatoes at about 10am one morning, saw Seán Treo passing and saluted him, but he got no reply from him and reported this at home. It transpires that Seán Treo was dead when his neighbour met him. He had drowned at sea while sailing home from Youghal. This was in 1886

The Power of The Sea

The sea shows its immense power from time to time. There has been much coastal erosion in the area with two schools, a coastguard station and two roads being swept away. Incidentally as a result of erosion the Ardmore Crannóg made a brief appearance in 1879, long enough to have it measured and documented by R. Ussher. The building of the storm wall early in

94

the 20th century with various additions at different times since curtailed the erosion.

In Whiting Bay, havoc has been wrought with two houses Jameson and Byrons being swept away in mid-century and also a road and a bridge.

In 1997 a large aperture was made by the sea under the promenade in Ardmore, and this extended under part of the road but the sea wall remained intact on top, the sign of this depredation can clearly be seen still.

Over the years Jimmie Rooney has noticed certain indications of bad weather. Seeing seals under the storm wall or fairly near the shore is a sign of bad weather; the sea 'walloping' against the old parish cliffs is another bad sign as distinct from having a pencil line between the sea and cliffs. Occasionally when fishing out towards Ardmore Head the sound of the Angelus Bell ringing in Old Parish was audible and that too was a bad sign. "Whiting Bay roaring and bawling" was another indication of stormy weather as were the sounds from Carraig Aodha i.e. the rock between Curragh and Ballyquin strands.

Jimmie foretells the time when the sea will again regain its former course and sweep over to Whiting Bay making Ardmore an Island once again as it was in the time of Declan. I think however, both Jimmie and I will be at rest beside the Round Tower long before then and I end with the words of an old Ardmore boat song.

By the side of a hill quite close to the shore
There stands a neat village by the name of Ardmore.
It's the burial place of St Declan whose fame is well-known.
He flourished in Ardmore a long time ago.

So row away hearty boys, row to the shore

And we'll all drink a health in the town of Ardmore.

In Ardmore graveyard there is a High Tower
And the ancients who built it they built it quite round,
With four lofts to ascend and a window to look out
Upon the broad ocean and the land all around.

So row away hearty boys, row to the shore
And we'll all drink a health in the town of Ardmore.

Life and Work

My Teaching Days

In June 1939, I finished my course in Teacher Training in Carysfort (Blackrock, Dublin). In July, the late Mrs Waide asked me to do duty for her for three weeks in her one-teacher school in Tinnock, high above the mouth of the Blackwater, so I cycled there every day and quite enjoyed the experience. I can't have looked too impressive (at the age of 20) as one day when the parish priest paid a visit he asked me where was the teacher!

24 The author with some of her pupils just before retirement in 1984.

At that period, it was difficult to get permanent and pensionable teaching appointments. In September, I was appointed supernumerary teacher at Presentation Convent, Youghal. This was a well-known teaching category at that time. It meant one was under the same rules and regulations and inspections as anybody else, but the appointment was not pensionable (the Irish National Teachers Organisation sorted out that general problem later) and as long as one remained in that position, one received the basic salary from the school authorities, not from the Department of Education, so I got my cheque for £11.4.0 every month.

While in Youghal, I was in charge of over fifty small boys in Senior Infants from 10a.m. to 2p.m. But my day began at 9.20a.m. when I went up each morning to take the Intermediate students for Geography and on Wednesday evenings took three Leaving Certificate pupils also for Geography from 2-3.30p.m. On the other four evenings I had 4th and 6th classes for Needlework.

I lodged in town from Monday to Friday, but in the summer I preferred to cycle in and out every day, frequently using the ferry-boat which operated every half-hour and one paid 2d for oneself and 2d for the bike. If one arrived late at the ferry point and the boat was already on the move, Moss Geary the ferry man always turned back to pick one up.

Then in January 1943, I was appointed to the one-teacher school at Ballycurrane and was there for over two and a half years, cycling to and from each day in all kinds of weather, a journey of roughly one hour.

Incidentally, I don't think there can be anyone else in Ardmore who has cycled as much as I have, between regular trips to Youghal, up and down to Ballycurrane as well as cycling holidays in Donegal, Sligo, Achill, Connemara, down to the ends of Kerry from Dublin and various other trips I cannot now recall.

In winter, the first duty in Ballycurrane was to light the fire; the girls and boys were accustomed to bringing in bundles of sticks which would have been drying beside it since the previous day. There were two deep hobs at either side and the children placed their bottles of milk there to heat them. Need I say they ate bread and butter; the age of crisps had not yet arrived. There were 16 boys and girls. Sanitary conditions were of course the same as at all national schools of the period i.e. a dry closet in a building apart from the school. Ballycurrane School is now a far different place; it is a newly built two teacher school with all mod cons.

For two and a half years, I officiated happily in the old establishment. That was until my retirement before my pending marriage. A rule had been introduced, I think in the 30s, which compelled all female teachers to retire on marriage. So when I left Ballycurrane in 1945, I certainly never expected to stand in front of a class again. There was no Women's Lib. Movement then and we just accepted these things meekly.

Then in 1958, the marriage ban was lifted. A vacancy arose in Clashmore School (i.e the old school near the church), and I applied and was appointed. One of the conditions was officiating at the choir. I forget now how often it was necessary to go to Clashmore for this. By this time we had acquired a family car, so I was driving not cycling.

Three weeks after my appointment in Clashmore after my thirteen years absence from teaching, my husband died suddenly beside me in bed one night. That need, I say, altered life considerably for me.

It was strange going back to school after such a long absence, but I soon got used to it. Michael Moroney from Dungarvan was the principal in Clashmore. There were two rooms and the usual conditions, with the fire having to be lighted every morning in the winter. The playground was above the church, that is apart from the school, and I remember vividly the school porch being full of children's sandals in summer, as they threw them off at lunch time, in order to feel free at play.

A few years later, in 1964 a vacancy occurred in Ardmore and there I remained for twenty years until I had reached retirement age in 1984. One of the happy memories I have is the summer of 1981 when the parents rallied around and did a splendid job in painting and decorating the interior of the school during the holidays. I was of course, in the thick of the chaos which lasted all summer. The colour scheme was by Mary my daughter-in-law and was regarded as a trifle unconventional. However, a visiting kindergarten inspector later remarked that it was the only school she knew where the colour scheme seemed to be devised for the children themselves.

In 1983, the Year of the Tree was celebrated appropriately when an elevated waste part of the school grounds was planted with trees, each parent bringing a tree, and extra ones were also presented. It was a festive occasion with the then minister for Agriculture, Austin Deasy (whose family had strong Ardmore connections) partaking and everyone having a buffet tea later in the school.

When I retired in June of 1984, I was absolutely overwhelmed by the farewell party in the local hall and particularly by the extraordinarily generous presentation given to me of a ticket to Hong Kong. It is a wonderful memory.

Tigaluinn

25 Tigaluinn Hotel c1925 (Courtesy Horgan family)

Tigaluinn was my home from the late 1920s until my marriage in 1945 and again from 1955 to 1965 when I sold it. My sister Eileen was born there in January 1921 and later on my brothers Michael and James (I was born in my aunt's house, Mrs Quain of the Cliff, before my parents finally settled down in Ardmore).

When we acquired the house, it was two storeys with a flat roof and breast-high wall all round. My parents proceeded to make that a third storey. Paddy Troy of Grange and Charlie Power of Old Parish worked on it. My father went for bricks to Youghal brickyard with a pony and cart. I do remember seeing through the school windows, buckets of cement being raised by pulley.

This was the period of the Irish courses, when there was a considerable number of visitors staying at Coláiste Deuglán and several other houses in the village. We had 30 teachers staying for the four weeks of August every year. They paid £10 each i.e. £2.10.0 per week and the £300 was immediately brought to the bank, to help alleviate the debt incurred in building.

I have vivid recollections of every-day life in Tigaluinn during that period. The standards of accommodation would appear horrendous to present day visitors, but I feel absolutely sure, our standards were very high, knowing my mother had very high personal standards. In any case she had had experience of hotel work in Tuam, in Vaughan's Hotel, Dublin and Kelly's of Rosslare, where she spent several happy years and had a close personal friendship with the family, which lasted through the years (as a matter of fact, we contributed some photographs to their centenary celebrations in 1995. I want to mention this just to show what high standards of which my mother was accustomed.

The bedroom accommodation meant, that there were two people per double bed and two double beds in a room. There would have been correspondence with the incoming guests and they knew precisely what the conditions were. Each room had a washstand with basin and ewer of water, towels, chamber pots and slop buckets. These slop buckets had to be carried down daily and emptied down the drain my father had installed at the back of the house and which made its way down along the backs of the houses in the row, towards the sea (this same scheme is still in operation). Candles in candlesticks gave light and these had to be cleaned every day as well, so all in all the daily cleaning of the bedrooms was no sinecure.

The toilet facilities consisted of a dry lavatory out in the back yard, its wooden seat scrubbed daily, and chloride of lime used in the aperture itself. For this purpose, there was a bucket of sand and a shovel kept in the lavatory also. The toilet paper consisted of neat squares of old newspapers replenished each day and there was no such thing as ladies' and gents' apartments. All lined up for the use of the one premises which looked quite attractive with the rambler roses growing around it.

In the dining-room, there were four tables, which I remember well, having been laying the tables there from the age of four onwards (i.e. placing the cups, saucers and plates in the appropriate places). There were two square tables seating six people each, a long one seating ten people and a round one seating eight people.

My father was always up first, even though the rest of his day was more often spent in other pursuits away from the house. He lighted the fire in the kitchen range and put on the kettles and the big double cooker for the porridge. The menu for breakfast was porridge and bacon and egg, the men being allotted three rashers and the ladies two. This was varied some days with liver or sausage. The next meal was at 12am, when all returned for lunch, a sit-down meal of tea with bread, butter and jam. Dinner was at 3pm, a four-course meal of soup, joint, sweet and tea. Tea followed at 7pm, tea, bread butter and jam again with fruitcake (huge slabs all wrapped up in 'silver paper' and bought in town). The jam was bought in big earthenware pots, which later were used for containing dripping, a good deal of which my mother dispensed to various people after the season.

Cleaning the knives in the big circular machine, which held 3 knives at a time, was a familiar chore in pre-stainless steel days, as was the transformation of pounds of creamery butter into small, dainty butter pats. A side of bacon was bought at a time and my father was really matchless in cutting this up into rashers; no present-day machine could equal his ability. If ever he happened to arrive home at dinnertime, he was always given the job of carving. The carving knife was kept very much apart and dare anyone lay a finger on it.

The teachers attending the courses did enjoy themselves. One of my memories is of singsongs at our piano and passers-by congregating outside on the road to listen in.

The photograph of Tigaluinn (Fig. 46.) was taken in the 30s, at a time when conditions were not quite so Spartan as in the initial days of the Irish courses, in so far as the bedroom accommodation was more generous, but there was no running water until 1937. In spite of that, we had several satisfied guests who returned on holidays year after year. Cliff House and Melrose tended to over-shadow the Tigaluinn picture but my mother's very high standards (observe the maid in black dress, starched apron and cap) overcame many of our drawbacks. Running water had come in 1937 and the dry lavatory in the yard was converted, and there was water in the kitchen taps.

The great leap forward was in 1938, when the new extension was put on and wash basins were installed in all bedrooms (i.e. 7) on the first floor, plus a bathroom and toilet with a toilet also downstairs.

Guests continued to come. I remember among several others Dom Wenoc Mertens Benedictine monk, and cousin of the Little Flower, Saint Thérèse of Lisieux; the Looby family (Mr. Looby was co-founder of Roches Stores), Seámus Dalton, first translator in the Dáil; the O'Connell family, one of whom became the wife of Benedict Kiely, the well-known novelist; the Clarkes of stained-glass fame, Dr. O'Flaherty and Madame Servais of the French Faculty in U.C.C.; Nano Reid, well-known painter from Dublin, and many others.

My mother was an excellent manager and we all had our assignments, but in the evening before departing to football field, céilí at the college or whatever, the Rosary had to be said. I remember well one evening, when my brother James had us all rounded up ready to begin and my mother asked him to drop in to Fr. O'Neill in the sitting-room with a jacket on which she had replaced a missing button. The door between was open and we could hear Fr. O'Neill inviting James to listen to a tune he was lilting, and we could hear James' agonised rejoinder, "Yes Father, yes Father, I'm in a bit of a hurry now Father." We were giggling to ourselves, as we understood James' discomfiture perfectly. He was on tenterhooks in case we all scattered again.

My mother's health was failing and my sister stayed at home to help and eventually moved to Melrose in 1955.

26 Cormac Murphy O'Connor now Archbishop of Westminster with his elder brother Jim outside Tigaluinn in the 1930s.

Attached is a photograph of Jim and Cormac Murphy-O'Connor eldest and youngest of the five sons of Dr. and Mrs Murphy-

O'Connor from Reading who spent each August in Ardmore in the bungalow now owned by Mr Billy Murphy. They were always in and out to us in Tigaluinn. Cormac used play 'Hot-Cross Buns' with one finger on our piano and when my mother asked him one day what he'd like to be when he grew up he answered a "Poke" i.e. Pope. He was later Bishop of Arundel and Brighton and has now been chosen to succeed the late Cardinal Basil Hume in the See of West Minster.

Conway's Farmhouse

One day when I was about 12 or 13 years old, I was in Ballinamertina, a place generally outside the compass of our ramblings. I looked across the valley to the north, less than a mile away and saw this fairy-tale like thatched house with farm buildings around. It stood at the entrance to a glen with the hills opening out behind. I looked and looked for quite a few minutes and wondered who were the owners of this seemingly magical place. And then I realised, it was Conways (now Flavins) Clerkstown, a house with which I was familiar since early childhood. My father had spent some years there with his aunt as a child, and we were closely associated with it and with our cousins there, all through the years. Alas, a modern two-storey house has now replaced it and the farm buildings are the modern conventional ones.

I have vivid memories of the big kitchen with an enormous fireplace and fire machine. Huge pots of feeding for animals were boiled here, being slung on a crane, swinging in and out over the fire. Baking was done in an oven in the wall at the side and of course, bastable bread was baked in a covered pot with live coals or pieces of turf on top. People still smack their lips at the memory of the wonderful bread which emerged from these pots. Over the fireplace, the black puddings were smoked. My brother James as a toddler, first seeing these, asked, "What were all those small tyres doing?"

The long table by the window looked out on the yard. A door below it gave access to a large porch off the yard and in this was a variety of buckets and pots and strictly utilitarian articles. That was the entrance we children always used.

Two dressers with big willow pattern dishes occupied another wall. At the bottom of one, was a chicken coop, on the fourth side was the settle bed and the staircase.

It was an L shaped house and at the right-hand side of the fireplace, were shallow steps leading to the dining room. Up above the porch framed by the steps, was an attic bedroom. The dining room was strictly utilitarian. I remember a large table and sideboard and gramophone with horn, and it was here, the maiden aunt, Mary Anne (my Godmother) presided and gave us our tea. We never penetrated the room above that.

At the opposite side of the kitchen, was a door giving access to a small hall and the front door. There were deers' antlers for hanging coats and there was also a small bedroom with very special furniture, which I'm afraid I can't describe. A door led into the parlour, a very formal room with a grand piano and formal furniture. The only other place we saw a similar piano was in Kinsale Museum.

From this hallway, the front door opened on to a formal shrubbery with sundial and there were steps leading down to a garden with blackcurrant and gooseberry bushes.

The large porch on the other side of the kitchen (previously referred to) led on to the farmyards, which sloped down to the river. The haggard was on a higher level than the farmyard and two long flights of steps led from one of the barns down to the yard below. As far as we were concerned, the haggard was the fun place. Where we climbed to the top of the hay in the big shed and played various other games. At haymaking time, we trudged cheerfully up to the high fields, in order to get a spin down the hill on one of the hay floats.

We paddled up along the river too. I seem to remember very faintly, some talk of a family death being preceded by the voices in the river coming down from Cor Uisce Finn. All the other voices are stilled now too, as we face the stern, utilitarian 21st century.

Curragh

Curragh had once a teeming population in the small houses clustered together at the northern side of Ardmore Bay. Access to Ardmore was down the boreen to Bun an Bháile and across the strand. Perhaps, at one stage, the boreen went further, say to Ardmore itself. It is quite likely that this boreen extended right across what is now Ardmore Strand and perhaps met up with the present Coffee Lane here at the Straoilleán. Certainly, the boreen did extend on the north side of Curragh across to Ballyquin.

Some years ago, my sister Eileen from looking out the kitchen window in Tigaluinn on Sundays, was always able to calculate how much time there was still to spare before Mass, by observing the moving lines of Curragh people on the strand. If the lines had trickled down to a short one on the Ardmore side, it was time to get up and go. Nobody walks across the strand to Mass now; people come around the road in their cars.

Below is an account of some of the families in Curragh, at the beginning of the century.

On the left-hand side coming up the boreen from Bun an Bháile was Hannah Monsell, a very pious, always good-humoured woman, in spite of the fact, that her shelter at one time was reduced to a covered car bed, with I think, some corrugated iron overhead. Next came Fletchers and Monsells, one of them called the Cailín as he had long black curly hair down to his shoulders. The Cudahys, on the opposite side of the road lived in a two-roomed thatched home like so many in Lower Curragh. Mary was a tall, rosy-cheeked, slightly stooped person always dressed as so many others in black, but Mary's black was impeccably black from head to foot. Her mother was a Lincoln woman from Grange and Mary remembered such family traditions as the Lincolns coming originally from Waterford and being friends of the Searlógs (Sherlocks) of Butlerstown Castle. How many other snippets of family tradition did she bring to the grave with her? The house is now a two-storeyed one, the property of the owner of Chez Hans Restaurant in Cashel.

Other names that I know of were Deugy Connery, Tomnín Harty and his sister; Miles Harty; Peaidín Siobhaínín (Kiely) and his family, Han Kiely, Johnny and Miky. Han lived in a thatched house which now belongs to Dermot O'Leary, leader of the 'The Bards' ballad group. Winter and summer Han traversed Ardmore strand daily to go to Mass.

Deugy Power was another well-known person as was Jack the Crathur (Creature?) who had a pig and piebald pony in the kitchen, and who was always saying his rosary made of twine with knots of twine for beads, Jimmie Rooney distinctly remembers him praying out loud in church using his home-made rosary beads.

The Lynches, who now have two fine houses in the area are of the old stock, as are the O'Briens also strongly based in the district.

There were Hurtins too and Keanes at the Cross, Patsy Power and Deugy Power.

Curragh, in the early days of the century had a Pipers Band. There was a second band in Ardmore bands - the Fife and Drum Band – and the rivalry between the two was intense. According to Jimmie Rooney, a bandmaster of the British Army taught the Ardmore Band. Their band-room was in the house farthest to the east in Chapel Row, the property of the Burkes. Nick Rooney, Jimmie's father, was in it and Jack Burke, father of John Burke, Cardiff, was the drummer. Other venues were used also.

These bands used play at Land League meetings, being brought to the venue by wagonette. When they marched in the street, evidently a popular tune was 'The Peeler and the Goat', in order to annoy the R.I.C. Ivy Lodge (on the western corner of Main Street and Coffee Lane) was originally the R.I.C. barracks. The barracks later moved to a site on the opposite side of the main street, next door to the present White Horses Restaurant.

According to an account in the 'Times Past' column of the *Irish Times* of July 9th, 1943, there were some 37 houses in the village at Curragh, though by that stage about a third were already derelict. According to this account:

'Fine specimens of early nineteenth-century carved dressers and settles, rich with classical decoration, are mouldering in outhouses in the Ardmore district of Co. Waterford.

This was one of the discoveries by three architectural students of U.C.D., who have just come back from a survey of cottages in this district, working on the same lines as the group at Lusk, whose survey was reported in the *Irish Times* on Tuesday. They selected as a base for survey, the village of Curragh, near Ardmore, a decayed fishing village.

"The outstanding characteristic of these houses, they found to be the quantity of handsome kitchen furniture, most of it made in the early 19th century. The typical dresser of the district has carved pillars at the side crowned with cornices and has decorated panelling on the lower portion. The pillars are usually painted white while the rest of the dresser is brown. The settles are similarly ornamented and there is also a peculiar type of canopied bed, called the 'covered car' found in many of the cottages."

Within recent years, many families have moved to new houses built with the help of Government grants, and in some cases, despising the furniture of the old home, they have left it behind and used the old cottage as on outhouse.'

There are many new houses now across the bay. Deug Donovan of Curragh said on one occasion "The end of the world must be coming when the gentry are coming to Curragh". Well, for some years past, gentry alias visitors have been delighted to buy sites and build houses there, in incomparable positions, facing Ardmore and its bay.

Health Services

Dr. Poole, dispensary doctor lived in the house now known as Carraighdhoun at the end of the Rocky Road. It was occupied by successive doctors, until its sale by the Board of Health in 1963 (it has since been the property of the Cashman family, the late John Cashman having been principal teacher in Ardmore and Grange). The Ordnance map of 1841 shows a dispensary at Monea Lodge.

The new Health Centre was built in 1954 at the same end of the Rocky Road and excellent nursing and medical services are centred there. The former dispensary had been in the village street, in the eastern portion of the house now occupied by the Misses Alice and Kathy Flynn next to the village hall. Earlier in the century, two sisters, Mrs. Dawson and Mrs Sealy lived in the house now known as Byron Lodge and run as a guesthouse by Mrs Byron Casey. Mrs Dawson was an excellent gardener; Mrs Sealy had a room in the house, set aside as a dispensary and ministered there to callers with sores, bruises or other ailments.

The Nursing Association was founded by Lady Clodagh Anson when she returned to live in Ardmore in the late thirties. It did wonderful work in the dispensary district of Ardmore, various functions and collections being held by an industrious committee, to help finance it. These functions were generally held in the school, both the boys' and girls' schools being taken over, for preparation of tea and sandwiches. John Mansfield was in charge of the huge Tigaluinn primus stove, out in the shed. It made a noise like a tractor and John highly enjoyed the curiosity occasioned by the noise, and pumped it up more and more, to impress the callers. Dancing took place in the boys' school, with Lady Clodagh sitting in state at the top, resplendent in her magnificent diamond and pearl necklace.

The district nurse lived in a rented house in the village and cycled to her patients every day, often working in extremely difficult conditions, in bachelor households without water or light. The last two district nurses settled down in the parish, the late Mrs. Angela Keane of Duffcarrick and Mrs Catherine Veale of Youghal Road. They were the last of a line of dedicated unsung ladies, who went about their work quietly and unobtrusively and the people of the parish are deeply indebted to them.

It is difficult to remember how inadequate the health services were, in the early decades of the century. There was great poverty, poor living condition and tuberculosis was endemic in the country, and that meant Ardmore too. Many people were known to be, what is euphemistically termed 'delicate'; that

112

meant suffering from tuberculosis and sadly many of us older ones, knew several adults who died of it.

The late Noel Browne says in his book *Against the Tide*, "there was at the time, no known medical treatment. Hospital cases had to be paid for. Since there was no hope that the out-of-work patient could pay, he would be sent home to die and in the process he would infect one or more of his family." As is universally known when Noel Browne got elected to the Dáil in 1948, he proceeded to change all that, and did effect a revolution in three short years, with a massive hospital building programme; the finance needed was available from the Hospital Sweeps funds, so the elimination of 'TB' was achieved, and the infra-structure for a good health service was established.

Perhaps, there are several discrepancies in today's Health Service, but by and large, we do not realise what a wonderful Health Service *does* exist, available at all levels, to all members of the community.

Making A Living

Bakeries

The Quinn family (no relation of the present Quinns) owned the site of the present post office and had a bakery there. Much later on, Tommie Mooney started a bakery on their site near the strand; there was also a short-lived bakery at Sun Lodge beside Tigaluinn.

Shoe Making

Ned Quinn another member of the Quinn family (who had the bakery) was a shoe-maker and lived just to the west of Paddy Mac's. His long beard is a childhood memory of mine. William Mockler's brother, also a shoe-maker plied his trade in a work-shop opposite the Mockler household, now The Cottage and the property of Mrs Sutton. I remember going there with my father, one day with some shoes to repair.

Butcher

27 Parson's Hill, Ardmore, c1910.

A resident butcher lived to the north of the Boathouse. The site would have protruded on to the present Main St. and is long since gone. The O'Shaughnessy family were the proprietors; we always heard him referred to (presumably the last resident) as Mr. O. Patsy O'Shaughnessy later lived in what we called the Courthouse, the building now owned by the Perks family, and which contained the last Tourist Office and had previously been used as a Courthouse. He had the keys of the old Cathedral in the graveyard. There was another period, when part of his occupation was something in the nature of a sanitary officer i.e. an inspector of drains (á la Percy French). Byrons (now owned by Quinns) had a victualler business later, at the foot of Parsons Hill in the late 30s.

Net Making

Troys of the Cliff (besides being engaged in the actual fishing) made nets for themselves and other fishermen.

Forge

Moloneys had the forge in the village. When they came to Ardmore first from Aglish the forge was opposite the graveyard in part of Ronayne's farmyard, but that was for a short period. The clang of the anvil was one of the familiar village sounds, now heard no more. It ceased in 1951. (See *Ardmore Journal* 1991.)

28 At the forge, Tommy and Jimmy Moloney with Dick Pollock in riding gear.

Nowadays things are quite different. There is a hairdressing establishment in the village. There are two hotels, guesthouses and restaurants in a place, where once it was difficult for a visitor to get a simple cup of tea.

The building boom has extended to Ardmore and there is a plethora of new houses on the New Line, out the Youghal Road and in Whiting Bay, so we have builders, electricians, plasterers, painters and most efficient tradesmen of every genre.

Three very busy joineries turn out excellent furniture. The Pottery on the Cliff is a source of great interest. There one can see the potters at work and also select from a most superior range of crafts from all over Ireland and solely of Irish manufacture.

Working The Land

No aspect of Irish life has shown such a revolutionary change in the century as agriculture. We think of the early days of the century, indeed practically into the forties, as the days of horses and donkeys and carts; of haymaking, mowing machines, threshings.

All this has changed completely. A few years ago, on a school tour, the children were brought into an Art Gallery, and a local farmer's son asked his mother "What are they"? Indicating a field of haycocks.

Hay is certainly grown but what used to be regarded as the idyllic days of haymaking are now gone. Instead, the hay is generally not allowed to go to seed or ripen. For silage, it is blown into trailers taken to the haggard, to the silage pit on a concrete base; the trailer goes up and down to pack it, a plastic sheet is placed over it and old tyres placed on top to press it.

Many of the farmers in this district base their viability on their milk quota. In former days, the milk was brought in churns to the creamery, where it was separated and the skimmed milk then brought home. So the creamery was generally a great social centre.

Since about 1983, the milk quota became important, one's viability depends on it, but one is penalised for exceeding it. Cows of course are no longer milked by hand, but by machine in milk parlours. The bulk tank comes to collect the milk, which used to be brought to Dungarvan, but now goes to Glanbia headquarters in Co. Kilkenny.

Other farmers in our area grow corn, which is threshed and dealt with by combine harvester. Gone are the days of threshings and threshing dances.

There are still other landowners who grow beet and also carrots. These are washed and graded and dealt with scientifically before sending to the big city supermarkets. Indeed, it is precisely in these supermarkets that the farmers' wives buy their potatoes and vegetables. So the wheel has turned full circle.

Farming In The Decies Within Drum In Ardmore Parish

I am indebted to Mr T. Gartland of Dysert for the section which follows.

Agriculture is the chief industry in this parish. There have been many changes in the farming scene since the beginning of this century. The number of people employed has dropped considerably. In the earlier years when emigration had taken its toll the remainder of the population took up employment on the farms. Hand labour was used entirely in the case of livestock and also in the work in the fields. Horses supplied the power for carting and tilling the land.

All cows were milked by hand. The milking machine did not make its appearance until the second half of the century and then only gradually in the fifties and sixties. Home-made butter was to be had in many farmhouses. Cream separators were not used in many cases as the fresh milk was put in large milk pans and the cream skimmed off after a day or two. At this time dash churns were used; the end over end barrel churn was not used until a later date.

Cattle were driven on the road to the monthly fair ten or fifteen miles to Youghal or Dungarvan and sold on the fair green or on the side of the street. Cattle marts replaced fairs in the 1950s and cattle were transported by lorry or trailers.

The crops generally grown were potatoes, and vegetables - cabbage and smaller quantities of carrots etc. The potatoes were planted in ridges or beds and drills.

Root crops grown were swede turnips and mangolds - mainly for livestock. All thinning and weeding of root crops were done by hand.

The sugar beet crop was grown from the thirties and was pulled and 'crowned' by hand labour. The mechanical beet harvester arrived in the late fifties.

All this has changed with the use of single beet seed - no thinning; weeding reduced to a minimum by using chemical sprays, lifting is done by mechanical harvesters; and tractor and trailer to draw the beet to a loading site.

With the arrival of sugar beet the use of chemical fertilisers increased. In the early part of the century and up to the end of World War II, Farm Yard Manure was the fertiliser used except near the seashore when seaweed and sea sand was used.

The cereals grown were malting barley, oats and a small acreage of wheat. In the early part of the century the corn was reaped by scythes and mowing machines drawn by horses. Then the sheaves were bound by hand. The reaper and binder was used on the larger farms. Small acreages of corn were threshed by flail on the barn floor and when the straw was required for thatch it was 'slashed' by hand against a stone. The grain was separated from the chaff etc. by using a hand powered winnowing machine.

Threshing machines drawn by steam powered engines were used on the large farms. Oil powered tractors replaced most of the steam engines during the 1940s.

It was during the 1950s that tractors replaced the horses for ploughing and tilling the land. Home produced wheat, oats and barley and potatoes were grown by the farmers under the Compulsory Tillage Order from 1940 to 1948. This order saved the population from starvation as very limited imports were allowed by the Allies. Ration cards were issued to everyone by the government for bread, flour, sugar, tea, etc., and for clothes, shoes and boots. At least no case of death by starvation was reported.

Farming During the War Years

During the war years in the forties the natives in Ardmore village planted potatoes and vegetables in their land in Dysert townland. Most families had plots of one to three acres which they acquired from the landlord in earlier times. There are 237 acres in Dysert and more than thirty people owned land there at the early part of the century.

At present the number of landowners is reduced to less than half of the original. Many dwelling houses are built there. At least fifty percent of the land is under tillage at present. The remainder is under grass. In the earlier years hay was cut by scythes and horse drawn mowers.

The hay was made into cocks by hand and stored in large ricks or cocks near the farmyard for winter-feeding. Hay is baled now and stored in hay barns. Most of the winter-feeding is now grass silage and is not so dependent on weather conditions at cutting time.

1947 was very nearly a disastrous year. There were long periods of wind and heavy rain during late summer and early autumn. Corn crops were lodged and in danger of being a total loss. The government of the day encouraged every bodied man, including soldiers to help to save the harvest. Migrants from the southwest and west of Ireland were drafted in to the tillage areas under a special scheme.

The rural electrification scheme in the early fifties brought many improvements in farming - light and power for milking machines and water pumps and many other uses including electrified wire fences for controlling the livestock.

After World War II farming was nearly in the doldrums. In 1949 the Irish Government got a loan of fifty million dollars under the Marshal Aid Scheme to improve agriculture. For the next forty years grant aid was given to farmers to improve their farms by reclamation and drainage and to encourage the use of ground limestone and fertilisers. The results were amazing. The area of arable land was nearly doubled, and the number of livestock was trebled. Sales of beef and butter did not match output and the country had mountains of beef and butter.

Food On the Table

When we think of farming, we think of the production of food (at least we used to). Certainly, for more than half of the century and into the 50s plenty of food was produced in our village.

I think of the late Tom Moloney, on the corner of the New Line who produced potatoes, lettuce, and various varieties of vegetables which many visitors were delighted to buy from him. It was he who initiated me into the setting of potatoes and for a good many years I grew them as well as lettuce, onions, carrots, peas, strawberries, and raspberries.

Behind Melrose, potatoes and vegetables were grown as well as tomatoes and cucumbers in the glasshouse. My father kept pigs in the outhouse behind Johnny Mulcahy's i.e. near the Boathouse. These were fed mainly on the waste from Melrose. (One wonders what happens to all the edible waste from hotels and restaurants). The late Frank Nugent also had pigs and his aunt, Mrs Kelly had fowl over beyond the former tennis courts at Cliff House Hotel.

The late Mrs Crowley at what was the Post Office kept hens as did Johnny Fitzgerald in the middle of the village. I remember Nanny Rooney who used live in Brisen calling "Tioc, Tioc" to her hens behind the house; Mrs Norry Brien further up the road kept fowl too.

Some people in the earlier part of the century tended to set some corn, slashing the sheaves later across a half-tierce barrel and bringing the grain to the creamery to be ground. There had been a corn mill at Pilltown, another in Glenlicky; my father's family owned a mill and he often worked in it as a youth (that was at Killishal to the west of Dungarvan).

People beside the sea had barrels of salted fish put aside for the winter. The Curragh man who hadn't done so was regarded as a lazy fellow.

Quite a few people produced butter at home. Jimmy Rooney tells of his mother churning two to three pounds of butter in a 'dandy', a small earthenware barrel with a wood lid. I often saw my aunt, Mrs Quain, churning. Flynns of Dysert also produced butter and probably several other people also.

Food just wasn't readily available in shops. In the late 30s I remember being sent out regularly to Keevers of Ballinamona for cream and of course, there was no such thing as milk in bottles or cartons.

Up to fairly recent times anybody having a back garden just didn't think of not tilling it and producing vegetables of some sort. My father had bought the ruins of the old Barracks now the White Horses Restaurant and besides the ordinary vegetables in the garden behind, I remember vegetable marrows and huge pumpkins.

29 Police Barracks in ruins in the 1930s.

Mrs Crowley had two gardens across the road from the old post office, where Perks were formerly and these she and Jerry her son diligently tilled. One of the plots was rented by Lady Clodagh

Anson when she was in Mrs Crowleys house at the top of the village, in the forties and her daughter Miss Clodagh could be seen regularly tilling it.

Johnny Mansfield, Patsy Walsh, and Henry Reilly did likewise. John Cashman was a great gardener too. In the 40s we remember Captain Jameson always up and down to the strand for seaweed for his gardens above Rock House. Tilling the gardens was very, very, important. Now we just pop down to the shop for most of our food.

Every household in the village got a plot in Dysert at the end of the 19th century when the Odell Estate was sold. They were used for grass for cows or perhaps for growing potatoes. These plots whose boundaries were rather tenuous have changed hands over the years. Some have been sold as building sites and others are still used for producing vegetables. We have a vegetable Co-op in Ardmore and some of the owners produce vegetables on a large scale.

Cows, Hens and Chickens

Up to quite recently, we shared our village with numerous flocks of animals and domestic fowl.

Mrs Byron lived in the present residence of the Quinn family at the foot of Tower Hill. She had ducks, who having negotiated the crossing at the tip of the village (not too hazardous up to about thirty years ago) took to the stream, which at that time flowed down the right side of Bóthar na Trínse (it is now covered in) to its junction with the river at Walsh's bog, and from there explored the rest of the stream, behind the village street. The ducks are long since gone, but it was nice to see a flock of geese across the way occasionally, in Powers' field until fairly recently.

Byron's had cows which were milked in the yard opposite the Round Tower. In the summer, Mrs Byron drove round in a special milk car, and measured out the milk to her visitors and other customers. Mrs Crowley (first house on the left out the Youghal Road, a former post office) kept hens. The Crowleys also kept cows and Jerry drove them down and milked them in the garage on Parson's Hill where Miss Mary Power now keeps her car. Gearys were the occupants of Tigaluinn up to the 1920s and they milked cows in the back yard.

Dick Pollock, Maycroft, had a donkey, later a horse and hounds in part of 'The Coachhouse'; and John Keevers had hay and a horse in the house now occupied by Caroline and Ian Sullivan. This was previously used as a garage for Tom Foley's hackney car.

Next down the road was Mrs O'Brien in what is now Dunne's showhouse and she had chickens behind the house. Nanny Rooney, Jimmies' grandmother had chickens behind her house (now Brisen) at the end of the row and I well remember her "tioc, tioc, tioc" as she called them for food. Johnny Fitzgerald in the village (now Carltons) had hens also.

Rooneys had land in Dysert and up the Glen, so Jimmie was constantly up and down, bringing them to be milked in their yard in the village behind the pub. It should be mentioned that all the householders in the village had a plot of land in Dysert (pronounced Dessert)

Quains drove down the cows from the land beyond the coastguard station and they were milked in the cowhouse opposite Cliff Cottage.

Mrs Fred Keane of Star Cottage drove her cows up and down the Cliff also and presumably they were milked in some area now incorporated in the dwelling. Ciss Quain still remembers her conical hat. Incidentally, up to about thirty or forty years ago the women coming into the village always wore shawls, generally but not always black and tasselled. It seems they're coming into high fashion again.

Johnnie Mulcahy who lived between the Boathouse and the church and Mike Troy who lived in Chapel Row, were also constantly on the move driving cows up and down from Dysert to be milked behind their houses. The McCarthys at the end of the village were always doing likewise.

30 Star Cottage, Ardmore being renovated, c1920.

Catherine Fitzgerald (Odell) of Odell Lodge, now Melrose had about four cows in the big field to the east of the Health Centre and she sold milk.

Lady Susan Dobbs of Camphire owned the house on the New Line now known as 'Ringsend'. When she came to Ardmore for her annual holiday, my father Martin Hurley went with his lorry to Villierstown Pier. There the ferry boat, a large flat one, still operated and brought across Lady Dobb's cow, which was then transferred by lorry to Ardmore.

All the bovine traffic I have described seems incredible now, but I remember it very well. One refrains from comment on the condition of the roads in the village after this constant passage of animals. At any rate, we had a frequent 'moo moo' here and a 'quack, quack' there in the Ardmore of not so long ago.

Holidaymakers

Tourism as a facet of Ardmore life, took a long time to grow. In the first place, ordinary people didn't have holidays; it was years and years before the concept of an annual holiday began to materialise. The army officers from Cobh who came for weekends to the Hotel at the end of the century were probably our first tourists. See article *The Hotel*.

In 1988 there was a most interesting article by Clodagh Anson in the *Ardmore Journal*. She speaks of coming to Ardmore on holidays each summer, the excitement as the 'convoy' of horse and donkey-drawn vehicles set off from Ballysaggartmore; and the further excitement when they came in sight of the Round Tower. They rented Ardmore house (now Stella Maris) and enjoyed themselves immensely. She mentions the people with whom they played, the Daniels, the Curreys, the Jamesons, the Musgraves and the Powers who lived in Cliff House. They were of course all of the gentry class. They sometimes went swimming in the Boat Cove and she quoted an article in the *Dungarvan Observer*, which said, "The disgusting British habit of mixed bathing is being carried on in Ardmore, corrupting the morals of the children in the nearby houses". Sir John Keane's family, the Pollocks, and the Dawsons were other gentry families who came and spent the summer in their Ardmore houses, right down throughout the 30s and 40s.

31 Coláiste Deuglán, The Irish College, Ardmore c1930

However, the greatest milestone in the tourism industry in Ardmore was the foundation of Coláiste Deuglán in the early 20s and there was a big influx of teachers doing Irish courses, in the beginning days of the state. They stayed both at the college itself and at numerous houses in the village. This phase abated somewhat towards the 30s, but people still came attending courses and rented houses in the village, so that children could attend Irish classes. It must have been about this time that holidaymakers began to be referred to as 'eolaishers' (coming from the Irish word *eolas*, meaning knowledge). Gradually the idea grew of coming merely on a seaside holiday. Religious orders too began to rent houses and come on summer holidays to Ardmore.

There was a big influx of visitors from Cork. Their precursor was Mrs Barry (née Dwyer) who had based herself on the Cliff in the early days of the century and spent half the year in Ardmore. She was in Rosary Cottage and helped to bring up the family of her brother, Walter. He had married three times. Sr. Colette, the nun who is well known for her work with travelling people belonged to one of those families.

Other Dwyer houses were Ard Carraig, the Anchorage, Star Cottage and Monea Lodge after the departure of the nuns to Stella Maris. Two others were built for them: Four Winds and Green Shutters. Lady Dobbs had a house built on the New Line.

The Murphys (relatives of the Dwyers) built Timber Tops. Other Cork-based families (merchant and professional) all closely associated with the Dwyers were the Maddens, Byrnes, Kearneys and the Murrays all came annually for summer holidays.

The bus service came in the 40s; it was in to the 50s before cars became universal and these factors were a great fillip to the tourist trade. There were a few hotels and guesthouses but it is only quite recently that restaurants have been firmly established.

There are three caravan sites and these bring a big influx of summer visitors. Perks Amusements in the 70s and 80s were very much appreciated by the younger folk, who look forward to their possible re-establishment. Bathing, boating, and angling are of course important.

32 Carved stone panels on the west gable of Ardmore Cathedral depicting events from the psalms.

A major focus of tourist interest is the Round Tower, the old cathedral and Beannachán with special emphasis on what has been described as 'the most extensive collection of architectural sculptures to survive anywhere in Ireland since the 12th century'. This is the array of carvings on the west gable of the ruined cathedral. St. Declan's Well and the old, ruined church on the cliff is another tourist venue and this is on the well-known cliff walk, a wonderful scenic trip (way-marked) which in the space of about an hour, bring one round to the Round Tower at the other end. Even in the middle of winter, one finds walkers on this route every day, and indeed in the middle of winter one finds visitors at the Round Tower complex.

33 The Cliff House Hotel, Ardmore c 1950.

So we really have the basis of a very good tourist trade in Ardmore; sea, sand, superb cliff scenery and interesting historical remains. We have the best of several worlds, and it behoves us to keep a watchful eye on our treasures.

The Tidy Towns Association

The history of the Tidy Towns Association is a long and eventful one and deserves to be recorded. It falls into four distinct phases.

The different climate of the times in the various periods is worth noting.

1963 - 1973

It was through the efforts of the I.C.A. that the Tidy Towns Association was formed in Ardmore. As far back as 1954, they were concerned with the image of the village. At the June guild meeting in 1959, it was decided to ask the Co. Council to retain the services of the council man in the village, instead of taking him off street cleaning services as had happened the previous summer (note far different circumstances of 1999). A few litter bins were also requested. In September the council was written to, as regards the objectionable condition of the Cúlam, (the cliffs on the way to Fr. O'Donnells Well) owing to the system of disposing rubbish there (on the part of the council).

In October 1962, the question of entering for the Tidy Towns competition was discussed. Bord Failte was also contacted and on Tuesday 23rd April 1963, a public meeting took place in St. Declan's Hall, attended by a representative of Bord Failte who showed relevant slides. Fr. Griffin C.C. chaired the meeting and the Tidy Towns Association was founded.

Ciss Quain was vice-chairman, but for most of the first year acted as chairman, as Fr. Griffin was changed from Ardmore, Desmond Connery was secretary, Donal O'Brien was treasurer, Michael Moroney was press representative and Sergeant Quinn was liaison officer. From 1964 to 1973 Frank Nugent became chairman and treasurer, Siobhán Lincoln became secretary and John Cashman became vice-chairman.

It was gratifying to become recipients of a Tidy Towns award in 1964, for the best seaside resort of under 500 in population. C. Quain, Kathleen Keane and B. O'Brien went to Virginia, Co. Cavan to bring home the certificate. The prize itself of £75 would not be paid until plans were drawn up for spending it. The Tidy Towns Association added £50 to it and this was further augmented by the Co. Council.

34 The Boat Slip, Ardmore, c1920.

The plans provided for the improvement of the graveyard area, more public seating, and improvement of the flowerbed on Bóthar na Trinse and it involved on-going negotiations until 1966. The association was also pressing for the improvement of the Boat Cove. The existing wide slip leading down to the beach area, had, at this stage, a large area of rough stones extending towards the cliff to the right and it was 1972 before the association succeeded in having the concrete area extended, so that boats could also be pulled up there.

In 1964, John Walsh, horticultural advisor came and suggested types of trees for the stretch along the river behind the village and these were planted.

The question of the derelict sites at Ardmore was always a bone of contention and in February 1965, the association did suggest to the council that those in the street be used for housing and this was done at a later stage. It was involved very much in the housing problem since 1965 and away into the 70's. There is voluminous correspondence with Charlie Curran, local councillor. For a long period houses would not be built, because of a lack of suitable applicants and also because the council was not aware, it owned a site at Ardmore.

In 1970, a letter from Mr. Hally, Co. Engineer to C. Curran says, "With regard to the Ardmore organisation's assertions that the council has land at Ardmore suitable for housing sites, I shall be grateful if you will be so kind as to indicate where the land is situated." Eventually, after a meeting in Rev. Fr. Power's P.P. house, the county manager, John Cashman, and Siobhán Lincoln brought the manager to the school grounds. From there the extensive site behind the existing row of houses was pointed out to him and Fr. Power undertook to make a stretch in the eastern side of the school grounds available, in order to make an access road. The top terrace was eventually completed in 1976.

From June 1964, an annual dance to raise funds was held during the summer in the local hall. It is interesting to note the fee for the bands; the Royal Aces in 1965 cost £13 and admission fee was 3/. Their fee increased through £20 to £25 in 1965, when the admission fee was 7/6. The Musketeers charged £30 in 1971, admission fee 35p. The Double Unit came in 1973 and on several other occasions. A fact worthy of note is that Mary Hegarty (daughter of the band-owner) the well-known Cork singer came with them usually and sang with the band, when she was but a slip of a girl. She became a well-known singer later.

The climate of the times was completely different and has changed immeasurably since those early days. For instance, in April 1964, the committee was informed that the council had no function in the building of walls. In June 1964, they would not accept responsibility for tubs on the footpaths (donated by Rus Perks). In June 1964, they were written to, asking that the streets be swept three times a week, during the summer months. On 22/9/64, the council was asked to collect and remove rubbish by lorry twice weekly, instead of dumping it over the cliff at the Cúlam.

Achievements 1963 - 1973

- Survival in a climate of indifference and apathy.
- 1964 award
- 1970 award, a special prize of £25 from S.E.R.T.O. for being the most improved area in Co. Waterford, in the Tidy Towns competition.
- Flower plot at Bóthar na Trinse, also at graveyard.
- Approach slip at the boat cove extended to base of cliff.
- Improvement of Goat Island road.
- Gateway at northern end of graveyard.
- Wall and gateway leading to St. Declan's Well, rebuilt.
- Housing problems addressed in the 1970s.

These were achieved in the difficult times of the 60s and 70s with such a lack of enthusiasm on the part of the public, that disbandment was proposed at times, so it was a commendable and praiseworthy record.

Achievements 1973 - 1985

There followed a period of expansion, with increased interest on the part of the local authorities and also an increased interest on the part of the community.

The officers were as follows:

Chairperson
Desmond Connery
Mrs Caroline Bowen-Walsh 1981-85

Vice Chairperson
John Fitzgerald
Richard Lincoln

Secretary
Tommie Mooney
Tom Walsh to 1981
Siobhán Lincoln 1981-85

Treasurer
Frank Nugent
Mrs Caroline Bowen-Walsh
Paul McCarthy to 1983
Ann McCarthy 1983-1985

Both Chairpersons Desmond Connery and Mrs Caroline Bowen-Walsh were worthy leaders, and a heavy programme of work was carried out enthusiastically, bringing major awards, first in 1978 and then in 1982, 1983, 1984 and 1985.

Achievements 1973-1985

- National awards in 1978, 1981, 1982, 1983, 1984 and 1985
- Bóthar na Trínse flower bed; plot near Quinns.
- Initiation of flower bed behind the car park opposite the school, planted in 1985.
- Housing and derelict sites; 1976 top terrace, then lower ones and finally houses in street.
- Prizes for well-kept houses and gardens; window boxes.
- International students 1976 and 1977
- Trees at school 1983, also at graveyard, along street and in front of new terrace of houses.
- Co-operation with G.A.A. in 1978, paying for leveling of school playing pitch.
- Advance signs for Ardmore 1980, costing £468. Tourism promotion.
- Elimination of insensitively placed wiring at the graveyard 1984.
- Railing along the Straoilleán,
- 1983 *Marechal de Noailles* anchor brought ashore and placed in position in 1985.
- Extra lights, seats and bins.
- Barrier erected at the roadside in front of the school.
- New entrance to the graveyard.
- Elimination of motor traffic on the strand.
- 1984 and 1985 a band recital by Youghal Brass and Reed Band on the promenade on Pattern Sunday, sponsored by the Tidy Towns Association. Tea and sandwiches afterwards in the I.C.A. room.
- Cleaning of St. Declan's Well at Pattern time.

35 Saint Declan's Well, 2021.

Achievements 1985 - 1992

At the A.G.M. in 1985, there was a big and welcome influx of new members from the Youghal Road area. The officers elected for this period were the following.

1985-1989

John Fitzgerald Chairperson
Rus Perks Vice Chairperson
Mrs Caroline Bowen-Walsh Secretary
Miss Cantwell Treasurer

1989-1993

Mrs Caroline Bowen-Walsh Chairperson
Breda Hennessy Vice Chairperson
Mary Flavin Secretary
Miss Cantwell Treasurer

36 The late medieval carved stone crosses on Saint Declan's Well.

Ardmore was approved as the village entry for the *Entente Florale* competition, and this meant there was much interest at a higher level. There were various meetings with Bord Fáilte.

The formation of KATS (Keep Ardmore Tidy Society) was an interesting development. These were the children organised by Billy Harty and Currie Hosford, who formed a junior association who painted window boxes, took part in painting competition and arranged teams for collecting litter during summer.

On 24th July (Pattern Day), the judges from the seven participating nations in *Entente Florale* came to judge Ardmore. The sun shone, the KATS wearing their KATS t-shirts, were lined up to meet them. At the Cross, on the Perks property were seven flower beds in the national colours of the seven countries. From the Straoillèan to the Boat Cove, the seven flags flew proudly, and the entourage gradually wound its admiring way to the Cliff House, where there was a reception. In October, Mrs Perks and

Mrs Hosford went to Austria, to be presented with a green and white crystal vase, the trophy for attaining 4th place in the competition.

1986 was the year Ardmore won the title of Ireland's Tidiest Village, being just one mark below Kinsale, the overall winners.

The £5000 grant of the previous year had been spent on:

- Constructing 10 pairs of stone piers on the approach roads to the village and on the New Line.
- Erecting rail fencing on the hairpin bend on the New Line (£650)
- Shrubbery and additional kerbing on the Youghal Road.
- Constructing a stone wall at the sea front car park.
- Constructing a fountain in the roundabout.
- 24 large sycamore trees were planted at the G.A.A. field.

The cubs and scouts this year were very co-operative and a draw for a bicycle was arranged for the end of the season.

In September 1992, the president, secretary, and others of the committee went to Dublin for the announcement of the prize winners in the Tidy Towns competition; not really daring to hope.

D-DAY September 1992

The excitement of the occasion is best portrayed by Mary Flavin in her account in the *Out & About*, the tension of the waiting at the reception in Dublin Castle, until at last, the announcement was made. The T.V. cameras, the interviews, the congratulations and leaving for home at 6pm. Then the euphoria of the arrival in Ardmore, when the entire village were out to meet the victorious home-comers.

The following day, the excitement continued, when all marched in the evening to the Beach Park, where there was a huge bonfire and barbecue with Mary Lincoln and John Brabazon being kept busy for hours, cooking sausages and hamburgers. Mary Flavin says "There was not a night like it all through the summer, a calm night with the harvest moon shining over the bay. Music, song and dancing around the blazing bonfire. Jim Lane was leading the team of local musicians. Such excitement, such joy was had by all, a night to be remembered." It was a fitting end to 29 years of endeavour, but the end was not yet.

37 Unveiling the Tidy Towns Plaque. Front; Michael Smith, Minister of the Environment with Mrs. Caroline Bowen-Walsh, Chairperson Ardmore Tidy Towns Committee. Also Matt McNulty, Seamus Scully, Brian O'Shea TD, Min. of State, J. Palmer, Cllr. Billy Kyne.

National Tidy Towns Day was arranged for May 2nd, 1993, and the village was again *en fête*, even though it wasn't possible for President Mary Robinson to attend, on account of a state visit to Spain. A reception had been arranged at the Cliff House for the Tidy Towns Committee, former officers and present patrons, after which all left for the sea-front where there was live entertainment, before the speeches of the Chairperson, Mrs Caroline Bowen-Walsh, Mr McNulty, Director General of Bord Fáilte, Mrs S. Scally, chairman of Super-Valu, national sponsors of the Tidy Towns project, Minister Smith Minister of the Environment, Joe Palmer, Manager of S.E.R.T.O., Austin Crowe, Chairman of S.E.R.T.O. and Brian O'Shea Minister of State at the Department of Agriculture, Food and Forestry.

Then led by the Castlelyons Pipe Band, the local Scouts, Cubs and Beavers, all marched up the street to the cross, where Mr Smith aided by Mrs Caroline Bowen-Walsh unveiled the engraved bronze plaque marking Ardmore's big day.

President Mary Robinson came on Pattern Sunday 1993 and was accorded a tumultuous reception by the huge crowds, gathered for the occasion. She had been welcomed by a guard of honour of Civil Defence members under Colm Bannon C.D.O., then by the 34th Waterford C.B.S.I. Troop together with Girl Scouts, Cubs and Beavers, all under unit leader, James Moloney.

The Presidential Salute was performed by Dungarvan Brass Band and Mrs Caroline Bowen-Walsh made a welcoming speech which was responded to by the President. After this she walked up the street and inspected the memorial bronze plaque at the top, marking Ardmore's wonderful achievement.

Awards

- 1986 Tidiest village in Ireland (one mark behind Kinsale, overall National winner)
- 1987 County Award.
- 1987 Zanussi National 'Wash-day' Award, £200, children picking up stones and cleaning park near strand, in course of its conversion from derelict site to park.

- 1988 County Award, 9th year in a row.
- 1989 Clean Watch award, £500.
- 1991 Regional Award for South East.
- 1992 Overall National Award.

Achievements

- Floodlighting of the Round Tower from June 1986.
- Telecom and ESB wires in village put underground in 1990.
- Development and planting at car park opposite school.
- Development and planting of strand park behind 3 new houses in village street.
- Stone walls and piers on approach roads and New Line.
- Hundreds of trees planted.
- Slogaire tidied and planted.
- Roundabout erected at end of the village street, planted in 1991, provided with a fountain in 1992.
- Erection of post and rail fencing on Rocky Road, Bóthar na Trinse, at dangerous bend on New Line.
- Ardmore approach signs (sponsored by Waterford Foods).
- Seating and picnic tables.
- Litter problem dealt with efficiently.

All these achievements meant that besides being a period of immense activity, it was also a period of immense expense. Thousands and thousands of pounds have been spent on the improvement and embellishment of Ardmore over these years. This money came from:

- Prize money from the Tidy Towns awards.
- Prize of paint for e.g. From H. Goodlass & Wall.
- Sponsorships from firms like Currans, Dungarvan.

- Sponsorships from Waterford Co-Op Society, Bank of Ireland, AIB.
- Local donations from societies e.g. G.A.A., Angling Ass., Ardmore Enterprise Co-op and from individuals.
- Annual American Tea Party, church door collection and annual cake sale.

1992

1992 marked not alone, the distinction of winning the national award after twenty-nine years, but also the inauguration of another phase of endeavour.

Planting proceeded: 24 elegant black litter bins were bought; a section of roadside bank out beyond the school was tidied and planted; window boxes appeared as usual at the appropriate times; five Irish signs were erected in the village precincts. The two large stones with Aird Mhór inscribed on them were placed in position at the two entrances roads to Ardmore.

The Fás scheme continues to be a great boon to the association, with men constantly at work cleaning, tidying, weeding, and planting. The considerable 'Red Tape' work devolves on John Fitzgerald.

Awards were:

- 1993 Runner up in Category Award Ist County Waterford. Regional Award.
- 1994 Second in County Waterford.
- 1995 Second in County Waterford.
- 1996 Second in County Waterford.
- 1997 Second in County Waterford. Second in County Environment Award.

- 1998 Third in County Waterford. Third in Waterford County Council Environment Award.
- 1999 Second in County Waterford. Overall winners of Clean Crystal County competition.

The 1999 A.G.M. was held on 6th May at the Round Tower Hotel. Mrs Caroline Bowen-Walsh resigned from being chairperson but remained on the committee. The meeting bestowed the title of Life President on her in gratitude for her many years of dedication to the Association. The officers of the new committee are as follows.

Billy Harty: President
Desmond Connery: Vice-President
Don Brockie: Secretary
John Fitzgerald: Treasurer

Plans for the coming months were arranged and so the good work goes on. S. Lincoln and E. Colbert happen to be the only two who joined in 1963 and have been members ever since. An A.G.M. for 2000 has been held. John Fitzgerald is now President, Desmond Connery, Secretary and Aidan Quirke, Treasurer. A millennium garden has been inaugurated at the Slogaire, Ardmore is again being entered the Tidy Towns Competition so a busy year looms ahead.

The Ardmore Enterprise Co-Op

The Ardmore Enterprise Co-Op was founded in 1989 and has gone from strength to strength ever since, there being a lively and energetic committee.

Among the projects it undertook was a study of storm damage in Ardmore. A Tourist Plan gained a National Merit Award of £2000 in October 1996.

The organisation has been very successful in liaising with and procuring grants from national organisations, such as, the National Heritage Council. As a result, two thatched cottages were re-instated in the village.

38 Thatched cottage, Ardmore, 2021.

The opening of a Tourist Office (in Mrs Perk's premises, formerly known as the Courthouse), the production of two tourist brochures and the initiation of the Cliff Walk took place in 1991. The Cliff Walk has ever since, been a major attraction in Ardmore.

In 1996, St. Declan's Way was opened. This was the culmination of years of preparatory work and on a sunny July Sunday, the minister Bernard Allen officially declared it open. Richard Lincoln, James Moloney (founder of the Ardmore Scout Group) and a group of scouts, took three days to walk the route from Cashel to Ardmore and were present at the offical opening. A guide and map were also produced. Discussions are ongoing and quite a few meetings have been held with the Heritage Council about upgrading the walk as part of their Pilgrims' Path millennium project. Separate Co. Waterford and Co. Tipperary committees have been formed. The Ardmore group has been carrying out maintenance between here and Ballinameela.

The different aspects of Ardmore life that have been catered for by the organisations are quite extraordinary, from the funding of the Vegetable Growers Co-op, to helping to finance an all-weather playing pitch for the local school, to the provision of a branch office of the Youghal Credit Union and the initiation of a tourist stand on the Rosslare Stena ferry, this last development having now been taken up by Waterford Tourism. The Twinning Association was another interesting association helped into being by the Ardmore Enterprise Co-op.

In 1996 the innovative beach facility (incorporating lifeguard tower, tourist office, and toilets) the building known more familiarly now as the Sandcastle occasioned a great deal of comment. In the *Dungarvan Leader*, November 29th, 1996, there was a short article as follows: -

"The innovative beach facility building in Ardmore designed by Dungarvan base architect, Damien Dillon & Co., was recently featured in a number of major architectural publications.

Architects' Journal, an English publication seldom gives coverage to Irish architects or buildings but in their October edition, the *Journal* carried a full colour photo of the Ardmore Lifeguard Tower/Tourist Office. The photograph complete with write-up was shown alongside competition winners and substantial building projects such as a design for the German Foreign Ministry building in Berlin."

Such valuable coverage is indicative of the reception that this small project has received. Ardmore's Sandcastle building which was commissioned by Waterford Co. Council in co-operation with the Ardmore Enterprise Co-op was featured in the most recent publication of *PLAN*, the Irish Architects magazine. It was the only other building featured apart from the winners of the regional awards for 1996. The Enterprise Co-op was responsible for its innovation.

According to an agreement entered into by Ardmore Enterprise Co-Op with Waterford Leadership Partnership, a new Local Employment office was set up in Ardmore in 1997.

St. Declan's Community Association was formed with the help both financial and otherwise of the Ardmore Enterprise Co-op. The seating and other accommodation in the I.C.A. room was improved in order to make it a comfortable meeting place for the elderly people to get together once a week. The Health Board co-operated in this valuable social initiative.

Access from the lower to the higher levels of Ardmore has been much improved by the Dá Thig steps and the continuation upwards of Sir John's Steps.

An Arts weekend took place in 1998 and also the presentation of the Molly Keane Creative writing award (this also took place in 1999). Besides these there is also the more mundane work of the improvement in the water supply and sending a delegation to Minister Dempsey re our sewerage problems.

The opening of the Round Tower in Pattern Week 1998 was a fantastic success and it was repeated in 1999. This was done in co-operation with Dúchas and about 5000 people visited.

The initiation of an Ardmore Enterprise Centre is their most recent venture. Following prompting from the group, the County Council purchased three acres of land near Ardmore school, land zoned for industrial purposes to enhance the employment prospects of the area.

So our Enterprise Co-op seems to keep a watchful outlook on all aspects of Ardmore life. We never know where next they show their hand.

Reminiscences Of Jimmy Rooney

39 L to R Jimmy Rooney, Johnny Foley, Jack Farissey. Photo by Paul Quain.

Jimmie Rooney is now 90 years old in 1999. He spent long years salmon fishing and his fishing reminiscences are recorded in the account on fishing. He also has memories of farming life in his youth.

As a young man, he was occasionally sent to Grange Creamery to order a load of slag or manure; this was 50/- a ton. The other manure with which he and everybody else were familiar was called 'truc'. It consisted of seaweed and sand; seaweed was placed on a base of sand and one continued building up alternate layers of seaweed and sand, which were then left to rest. The resultant heap was black and was cut down through with a hay knife in order to remove it and convey it to the crop. People were very particular about the seaweed when it was blown in and guarded each section of beach diligently; one dare not encroach on the neighbour's section. At the far end of Goat Island cove, there was a derrick for raising up the seaweed as the approach to the cove itself was rather difficult.

The first mowing machine in Ardmore was bought before the first World War by Mike Troy, Chapel Row and Johnie McGrath of Dysert. The two of them combined in buying it. However, after the first World War, Fr Enda Ducey, formerly of Crossford, remembers his father paying £45 for a reaper and binder to replace his mowing machine.

I remember my father-in-law, William Lincoln, Lios an Uisce, extolling the professionalism of Seáinín Curran, who was terrific for making stacks. He made a stack of four acres of corn and finished up with two sheaves on top, which never stirred in a storm.

Jimmie remembers a threshing machine drawn by four horses. This was in use at Deugy Powers of Curragh and the extra horses would have been loaned. The machine was a huge wide drawn one with heavy projecting beams about 14/15 feet long at either side. Two horses were tackled to each beam and kept going round, while a few men fed in sheaves from the stack of corn.

Bigger threshing machines were used later. All the local farmers either came themselves or sent a man to represent them on the big day. Water had to be drawn for the engine, two barrels at a time; the sheaves had to be piked from end to end of the rick up to the men feeding the machines. It was a very complicated process.

The threshing day was a very busy day for the ladies of the household too, with so many men to feed. I remember, when teaching in Ballycurrane in the forties, children being kept at home on threshing days to keep turning the fire machine to keep a good fire under all the pots. When the men came in for the midday meal, there was often segregation; the farmers being directed to the parlour and the labourers to the kitchen.

And then we came to the era of combine harvesters. In the forties we walked out from the village to see our very first one, operating in a big field of Walshes at Rodeen near Powers Cross on the way to Youghal.

Jimmie Rooney had a contract for malting barley during the war and wheat had to be set at that period also. He had a contract for beet in the fifties and spoke feelingly of the hardship involved. A double-boarded plough (horse-drawn) was used to open drills. The seed was set by a hand-held machine, you went on your knees to thin it out, crown it and leave it in little heaps to be conveyed to the side for collecting. Jimmie had five acres of beet; £3 a ton was the price paid and he had perhaps sixty tons. A high sugar content raised the price. Now all is done by machine. There is precision sowing, so no thinning is required. Chemical spraying reduces weeding to a minimum and lifting is by mechanical harvester.

In the days of the landlords, Jimmie holds that the landlords' agents were even more difficult to deal with, than the landlords themselves.

The Landed Gentry

The Odells

The Odells had a long connection with Ardmore, the family having been in county Waterford for two centuries. The Ardmore property (until its sale in 1888) comprised the townlands of Ballinamertina, Curragh, Duffcarrick, Dysert, and Farrengarret.

'A deed, dated 20th February 1837 was made between the Ecclesiastical Commissioners for Ireland on the one hand and John Odell on the other part, whereby certain lands at Duffcarrick containing 135 acres, 3 roods and 25 perches, and certain lands at Ballinamertina containing 336 acres, 2 roods and 15 perches, and certain lands at the Curragh containing 291 acres, 35 perches all situated in the Barony of Decies within Drum and County of Waterford, previously belonging to the ancient See of Lismore were conveyed by the said Ecclesiastical Commissioners to the said John Odell.'

Note Dysert and Farrengarret are not mentioned in this deed, so seemingly the Odells were already in possession of those townlands. There was an Odell presence in Ardmore in 1829; John Odell was one of three present at a vestry meeting of the Protestant Church, which took place in the eastern section of the ancient Ardmore Cathedral. That section still had a roof at that time, and Divine Service took place there.

In the *Griffith Valuation* of the early 1850s, the property which later became Odell Lodge, later still the property of Lady Clodagh

Anson, still later St. Catherine's Convent of Mercy, was then occupied by Nelson Foley with Edward Odell as Lessor.

The Odell family was well-established in the Dungarvan area around Ballintaylor and Carriglea. Carriglea was built after the marriage of John Odell in 1827. There was a close liaison between the Ardmore and Dungarvan sections. Loads of sand and gravel came from Ardmore to Carriglea - at 1½d a load it is said. People were sent on messages from Ardmore to Carriglea quite often.

James Flynn of Dysert had to work at Carriglea in Spring and harvest-time as part of his rent. He ploughed for about two weeks every year with no pay; left the horse in Carriglea overnight and walked up and down himself every day. He died in 1937 at the age of 97

The Odells who figured most in Ardmore were Catherine and her family, she was daughter of Edward Odell, and had eloped with her cousin Thomas Fitzgerald of Ballinparka, but the marriage didn't turn out well and she returned to Carriglea with her two children. Edward Otto and Geraldine Agnes (who later married John Peddar Furlong of D'Loughtane). She then came to live at Melrose, Ardmore and changed the name to Odell Lodge.

Incidentally Catherine Fitzgerald and Captain William Odell were sister and brother, daughter and son of Edward Odell and Harriet Nugent Humble. (Harriet was adept at managing the estate, Edward wasn't.)

The story is told that when Edward Otto (later known in the village as Master Otto) was born, Declan was suggested as a name for him, but rejected as every tinker in the Co. Waterford was called Declan. This was recalled (or perhaps invented) later, when he became an associate of the tinkers and bought and sold donkeys and kept them in Ivy Lodge. He also went around "jolting (selling) herrings". When he died in 1899 at the age of 29, his mother kept the grave open and guarded for days, in case he wasn't really dead. An aunt of mine told me how she and other girls went up to the graveyard to investigate this, but were shooed away by the men on duty.

The Odells were responsible for laying out the village, probably in the second half of the 19th century and they are to be complimented on it.

It is said that a good many of the houses were built from the stone of Ardmore Castle.

John Peddar Furlong was estate agent for the Odells up to 1893, Cliff Row, Miles Row, Coffee Lane, Church St., Chapel Lane (also referred to as Chapel Row), and Thomas Row are the addresses of the tenants in his Rent Book. There is no mention whatever of Sleepy Lane, perhaps Thomas Row was then the name of Sleepy Lane?

The family names are all the usual ones still in the district to-day. Some of the more unusual ones are.

> John Deacon, Rent of £6.6.0, a Protestant who had land near the coastguards station - landlord agent.

> Dr. Poole, Church St., rent £6.12.0. Apparently, he was the dispensary doctor, who lived in what is now Cashman's house.

> Miss Inchendun, Dysert, rent £1.0.0 (note she is referred to as 'Miss').

> James Plunkett, Thomas Row, rent £1.2.6

Richard Weymouth, Ardmore, rent £1.15.0 - Protestants and living on the site of the hall.

Garret Keane, Main St., rent £1.5.0. He taught Countesse de Freney's father to sail and professed not to know any English.

Charles Thornton, Ardmore, rent £3.0.0

Lucy Davis, Ardmore, rent £2.5.0. She was a teacher in the local school.

William Scott, Curragh, rent £3.4.0, I remember a man named Scott, home from U.S? who in the early thirties stayed in Tigaluinn, a guest house run by my mother, he went over to Curragh every day, no matter what the weather and spent the whole day sitting on the site of his former home.

Captain Dawson, Ardmore, rent £2.0.0 The holding of Mrs Triphook is under the heads in the rental of Miss Lawlor.

Rev. J.B. Wallace, Thomas Row, Dysert.

Rev. J.B. Thirrill, £1.1.3.

Captain Triphook, Duffcarrick rent £2.6.0. This holding used to belong to Miss Lawlor.

Richard J Ussher, Dysert rent £8.5.0, ornithologist and archaeologist, was involved in the discovery of the Crannóg. Countess de Freney says John Power used accompany him even on visits to the continent, where they climbed cliffs and explored caves in pursuit of bird's eggs, and she says cases of these eggs are in the museum in Waterford.

James Plunkett, Miles Row, rent £1.2.6

Rev. A Power, Ardmore rent £6.10.0

Coastguard Station, Rent £5.10.0

Claude Bolliense, Cliff Row, rent £1.5.0

Capt. Odell, Monea, rent £75 (Ballinamertina - gave it up in 1885).

Capt. Odell, Farrengarret, rent £23.15.5

Col. Cotton, Dysert, rent £3.10.0.

Master Otty's sister Geraldine Agnes married John Peddar Furlong of D'Loughtane in 1884. He had been in the army, had land in D'Loughtane and became estate agent and collector of rents for the Odell estate.

When Thomas Fitzgerald died, John Peddar Furlong sold D'Loughtane (1907) and went to live in Ballinaparka. Their son Gerald Furlong also served in the army, Countesse de Freney is his daughter.

Catherine (of Odell Lodge, Ardmore) died in Ballinaparka in 1923 and left Odell Lodge to her granddaughter who sold it the same year. Myrtleville and Ivy Lodge, two houses in Main St., she willed entailed to her grand-son Gerald Furlong.

My mother, Johanna Hurley was a tenant of Catherine in Myrtleville in 1920 and kept an occasional paying guest. Mrs Fitzgerald asked her to give accommodation to a friend of hers but my mother declined very politely, as she knew it would be impossible for her to manage hot water in hip baths upstairs. Later on, she had another guest and Mrs Fitzgerald heard this and sent my mother a most irate letter, "How dare you put a common man sleeping in my good box-spring bed".

The Strand Laws were strictly enforced by the Odell landlords. There were local agents; and one paid for removing sand or gravel. It was also forbidden to go on the strand if the Odell family were bathing. A relation of mine, a Morrissey of Crossford spent a period in jail for infringement of these laws.

Bagges were the landlords who lived in Monea House and there were one or two Bagge/Odell weddings. Capt. William Odell (1849-1916) married Emma Bagge. His son William was also in the army and killed in Mesopotamia in 1917 and his grandson Edward was killed in Cyprus in 1941, during World War II. After the death of Emma, he married Isabel Ussher of Cappagh and had two daughters, Mary who died in 1976 and Ruth in 1974.

In 1917 Captain Odell and family moved from Cappagh (Ussher home) to Monea House (Coláiste Deuglán later), where they lived till 1914, quite a spartan life, judging by what Mary told me of her duties in the dairy there. It was she also who told me that the former Odell dwelling in Ardmore was in the complex of farm dwellings at Farrengarret, opposite the graveyard. It was evidently during their sojourn there that the rector was compelled by them to remove the top story from the rectory.

Note: The Gee family is also credited with having lived here.

The family moved to England for some years, but after Captain William Odell's death, Isabel and her daughter Mary returned to Ardmore and in the mid-thirties, built Aisling on the Rocky Road opposite Melrose. Both Isabel and Mary were talented painters. Among the visitors to the house during this period were Norah McGuinness, the well-known painter, Nano Reid also a well-known painter, Arland Ussher (a cousin) the writer and philosopher and probably Samuel Becket.

Isabel is buried in Ardmore, but both Mary and Ruth died and were buried in Dublin. They were in rather straitened circumstances in their later years.

Much of the basic information contained above was condensed from James Quains' article 'The Odells of Carriglea' in the *Ardmore Journal* 1986.

The Bagges

The Bagges were the other landlord family in the area. Their estate papers are not extant. However, in *Waterford: History and Society, Principal Inhabitants in 1746* by Henry F. Morris, there is the following Bagge reference "He (Isaac Quarry) was presumably the father of John of Ballymulalla (will proved 1680) who married Elenor, daughter of Robert Bagge, the son of John, who had come to Ireland c. 1620." The Bagges remained a prominent family in the Ardmore area and John Henry Bagge of Monea appears in the 1890 edition of *Walford* with 3016 acres and a rental of £2370.

The Bagges are generally regarded as having been stern, in fact conforming to the general perception of the landlord class. There were many evictions from their lands at Monea i.e. in the huge area of land bounded on the west by the Youghal Road and on the east by Bóthar na Trínse. They also had lands at Ballylane, Ballinamertina and Knockmealmore. Fairly early in the 19th century the Lincoln family consisting of seven sons and one daughter were evicted from their holding in Knockmealmore, Grange.

Micheál Ó Foghlú (who founded the Irish College) as a child, had lived in the farm at the very top of Bóthar na Trínse, more or less where Powers new house now stands, and his family were evicted from there. Mrs Keane (née Ducey) who lived in their farm a little over the road in Duffcarrick, saw it take place. The family went over to their cousins' barn (Paits Mhici) at Keanes of the Lough and it is said that the ousted lady never spoke again.

Micheál Ó Foghlú used to talk of the mass evictions earlier when forty tenants were given a week's notice and their passage money to Canada. This might have been in the wake of Catholic Emancipation (1829) when the 40/- free-holders were deprived of their votes.

Eddy Mansfield (born in 1920) speaks of his grandfather and other men in the village making an effigy of the landlord and carrying it from the road in front of his residence, down the village street and dumping it over the storm-wall.

My father-in-law, William Lincoln, born 1874, at Lios an Uisce told me of the tenants being brought in to set trees at Monea House (later Coláiste Deuglán) and earlier called Ardmore House. The men all got liquid refreshments at Bailys (i.e Keevers) at midday, but he was younger than the others were, and he got a meal.

Seemingly, some years before that, one of the Bagges had died in Dublin; his remains were brought to Dungarvan by train and the tenants were requisitioned to go in to Dungarvan and carry the remains to Ardmore, and we are told, it was one of the wettest days that ever came out of the heavens.

He is probably the Bagge member buried at the right, inside the entrance to the old Cathedral. There is a monument over him, and you will hear local people saying this was placed there, because no grass would grow on his grave; of course, the rest of us don't

159

believe this but it is symptomatic of the lack of esteem in which they were held. Various Bagge ghost stories are told too, for instance: After the death of one of the Bagges, his former coachman met him driving his coach along the road, he saluted him and put his hand on the coach. The story goes that his hand was scorched and always bore the mark.

Two matrimonial alliances were made with the Odell family, but I gather from the present Odell representative, the Contesse de Freney, that they were not highly acclaimed. Mary Odell lived in Monea House in the early years of the century, probably before it was sold and became Coláiste Deuglán in 1922. About that time, a member of the Bagge family came and disposed of the last of the family property. That was when my parents acquired the plot at the top of the village, where they planned to build a house and installed Ardmore's first petrol pumps there 1931. They also acquired a cottage there, with a rent-paying tenant. It is said that the last of the Bagges went to Canada.

Ardo House

40 Ardo House, c1900.

A very interesting account of Ardo House (by W. Fraher) appears in the 1990 issue of the *Ardmore Journal*. He says, "One of the earliest references to Ardo appears in the Civil Survey 1654-56. The proprietor's name was James Fzt Gerald gent, Irish papist. The property consisted of 280 acres and was valued at £23.15.0."

Local tradition records that a family named Costen was associated with the house in the 17th century. There appears to have been several subsequent owners and it was acquired in the later 17th century by Sir Francis Prendergast. Fascinating and sinister stories have been told about the place. One story tells of the young heir being wrongfully accused of appropriating valuable silver. He fled and was pursued and died on the cliff since called Croch an Oidhre (The Heir's Gibbet) having been hanged by his pursuers, or his horse failed to make the jump and he was caught and hanged in the reins. This story is well known but we do not know to what particular period if refers.

Much of our information on the history of Ardo is in an article written by Frances Currey of Lismore and published in 1853. The Coghlans of Ardo are listed as one of the principal families of Co. Waterford in 1710. "Henry Coughlan of Ardo, High Sheriff 1776 married to a widow Lindsay of the Co. Tipperary" appears on a list of the principal gentry of the county in 1775, compiled by the Right Hon. George Ponsonby.

The Coughlans must have fallen on evil days. There are several accounts of the Widow Coughlan and her smuggling activities, of her two handicapped children and her two beautiful daughters. One daughter became Lady Barrymore, and her sister Eliza went to live with her in London, where she met the widowed emigré Duc de Castries and married him and returned with him to France after the Revolution. The Castries family - was and still is - a prominent French family. At the coronation of Louis XVIII in Notre Dame cathedral in Paris, Eliza as the Duchess de Castries occupied a seat of honour. She never came back to Ardo.

Lewis' Topographical Dictionary of Ireland 1837 described the property as 'Ardo, the residence of P Lawlor...... a castellated mansion'. By the late 1830's, the Lawlors were gone from Ardo. *Griffiths Valuation for Co. Waterford 1848-51* notes the house as vacant and in the possession of the Directors of the National Bank. The house and offices are valued at only £1.15.0 which indicates it must have been in bad repair. A garden was occupied by the Directors of the National Bank but was owned by the Duc de Castries. The Duc also had four lots of land and an orchard valued at £103 and occupied by the Bank.

The Ardo estate came into the de Castries family through the marriage of Eliza Coghlan of Ardo and the Duc de Castries. It was later acquired by Marshal McMahon (President and Marshal of France in 1873) on his marriage to Elizabeth, daughter and heiress of the Duc de Castries (Marshal McMahon i.e. The Duc de Magenta deserves special mention and is dealt with by Renagh Holohan in her book, *The Irish Chateaux; In Search of Descendants of the Wild Geese*, in which the Ardo connection is mentioned.)

In 1985, my son, my sister and I were on a tour in southern France and visited the Tourist Office in Montpellier and happened by chance on a brochure of Castries, so went to visit it. There was an enormous chateau with appropriate gardens, and we were shown through the various apartments. In one place, were photographs of the family with the Pope, also with the present Queen-Mother who had visited them. There was a large portrait of Marshal McMahon.

It was Marshal McMahon who put the Ardo property up for sale, and Sir Joseph McKenna was the buyer. The McKenna family (who took over Ardo in 1865) was a distinguished one too. Sir Joseph (he was knighted in August 1867) was a ?Nationalist M.P. for Youghal 1865 - 68 and from 1874 - 1885, later for Monaghan. He had been born in Dublin in 1819, was educated at Trinity College and called to the Bar in 1848. The family was very proud of its connection with St. Oliver Plunkett through Sir Joseph's mother. (A nephew of Sir Joseph's, Reginald McKenna had a most distinguished career in English politics, having been Hon. Sec, to the Treasury, President of the Board of Education, Home Secretary; succeeded Churchill as First Lord of the Admiralty and finally became Chancellor of the Exchequer under Asquith). Sir Joseph married in 1842, Esther Lousia Horne of Dublin who died in 1871 and Tony Collis her great grandson says she is buried with her young daughter in Ardmore graveyard. There is a set of purple vestments in Ardmore Church, made from a ball-gown of Lady McKennas.

The tenure of the McKennas seemed to have initiated a period of refurbishment and prosperity at Ardo. Frances Curry (mentioned previously) writes in 1895 "of the scrupulously whitewashed walls, gleaming brilliantly in the sun". In fact, those years from the 1860s to the 1920s seem to have been the heyday of Ardo House. The photographs of the early 20th century show a delightful family home, well looked after as were the splendid out-offices of the adjoining farm. It exuded an air of prosperity and contentment.

The late Deug Connell (later to become owner of the place) spoke of a big ball given in Ardo (probably in the early part of the century) when the whole avenue beginning at the approach near his house, was lighted up with lanterns. That must have been the same one of which Mrs Pollock spoke. Her daughter, Mrs Dowson told of her father and mother bringing up cold sweets (refrigeration would have been a problem in those days), dancing all night and walking home at dawn. Mrs Dowson also spoke of going on one occasion with her father to visit Sir Joseph who was sitting up in bed wearing his tall hat. He died on 15th August 1906. He had re-married, and the second Lady McKenna died in July 1907. Both were buried in a vault in an adjoining field with a large stone angel on guard. Now the place is covered with briars. Lady McKenna had been noted for her dedication to the *Society for the Prevention of Cruelty to Animals* and the family was always resentful of the fact that this Society got most of the McKenna money and the place, as a result was not viable.

Sir Joseph McKenna had ten children six girls and four boys from his first marriage. One of his daughters married a grandson of Daniel O'Connell. Another daughter Magdalen Mary aged 13 is buried in the Ardmore graveyard, as also is Kathleen Elizabeth McKenna wife of Joseph who inherited the place in 1918.

Members of the family lived there for some years before going to England, Madeline who later became Mrs Collis was one of them.

For a period in 1920-21 it was let during the summer to the committee of Coláiste Deuglán, so Madeline's father, Joseph McKenna, had vacated the house by then. There was no caretaker, and the place was looted, eventually sold and deprived of its roof, so the final period of its desolation began.

41 The front facade of the remains of Ardo House photographed by Bill Flynn in 2006.

The Collis family (3 sons, Guy, Tony and Terrence) returned to Ardmore, bought Melrose and used it as a guesthouse in the late 30s, early 40s). They returned to England in the mid-40s (Martin Hurley, my father bought Melrose and there I spent the first ten years of my married life). Guy Collis was in an anti-partition league in England, moved to Leicester and became Lord Mayor of that city and was in frequent communication with me until his death a few years ago.

Traditions

The Irish Language

In 1900, Irish though not the language of the village, was universally understood, and most of the elders of that generation, spoke it fluently and naturally. Neither my mother (1885 - 1947) nor my father (1884 - 1953) spoke Irish, though it had been the language of their parents, and my mother felt that they conversed in Irish, when they did not want the children to follow the subject of the conversation.

42 Thatched cottages on Main Street, Ardmore, c1910.

Mary Walsh (died 1967 aged 93) of Whiting Bay, was custodian of many Irish prayers in verse. Incidentally, she lived in her youth, at a part of Whiting Bay to the north of 'The Quay', where there is a large stretch of flat rocks covered at high tide. This place was known as 'Paris'. It is impossible to know now whether it is a jocose reference or a derivation of an authentic Irish name. Fr. John Walsh P.P. at the beginning of the century (he was killed in 1901 as a result of a fall from his horse) gave his sermons in Irish and was known as 'Geallaim-se dhaoibhe-se, a bhráithre,' ('I promise you brethern') as this was such a popular phrase of his.

P Ó Foghlú of Whiting Bay knew 'Eachtra an Bháis', a long poem incorporating a dialogue with death. He got it from a Quinlan man who was picking potatoes in the area. These were very interesting sentiments surprisingly and poetically expressed in a potato field.

Death boasts of his prowess: -

> *Gabhaim don Róimh is do thír na nDéise*
> *Ar thír na dTúrcach, déanfad léirscrios*
> *I níos lugha ná nóimeat, bead in Eigipt*
> *Is mire mé ná an fiolar ná'n faoileán féin*
> *Nó an seabhac ar imeallaibh an tsléibhe*
> *Is mire céad uair mé ná an gath gréine*
> *Ná long faoi seol, lá is mó a bhí gaoth léi*

A literal translation might run as follows:

> *I go to Rome and to the Deise Country*
> *I Will destroy the country of the Turks.*
> *In less than a minute, I will be in Egypt.*
> *I'm faster than the eagle or even the seagull,*
> *Or the hawk on the mountain side.*
> *I'm faster a hundred times than a ray of sun,*
> *Or a ship in full sail the day*

she had the strongest wind with her.

Alice Broderick of Geata Bhóthair Aird, who died about 30 years ago was also a custodian of Irish lore. There were several others in Curragh. Many more of these stories, poems and prayers were collected from the people in question, by my late husband, Richard Lincoln, about 1936 for the Folklore Commission.

One of the poems he transcribed from Alice Broderick was a lament for a young man, Tomás Ó Dálaigh.

> *Ba dheise a dhá shúil ghlas*
> *Ná drúcht na maidne ar bharr féir*
> *Is ó síneadh ins an uaigh é*
> *Tá an fuacht ag fáil treise ar an ngréin*

A literal translation might go as follows:

> *His two gray eyes were more beautiful*
> *Than the morning dew on the grass*
> *And since he was stretched in the grave*
> *The cold is stronger than the sun.*

Martin O'Driscoll of Bawnard (my late husband's grand-uncle) and John Foley of Crossford (my grand-uncle) collected and interchanged manuscripts. While Irish was universally spoken, generally, people could not read or write it. My mother, Johanna Foley was born and reared in the bar formerly owned by Rooneys, now Paddy Mac's and she had heard many times of the wonderful books that were out at Crossford, her father's former home, just at the bridge. Then one day, she saw them and was utterly disappointed. Instead of the nice shiny books with pictures, which she as a child had envisaged, these were dusty, shabby looking manuscripts. Unfortunately, they are now scattered. I am very happy, though to have been able to acquire two of Martin O'Driscoll's manuscripts.

The Gaelic League was founded in 1893 and this brought about a great resurgence of interest in Irish. The first feis in Munster was held in Ardmore in 1899 and was addressed in verse by Liam Ó Beaglaoich of Ardo. These are the first lines of his address: -

> *Bail ó Dhia oraibh, a mhuintir na hÉireann*
> *Dir mhná is fhearaibh nbhúr seasamh le chéile*
> *Beag is mór, óg is aosta*
> *Is fíor gur fearra liom bhúr fheiscint mar thréada*
> *Ná an rí tá ar Shasana 's a chuid airm go léireach*

A rough English translation might read:

> *God's blessing on you, people of Ireland,*
> *Both women and men standing together,*
> *Small and big, young and old.*
> *It is true I would prefer to see you standing together*
> *Than the King of England and all his army.*

Arland Ussher, the well-known writer, essayist and philosopher who died in Dublin in 1981, was closely related to Mary Odell and her mother, Isabel (née Ussher). They lived in 'Aisling' on the Rocky Road and were visited there by their cousin. He learned Irish in Cappagh (outside Dungarvan) by following the ploughman up and down his fields, his notebook in hand. He published then in 1942, two classic books recording the way of life and the idioms of the Déise Gaeltacht, *Caint an tSean Shaoil* and *Cúrsaí an tSean Shaoil*. He made the first translation of *The Midnight Court* and was a former President of the Irish Academy of letters and a winner of the prestigious Gregory Medal, an award for outstanding contributions to Irish literature and learning.

In the early 20s, Irish colleges had been founded here and there throughout the country, and Irish courses were run during the summer months, in order to give teachers an opportunity of obtaining proficiency in Irish. Coláiste Deuglán was founded here in 1920 by Micheal Ó Foghlú and during the summers of 1920 and 1921, sessions were held at Ardo House, rented from the McKenna family.

Monea House was then acquired from the Bagge family and for nearly forty years, was a place vibrant with life and love and hope for the old language. Among its teachers were people such as Seán Ó Súilleabháin later to become Chief Archivist of the Irish Folklore Commission; Seamus Dalton, chief translator in Dail Éireann; Séamus Pender who had studied in Germany under Pokorny, a well-known authority on old Irish. Séamus Pender later became professor of history at U.C.C.; Philib Ó Laoghaire of Cor Cois Laoi; Deuglán Cullen of Grange, the first Headmaster; the very popular Michéal Ó Concubhair of Balinamertina and many, many others.

The passing of Coláiste Deuglán in the mid-forties coincided with a decline of interest in the Irish language.

Occasional flickers helped to warm the heart, for instance remembering as a very small girl in school, hearing the older girls calling teams for rounders, the leader on one side prefacing the proceedings by saying "Cuirim ort" and the other leader answering "Ligim leat".

Cáit Uí Leighin tells of a few Ballyquin ladies who always called to her aunt's house in the village on pension days and their whole conversation was in Irish. This would have been in the late 30s or early 40s. She also told me the story of the local man who while cutting furze for his fire from the fence of a neighbouring farmer, was apprehended by the owner. The furz cutter's rejoinder was in verse

> *Imeoidh a dtiocfaidh is a dtáinig riamh*
> *Ach ní imeoidh an grása ó Dhia*
> *Imeod-sa is tusa as an áit seo*
> *Is beidh aiteann ag fás 'nár ndiaidh.*

> *All things to come and that ever came, will go*
> *But God's grace will not go*
> *I will go and you will go from this place*
> *And furze will be growing after us.*

I remember going with my father in his lorry when he was delivering coal to Kate Kelly at Whiting Bay. She had no English and gave the money into his hand to count it himself, and she kept on telling us "Beidh Willie ag teach abhaile." Willie was a protege of hers who was due on a visit home from the U.S. that summer. This was probably in the 30s. The late Johnny Power, the Cliff, formerly of Curragh says his father remembers a local lad called Towler, emigrating to the U.S. and wearing a label as he had no English.

Quite recently, John Kennedy of Lisarow recorded a beautiful prayer from his father, John who died in 1947, a prayer to be invoked against nightmares.

> *Anna, a Mháthair Mhuire, a Mhuire Máthair Chríost;*
> *Naomh Elizabeth, máthair Eoin Baiste,*
> *na trí naomh agus fíoghar na croise;*
> *Idir mise sa leaba agus an trom luí.*

> *Anna, mother of Mary; Mary mother of Christ;*
> *Saint Elizabeth, mother of John the Baptist;*

the three saints and the sign of the cross;
Between me and my bed and nightmares tonight.

43 St. Declan's Well, Ardmore, c1920.

About 30 years ago my sister Eileen Colbert, heard two old ladies conversing in Rooney's pub (now Paddy Mac's) and one said to the other "Ná bí ag déanamh Máire Ní Ógáin díot féin" which meant "Don't be making a fool of yourself," Máire Ni Ógáin was the wife of a well-known Irish poet, Donncha Rua Mac Namara (1709-1814) and evidently it was well known that she had not done too well for herself by marrying the poet. This "throw-away phrase" of the old lady underlines the remarkable tenacity of the tradition of Irish poetry and lore in the locality. Sadly, one has to admit that in an area once so rich in song and story and poetry in our native language, that tradition seems to be gone for ever.

The traditional prayer at midnight, at St. Declan's Well, on the eve of the Pattern is still said there. Sadly, we wonder will we be the last who will do so.

Go mbeannaí Dia dhuit a Dheaglaín naofa. Go mbeannaí Muire anus beannaím féin duit. Is go dtí a thánga mé ag gearán mo scéil duit. Chun tusa á insint agus Dia á réiteach.

Tomás Mac Gearailt was the last native Irish speaker in the parish.

Irish/English

It is fascinating to observe how many Irish words are still used in ordinary every-day speech here in Ardmore, as well as phrases, the constructions of which are a direct translation from Irish. John O'Donohue in the chapter on 'Taste of Speech' in his well-known book *Anam Chara*, says, "One of the factors that makes spoken English so interesting is the colourful ghost of the Gaelic language behind it". I have put together a few paragraphs in this idiom, which of course is getting more out of date as we move from our Irish origins and as our speech is more and more moulded by radio and T.V.

A Seanchas (Chat) on the Bóithrín (Side Road)

I went down the *bóithrín* yesterday and saw Fitzgeralds had a big *carn* (heap) of beet there waiting for the lorry. Who did I run into but that *gligín* of a one of the Connors. Not a *splanc* (spark) of sense has she and she's an awful *straoill* (untidy person) into the bargain with her clothes hanging off of her, and a little bit of *taoibhín* (soft leather) wouldn't go astray on her shoes. Such an *áilleán* (good for nothing person) of a one, and what's more, she's an awful *cráiteachán* (grumbler), always *olagóning* (complaining) about this, that and the other, never stopped *cnáimhsealing*. Well, she put her *good morra* on me and there we were gabbing away for the best part of an hour and not a dish washed at home.

Well, of course, I had the news of the three parishes from her, about the wedding over the hill at Flanagans and young Flynn gone in there, a *cliamhain isteach* (son-in-law who takes up the father-in-law's holding). She told me, there was a big *meitheal* (gathering of helpers) at the threshing over at Foleys last week.

The old man over the road is only *ag stracadh leis* (struggling along), a great *amadán* (fool) of a fellow, and sure the father and mother there haven't a bit of *smacht* (discipline) on the youngsters. And, no wonder, how often did you see the father go up the road in the night and he *maith go leor* (good enough, i.e a little bit drunk), he's a right *cearrbhach* (gambler), playing 45 every night at the pub.

The poor *aindeiseoir* (pronounced ang-ish-eoir, wretch) Brigid Murphy passed along. God love her, there isn't a pick on her. She's in right *mí-ádh* (bad luck) since the mother and father left, only pulling the devil by the tail.

Who came along after that was Barbara Barron. She saluted us in her grand, stuck-up kind of accent. A right *seoinín* (one who apes foreign ways) that one is, and not meas madra has she on any of the neighbours. She's all for the other *seoinín* in town. The bridge and golf crowd. But sure, she's only making a *ceap magaidh* (laughingstock) of herself over-right the neighbours, sure all the world and Garret Reilly know well she hasn't a copper to her name.

174

Poor Noreen came along, all in *giobals* (rags) and right *aindeas* (ang-ish, miserable) looking, God help her. Sure, she's as *cract* (cracked, crazy) as *Pierce na Gaoithe*.

Well, the time went by, and do you know I was *mar eadh* (as it were) gone to the shop. Wasn't I the great *óinseach* to keep gabbing away to that *áilleán* instead and not a dish washed at home, but sure, we had a great *seanchas* all right.

Mary's New Look

It's Mary Drohan who has the great garden over. I passed by and there she was going setting with her bucket of *sciolláns* (a portion of potato containing an 'eye') going and setting them. Not so long ago, that field was a right *fásach* (place overgrown), full of *copógs* (dock leaves) and *buachalláns* (ragweed). There wasn't *deil* nor *deamhair* (appearance) on the way things were going on there before, no *riar* nor *eagar* (order) on anything, but now, there's not a *lúb ar lár* (figuritive, stitch left down), not a *máchail* (defect) on anything. Everything was *tré chéile* (figurative, upside down) up to this; now there's a new *buaic* (ridge) on the thatch and not before its time; it was being put on the long finger for ages. She has her chickens and hens and calves and *banbhs*. She's done a great *gaisce* (feat) since she came. It must be a great *sólás* to the old couple to have her there.

Mary's real *flaithiúl*. Nothing would do her but to give me a *slog* (swallow) of the fresh milk. A small *taoscán* (small quantity) would have done me but I had to drain it down to the *dríodar* (dregs), but sure, I was glad of the *sos* (rest) and the *seanchas* (chat) after walking over the *bóithrín*.

Ruílle Búille at Morrisseys

I called to Morrisseys yesterday and a *mhic-eo* (son, a familiar greeting) you never heard such *rí-rá* and *ruílle búille*. The young lad was wearing an *aghaidh fidil* (mask) he'd bought for Halloween, and he went fooling around with a *camán* inside in the house, and whatever way he managed it, he made *smidiríns* (little bits) of the mirror and made *brus* (small fragments) of the frame as well. His father gave him a good *palltóg* (a thump) so there was more *olagóning*.

The big lads came in then, all *sceitimíní* (excitement) after winning the match. I must say I couldn't give a *tráithnin* (blade of grass) who won; I had no *suim* (interest) at all in the match, but they were all excitement, talking of the great *poc* Seán gave right into the goal and that was the one that won the match for them.

A Few Phrases, Whose Constructions Are Based On Irish

Between two minds what to do: *Idir dhá chomhairle.*

With a long time: *Le fada.*

She let a screech out of her: *Lig sí scread aisti.*

I saw her and I going down the road: *Agus mé ag dul síos an bóthar.*

I was only after coming in the door: *Ní raibh mé ach díreach tar éis teacht isteach.*

I was just making for the gate when: *Bhí mé díreach ag déamh ar an geata nuair.*

Other Words

Mallacht: Curse, he put his *mallacht* on me.

Aguisín: a little additional piece (from the word agus, and)

176

Siabhra: Phantom or spectre, often used in derision, e.g. the little *siabhra.*

Piseog: A strange custom.

Leadránach: Slow dragging.

Bladar: Coaxing talk.

Goílín: Gully or small rocky inlet, pronounced guy-lean.

Féirín: A present. She got her fayrin for the Pattern.

Suarach: Miserable.

Sásamh: Satisfaction.

Feileastram: Iris, a bog flower.

Ag stracadh leis: Struggling along. Generally used as an adjective, sure she's only stracadh leis.

A mhic-eo, alanna, a ghrá, a stór, a chroi, a mhaoineach are familiar greetings.

*Sean Riabhac (*pronounced Shoun-dríoch*):* This refers to the early days of April. If the weather is bad, it is said April got a loan of a few days from March to kill the speckled cow who had been dying.

There are picturesque phrases, a few of which I recall. I remember somebody asking Paddy Flynn how was the fishing going and he answered "Sure I didn't wet a net with three days."

Then there was Jack Flynn who came in to see my father after a period in hospital. My father evidently waxed eloquent on the subject of his injections, and Jacks rejoinder was "Sure some of them nurses are that handy, they'd put an injection in a 'flay' (flea) for you!". What a wonderful picture.

I have merely touched on the subject here, and I hope it jogs your memories so that you can catch glimpses once again of what John O'Donohue calls, "the colourful ghost of the Gaelic Language".

Coláiste Deuglán

Many students have been disappointed in securing accommodation in existing Irish Colleges, and it has been decided to open a new one in the historic district of Ardmore. A magnificent house has been secured with residential accommodation for 40. Residential Accommodation £2 to £3 per week. Tuition Fee £1.

So, under the heading "Coláiste Deuglán, Aird-Mhór (St. Declan's College, Ardmore) ran an advertisement on a pamphlet, *Clock Labhrais*, which reported on the status of Irish in the schools of the Waterford and Lismore Diocese for the year ending June 30th, 1920.

Coláiste Deuglán held its first session from 16th August to 11th September that same summer at Ardo House, which had been rented from the McKenna family for the purpose. Classes also took place there the following summer.

Monea House was then acquired from the Bagge family and as Coláiste Deuglán, prospered until the mid-thirties. The influx of teachers (attending as pupils) then had declined, as most of them had by this time, acquired proficiency in Irish but several continued to come, to enjoy a holiday in congenial surroundings in the company of friends and of figures well-known in national circles. The clientele by then also included teenagers from various secondary schools, coming both to improve their Irish and to have some fun.

The residential accommodation in the college was always augmented by the guesthouses in the village and visitors rented houses in the district and sent their children to the classes each day. It is certainly true that Coláiste Deuglán gave its first fillip to the tourist industry in Ardmore, and for many years was its mainstay. It was only after the war, from the late forties on, that the industry began to develop, as we now know it.

The first wave of enthusiasm for Irish had waned by then and the writing had begun to appear on the wall. In an effort to re-vitalise the college, a limited company was founded in 1937 with Deuglán Ó Cuilliú, Grange and Liam Ó Míocháin, An Rinn, as principal shareholders. A new addition was built at the eastern side. This later became the property of the Dungarvan Mercy Convent. It then became the Round Tower Hotel, run by Michael and Mrs Ronayne, and is now owned by Aidan Quirke, formally of Clonmel.

44 Mr. Eamonn De Valera TD attending the Muintir na Tíre Conference at Coláiste Deuglán, in conversation with Mrs. Walsh N.T. at Glenbeg, Dungarvan.

The first rural week organised by Muintir Na Tíre was held in Coláiste Deuglán in 1937 and another one in 1938. These occasions brought it very much into the limelight, attended as they were by influential national figures and by no less a person than Dev (Eamonn De Valera) himself who stayed for the week, going to mass each morning in the local church, and taking time too, to visit an old neighbour, William Harris from Bruree who had a public house on the site of Harty's residence. One night, at the céili in An Grianán (a separate hall built for dancing and extra classes), Mrs Cullen asked him out dancing at a Rogha na mBan, and there was a general rush for the floor, everyone looking forward to meeting Dev in Fallaí Luimní.

Maud Gonne McBride also attended and spoke on at least one occasion at the nightly sessions. Canon Hayes, founder of Muintir na Tíre, was there of course; so was Dr. Ryan, the then Minister for Agriculture. Gertrude Gaffney, correspondent for the *Independent* and Aodh de Blacam for the *Irish Press* gave first-hand accounts of the day-to-day events, in their respective newspapers.

In the forties, a course for vocational teachers was convened at Coláiste Deuglán, two years in succession. Andrias Ó Muimhneacháin, iar-uachtarán of the Oireachtas helped to run that course; Caitlín Ní Ruairc also taught there. She was later to help Lady Goulding in founding the Rehabilitation Centre in Dublin.

These sessions evoked memories of the earlier years when the place was vibrant with life and hope and love of the old language. However, it was its swansong, and it was sold to the Tourist Board, who perhaps had visions of a hotel there, but all the villagers saw happening was the demolition of the high walls around the orchard and the opening-up of the big yard between new and old buildings, where aeríochta used to be held in the earlier days.

The building was sold in 1954 to Mr F Nugent and Mr J O'Brien. For the next four years, the I.C.A. held meetings there, in the big room at the right-hand side of the entrance hall. The G.A.A. later had the room at the left, and there was considerable liaison between the two groups. Then in January 1958, the tenancy was ended and the building was demolished. So ended Coláiste Deuglán.

To the local boys and girls who knew it in the thirties and early forties, it looked like an 'institution' that was always part of Ardmore and would go on forever. It seems almost incredible that it lasted less than forty years.

The memories of youth are wound round it inextricably, the wonderful céilithe at the Grianán each night; of endeavouring to direct Jim Murphy-O'Connor, brother of the bishop of Arundel and Brighton (now Archbishop of Westminster) through the intricacies of Rinnce an Fhéir, without revealing that he knew no word of Irish - he was being given directions in Irish by Fear an Tí; of classes with red-haired Micheál O'Conchubhair, the most popular teacher of all; of Micheál Ó Foghlú playing the bagpipes not alone in the hall but up and down the street with Seainín 'Coe'; of the Italian count who came to Muintir na Tíre rural week and spoke of his lands round Bobbio, the monastic foundation of St. Columbanus. Big Liam Moloney, the 'Gas', Pilip Ó Laoghaire of Cor Cois Laoi fame, Muiris Ó Faoláin, the renowned seanchaí, all flit in and out of the pictures conjured in my mind. Máire Ní Mhéara, one of the three Clonmel sisters, came year after year to teach Irish Dancing. Eilís Dillon, the well-known novelist, was Bean an Tí, once or twice.

Mícheál Ó Foghlú was the person associated with Coláiste Deuglán, throughout the whole period of its existence, being its secretary all that time. A local man, he spent some time in Scotland, was involved with Irish classes there and went to Wales in 1911 where he taught Connradh na Gaeilge classes with Pádraig Ó Mileadha, the Sliabh gCua poet. There was a life-long friendship between them and they corresponded frequently, mostly on poetical matters. Traditional music was the breath of life to Mícheál. *Saothar na mBeach*, *Cuisle Ceoil* and *Seoda Sidhe* were collections of songs published by him. He also founded a Piper's Band in Ardmore and brought them to aeríochta and feiseanna.

All members of the Cullen (O'Cuilliú) family were always deeply involved with the college. Deaglan was headmaster in Grange which he made an all-Irish school, and, as indicated in the initial advertisement at the head of this section, he was the first headmaster in Coláiste Deuglán and a guiding light in it down through the years. The family was very musical and played for the céilithe, Una (Mrs Prendergast, Dungarvan) on the piano and her sister, Máirín and her father, Deuglán on the fiddles. Mrs Harty played the melodeon as well. The musical tradition was well exemplified too in Labhrás Ó Cadhla, a native of Kilbrien who had a wealth of Irish songs, many of which were recorded for the Folklore Commission. He also played the uileann pipes. Deuglán Suipeál of Grange, another singer of note, was often heard on the sound waves, in the early days of Irish broadcasting. Séan Ó Suilleabháin, former chief archivist in the Folklore Commission and known internationally for his work on folklore, was a distinguished name connected with Coláiste Deuglán.

Séamus Ó Suilleabháin, more popularly known as the 'Gas' was 'ard ollamh' from 1923 - 1930, and after his death came Séamus Dalton (related to the Troys of Curragh), former chief translator in Dáil Éireann, who filled the post 1930 - 1933. With him on the staff were Micheál Ceitinn, Seán Ó Dúnái and Micheál Ó Concubhair of Ardmore, Muiris de Léis of Old Parish and Sean Ó hAlluráin of Clashmore.

Séamus Pender from Waterford followed Seamas Dalton. He had a travelling scholarship in history and studied in Germany under Pokorny, a well-known authority on Old Irish. He was lecturer and later, professor of history in U.C.C.

Sylvester Conway from Clare, headmaster in Cappawhite Vocational School, was ard ollamh later on and still in the thirties, there was an t-Athair Tadhg Ó Murchú who taught in Farranferris, established Brú na nÓg in Dun Caoin, and became Parish Priest of Carragi na bhFear, Co. Cork.

Liam Ó hUalaigh was a member of the staff in the forties; he was a pious Corkman and a teetotaller. Micheál Ceitinn, on being asked a few years later, how Liam was, said sarcastically, "Conas a bheadh se ach mar a bhí sé i gcónaí, ag ól tae agus ag léamh an *Messenger*". ('How else could he be except as he always was, drinking tea and reading the *Messenger*'.)

At the beginning of the war, a big Red Cross dance was organised by the local committee and held in the new building at the college. I have vivid memories of Séan Ó Dúnaí sipping his pint in Rooney's kitchen, shaking his head sadly as he repeated over and over again, "Coláiste Deuglán, Mick Delahunty's jazz band", that it should come to this!

The College grounds extended from Crowley's house (old Post Office) right out to the end of the row of seven houses. The orchard, surrounded by high stone walls, was at the eastern end. Then there was a spacious yard with separate entrance from the road. The house itself was somewhat slightly to the rear of Dr

McNamara's house and extended a considerable distance backwards. The lawn in front was surrounded by old trees and fumbling for the key of the big Georgian door, on a dark winter night, in pre-electricity days, wasn't an experience for the faint hearted among the I.C.A. The Grianán - where ceílithe were held - was to the west of the house, but nearer the road, and there was a separate small gate giving access to the grounds here. The principal entrance, but rarely used, was at the far end of the terrace of seven houses, and a long driveway lined by several old trees led over to the house. It was first the dignified gracious residence of local landlords and then for well over thirty years, fulfilled a very different role as a nurturing place of Irish language and music and culture. Sadly it has completely disappeared, but it is good to remember it and right that the present and other generations should be aware of that brief but brilliant and exciting period in the life of Áird Mhór.

The Oireachtas

Rulers of the ancient kingdom of 7th century Ireland formed the original Oireachtas or Assembly. In 1897 Connradh na Gaeilge founded what is now Ireland's longest running annual cultural festival, thereby reviving the noble tradition of assembly and discussion begun by our ancestors centuries earlier. The spirit of the Oireachtas is evoked by similar festivals in the countries of our Celtic neighbours, namely the Eisteddfod in Wales, the Mod in Scotland, the international Celtic festival of Lorient in Brittany and Yn Chrucnnaght in the Isle of Man.

The Oireachtas is a feast of Irish music, song, dance, and storytelling with numerous side-events such as cookery demonstrations, craft demonstrations, fashion competitions, and sports events, to mention but a few. It takes place at a different venue every year and in 1994 it took place in Ring/Dungarvan and was an outstanding success with well in excess of 20,000 visitors during the ten days.

Ardmore participated in the 1994 Oireachtas, and this involved attending regular meetings in An Rinn through the preceding year. The members of the Ardmore section comprised E. Mansfield, C. Lyons, C. Burke, E. Fitzgerald, the present writer and, of course, we were present at the official opening by festival patron Ciarán Mac Mathúna, the well-known broadcaster and collector of Irish music, and at various other events during the ten days. Sr. Deuglán of Aird Mhór gave 'léacht an Oireachtas' in Lawlors Hotel and E. Moinbhial was part of the choir for the televised Mass in St. Marys Church, Dungarvan.

The members of our committee were very busy before Monday 31st October, the special Oireachtas Day of Ardmore. It was a memorable occasion. The Oireachtas visitors were given a talk in Irish at the Round Tower by the present writer. St. Declan's Well and St. Declan's Stone were then visited. Refreshments were supplied at the Round Tower Hotel and E. Mansfield regaled the company with stories of Coláiste Deuglán, of which the hotel was formerly part. The late Mrs. M. Foghlú was guest of the committee, her father having founded Coláiste Deuglán.

The Youghal Pipe Band led the group to Halla Deuglán and an evening of music song and dance followed. It was contributed to by the Ardmore children, Nora Looby and her flute players; Mrs N. Walsh and her dancers; the Aglish group who won the Youghal Busking competition that summer, our set dancers; Don Brocky and his musicians and his truly wonderful choir, Canon Power who played the violin and Sr. Deuglán who sang, as also did E. Mansfield. We heard two tapes of Deuglán Supple singing. He was the first to perform in the very early days of broadcasting for 2 RN.

St. Declan's Well.

45 An engraving of Saint Declan's Well, Ardmore, c1840.

No account of the 1994 Oireachtas would be complete without a mention of Keith, not yet four years, who in his piper's uniform and carrying a real set of bagpipes, marched manfully with the band.

The Tidy Towns committee had the flags flying, both at the Cross and at the promenade, so it was really a gala day all around.

C. Burke and C. Lyons had done trojan work beforehand, preparing most attractive posters and other material for display, not alone in Ardmore, but at the functions in Dungarvan and they also arranged the photographic material displayed in the Round Tower Hotel.

These Ardmore committee members deeply appreciated having the hall at their disposal for functions, of the help given at the door and also behind the scenes by John Kennedy and naturally, of having had such a talented group of people providing entertainment.

Among the distinguished visitors present in Ardmore were Fr. Diarmuid Ó Laoghaire S.J., Íte Ní Chionnaith, Chairperson of the Oireachtas and Ciarán MacMathúna, patron of the Oireachtas.

Religious Knowledge and Observances

In school in our day the 30s & 40s we had the small *Green Catechism*, the *Red Catechism*, the *Manual* containing still more advanced knowledge of the matter and form of all the Sacraments, the Ember Days, and the Rogation Days. There was also *Schuster's Bible History*.

We learnt the 6 precepts of the Church: -

1. To hear mass on Sundays and Holy days of obligation.

2. To fast and abstain on the days commanded.

3. To confess our sins at least once a year.

4. To receive the Blessed Eucharist at Easter time, between Ash Wednesday and Trinity Sunday.

5. To pay dues to our pastors.

6. Not to marry at the forbidden times nor within the forbidden degrees of kindred and not to marry persons of a different religion.

We could list off the seven deadly sins, knew the Rogation Days and the Ember Days, what was commanded and forbidden by the Ten Commandments.

We were certainly well instructed in our religion. The present-day children do not learn in such detail. The information is presented in a much more attractive manner and has more of an emphasis now on God's love for us all, on our duty in return to love God, and all God's people, and to love our neighbours as ourselves.

As a matter of course, everybody went to Sunday mass in the old days. Fasting and abstaining on the days commanded was regarded as a very serious obligation. Every Friday was of course a day of abstinence; there are now only two in the year, Ash Wednesday and Good Friday.

46 Tigaluinn Hotel, where the author grew up.

The eves of certain feasts were days of abstinence too. My sister Eileen Colbert remembers this vividly. When she was in Tigaluinn and running it as a guesthouse in the forties, it must have been suddenly announced at Sunday Mass that the following day, Monday, the eve of the Assumption was a day of abstinence, and she had no fish for the mid-day meal. In a private household this would not have been a disaster, but in a guesthouse it was. It being Monday there was no fish to had in Youghal either, so Dick my husband drove to Cork to procure it for her guests.

188

People went to confession regularly and there were confraternity meetings once a month and practically everyone went to the sacraments once a month.

Jimmie Rooney speaks of the difficulty of getting into confession, the place being so crowded. One special time of the year when it was crowded was before Trinity Sunday as going to the sacraments at least once a year was obligatory and the time for this was between Ash Wednesday and Trinity Sunday; hence the phrase doing your Easter duty.

On one occasion my sister and I cycled to Melleray to visit our brother James who was at school there. On the way up, a car passed and one of the Sergeant boys from Cappoquin, whom we knew, opened the window, and waved at us in a sort of jeering way. We were puzzled but we soon found out the reason. We encountered a long line of the Melleray boys in the avenue and when we met James, he said, "What brought ye up to-day?" Evidently, it was the last day for the 'Easter Duty' and all the 'hard cases' were going to Melleray for confession that day.

Old Funeral Practices

Funeral Protocol has changed very much within the last forty years or so. It was thought necessary then to lay the dead person out in a brown habit bought at a draper's shop; now the personal clothes of the deceased person are used. In 1958, when my husband died, he was laid out in a habit, but my two sons in 1979 and 1982 were dressed in their own clothes. When my aunt Mrs Quain died in 1978, her daughter Ciss had her laid out in a beautiful white night-dress made by my grandmother. I know I can never, never again see such an extraordinarily superb example of needlework.

The corpse was always 'waked' in the house too, and there, neighbours came to pay their respects. Food or drink was generally offered. Wakes still take place at home, but people tend to make much more use of 'funeral parlours' now; the body is conveyed there and the mourners come there to pay their respects before the remains are removed to the church.

Up to about 30/40 years ago, the priests receiving the corpse at the church wore around their hats and hanging by their sides a long strip of white linen, which was donated by the family of the deceased.

At the period my husband died (1958) it was considered necessary to go into mourning and wear black clothes for a whole year afterwards and this I did. However, I didn't do so on the occasions of my sons' deaths in 1979 and 1982. The custom has changed completely in that respect. Very many things have changed as regards religious practise since then.

Lent

Lent long ago was most definitely a penitential season and church rules and regulations differed from diocese to diocese. The late John Cashman used to jokingly remark that in their household, the old home at Red Forge on the Tallow Road, they had the choice of two programmes because the borderline between the Diocese of Cloyne and of Waterford/Lismore passed through their house.

The law of fasting applied to those between the ages of twenty one and sixty and generally consisted of the allowance of one full meal a day and two 'collations'. The two 'collations' meant light meals. Invalids and those who had to do difficult manual work were exempt.

It was more or less taken for granted that children fasted from sweets for Lent (except for St. Patricks Day). I remember saving them up and looking forward eagerly to noon on Easter Saturday when we considered ourselves dispensed.

Public entertainment too came under Lenten regulations and again the rules changed from Diocese to Diocese. No dances took place in our Diocese during Lent but other Diocese were different.

Parish Missions

A feature of religious life in the parish was a 'Mission' run every few years. Two priests from a religious order came and worked hard to renew our religious fervour, instruct us and generally give us an in-depth course in our religion. There were daily masses, sermons both morning and evening and confessions going on for hours during the day. The missioners visited all the sick in the parish. A big feature of the week was the blessing of rosaries, statues and all kinds of religious objects. A stall was erected outside the church gate where all these objects were on display and could be bought.

The sermons in the church were followed with great interest and the different preaching styles of the two missioners commented on. The Wednesday night sermon was usually on the sixth commandment on chastity, and commanded a good deal of attention.

Mrs. Barry, the Cork lady who virtually dominated the Cliff in the earlier years of the last century was a keen apostle of Temperance and is reputed to have sent a message to one of the missioners to preach on the subject. It is also reported that the missioner responded in a most unmissionary like way "Tell Mrs Barry, *Go to hell*". One cannot of course vouch for the veracity of the anecdote.

A well-known local man is said to have shocked the priest in the confession box when he reported the length of time since his last confession; the confessor voiced his horror in no uncertain manner and the would-be penitent reacted by telling the priest out loud "We paid a lot of money to bring ye here and 'twasn't for abuse we brought ye".

Generally speaking, there was almost 100% participation in church devotions during the mission period. It was like a spring clean, and brought a revival of religious fervour in the parish.

The Pattern

47 St. Declan's Well, 1910. Photo by Thomas Mason. Dept. Irish Folklore, UCD.

Canon Power, the great historian of our Diocese; "The Pattern of Ardmore was perhaps the most remarkable celebration of its kind in Ireland and certainly the most ancient and notable popular assembly in Decies". This is fitting, considering St. Declan's Well is the most ancient Christian settlement on this Island.

A first-hand account of the Pattern in Ardmore was given by 'a gentleman of high attainments and undoubted veracity' to Mr & Mrs Hall, who toured the country in 1838 and 1840.

"After coming up to the Well the people knelt down and said their prayers. At twenty different periods, I counted the people as they prayed; they averaged fifty five a minute which gives a total of 12 or 15,000 persons. Eating, drinking, and dancing went on down the village so bloody knees from devotion and bloody heads from fighting is not uncommon". Fr. McGrath, Parish Priest, suppressed the Pattern in the 1830s, but it survived and later on, got ecclesiastical approval.

For generations, Pattern Week has been the highlight of the year in Ardmore. People aimed to have their whitewashing and general tidy-up done before the Pattern. Children looked forward to getting their Pattern Fayrin (féirin, present). It was exciting going down to see all the stalls and hurdy gurdies, which seemed to fill the lower end of the street. The public houses were of course full and there was a dancing platform out in Rooney's yard (Paddy Macs now) and also in Harris' garden. People would have gone up to do the Rounds at the well before this, gone under St. Declan's Stone, and paid a visit to St. Declan's grave in the Beannachan.

Clodagh Anson (now deceased) writes in her article 'Ansons at Ardmore' in the *Ardmore Journal* 1988 "We always looked forward to Pattern Sunday with the bands and stalls and people crawling under St. Declan's Stone. We watched from our drawing room window thinking someone very fat might try and get stuck." This would have been in the early years of the century, and they were watching from the house now known as Stella Maris.

In Tigaluinn (my home) as in other places, teas were served and I remember in the 30s and 40s being run off our feet all the evening. One of the girls helping in the house was from Limerick and when she saw all the food supplies being brought in, beforehand, she asked in bewilderment, "How long does the Pattern Last?" One had to be careful to put supplies aside for the breakfast the following morning. Another point to be noted, was, that home-made bread was not served to the Pattern visitors; they had too much of that at home. We were visited not alone by paying customers but by relations from surrounding parishes, whom we hadn't met since the previous Pattern.

St. Deglan's Stone, Ardmore

48 A postcard showing a man crawling underneath Saint Declan's Stone, Ardmore, c1920.

Pat Ormond, The Square, Dungarvan, talks of his grandmother and others walking from Dungarvan to Ardmore, up Towler's Glen and the old short cut which emerged at the Seanchaí and on to Ardmore selling what he thought was probably dried hake. They walked back again in the evening. My uncle Paddy from the

Dungarvan area says anything that had a wheel under it in Dungarvan and Cappoquin went to Ardmore for Pattern Sunday.

Some of the Helvick and Baile na nGall people often made their pilgrimage to Ardmore Pattern by boat. About 1943 or 1944 the two boats that came were the *Comhluadar* and *Betsie* with about fourteen to fifteen people in each boat. On that particular occasion one of the boats because of bad weather conditions could not manage to get into Ardmore Bay and had to continue right around to Youghal, leave the boat at anchor there and return to Ring on foot, a call to Flemings' Pub in Grange being the nearest they got to the Pattern in Ardmore.

The other boat had its adventures too. It went aground at the end of Carraig an Ánn. Paddy Flynn and Jim Quain ferried the passengers to the pier. In the middle of the night, P.J. Morrissey from Dungarvan, who had stayed on board, signalled for help to get the boat started. In response Dan Gallagher the local sergeant disturbed the slumbers of Jack Brien and Jimmie Rooney. Jimmie had to get a can of petrol and ferry it across hand over hand by rope to the boat, a somewhat hazardous undertaking since swimming was not one of his accomplishments. I have had these stories from both Jimmie Rooney and Nioclás Graves of Ring. I can't say they tally exactly in the details but 1943 is a long time ago. At any rate there were other pilgrimages by boat from Ring to Ardmore Pattern not usually accompanied by such adventures.

My mother speaks of once meeting two men from Kilmacthomas who walked from there and back, spending the night at the Well. She had them down for breakfast in the morning; this happened on at least a few occasions.

There was a Pattern Céilí at Coláiste Deuglán and tired and sore as our feet were, after the day, we always went over. There was also a dance at Halla Deuglán. In 1930 the *Dungarvan Observer* made the following announcement under 'Local Happenings':

'Ardmore Patron on Sunday next will enjoy a feast of music song and dance at the aeríocht Céilí to be held in the College grounds. The programme includes pipers' bands, contests, tugs of war etc. Three artistes from the Dublin Broadcasting Station will contribute to the programme'.

49 Pattern Festival activities, the Beer Barrel Race along Main Street, Ardmore.

Things are entirely different nowadays. Efforts have been made from time to time, to renew the sense of carnival. In 1967 and 1968, there were 3-day events incorporating football, greasy pole contests, wheelbarrow races, scavenging hunts, bands and ballads. The I.C.A. always has something special, like the Antique Fair and afternoon tea.

There was midnight Mass at the Well for a few years in succession, with a candlelight procession from the Church beforehand. On at least one occasion it was followed by an all-night Vigil with Fr.

Butler carrying the monstrance at dawn, across the New Line and down to the old cathedral in the graveyard, where we knelt and prayed. It was a very moving experience praying publicly there after some hundreds of years.

50 *Ardmore Cathedral, 2021.*

The bogey of insurance has now intervened, and Mass did not take place last year 1998, but the faithful came and said the traditional prayers there at midnight. The Whelan family and friends from Ballyquin had illuminated the place beautifully with lighted candles in the ground and so the tradition goes on.

A point worthy of note is that the feast of St. Declan was indeed celebrated with special ceremony in the local church but that until about ten or twelve years ago, when Mass first took place there the recitation of the prayers at midnight and any other ceremonies at the Well were solely carried out by the laity.

Crowds still come to the Well on Pattern Sunday (the Sunday nearest the feast); but the gathering at midnight on the eve of the Feast is much smaller. People also come and do the Rounds in the evenings during Pattern Week.

Old Irish Song (From Dungarvan Observer, October 1950.)

This hymn was composed by Tadhg Gaelach and the tune taken down from Síle Foley of Ardmore. Síle who was born in 1772, probably learned it from an older generation. The tune could be hundreds of years older than the words. In fact, this tune and the Rounds associated with St. Declan's Pattern Day were thought by a 19th century bishop to be relics of an ancient pagan superstition.

The bishop came to the beach and ordered a man called Diarmuid Ó Foghlú to break the stone with a sledge. Diarmuid answered, "Tabhair-se féin, a thiarna easpoig an chéad bhuille dí agus brisfidh mé ansan é." The stone is still on the beach.

Strangely, the tune is an almost perfect canon. It is fanciful to think that this tune evolved from the Rounds themselves, as harmony (or canon) did not exist in Irish tradition. It could have happened like this. As one group of people circled the tower or church, starting the tune as they did, they were likely to be overlapped by other groups who started later. So to avoid absolute cacophony, a song emerged which sounded well even overlapped on itself i.e. canon. We give the tune here as a strict canon, with ostinato.

Mo ghrá-se mo Dhia, mo Gharda, mo líagh
Mo ghrá gheal, mo Thiarna trócaireach
Mo ghrá mhilis Críost, agus gráim uile chroí
Mo ghrá 's tú Rí na Glóire.

This tune and commentary are unsigned, but it is more than likely they were provided by T. Horgan of Youghal.

Ardmore GAA Club

The G.A.A has had numerous ups and downs in the parish, from the Holy Terrors who were pre G.A.A to the 1898 team, the first team to play under G.A.A. rules. The members of the first 17-aside team are enumerated in Paddy Foley's article in the 1984 edition of *The Ardmore Journal.* However, until the 50s it was a lean period even though Martin Hurley provided a clubroom in Johnie Mulcahy's old house near the Boathouse and drove supporters to matches in his lorry.

In the 50s things began to perk up. In 1950, Ardmore won the Western Junior Football Final and were unlucky to be beaten by Kill in the county final. An amusing story of this match concerns my late husband's hat (Richard Lincoln) and it was remembered as recently as this year, when two of the Cullen brothers from Tramore spoke of it to Paddy Foley. Apparently Dick was on the sideline anxiously watching the match, his hands behind his back holding his hat. When the match was over, the hat had got such handling that it was completely unwearable and of course, was a great cause of hilarity among his companions.

In 1957, the club having lapsed, a public meeting was held and a new committee elected. Jimmie Rooney made a field available free of charge and Frank Nugent gave the use of a room at the college as a clubroom. In 1958 the departure of Fr. Phelan and the death of Richard Lincoln were serious blows to the club, but however, in 1960, the first Junior county final was won by Ardmore, so the tide was turning. Paddy Foley remembers Joe Curran being the person in charge of a flour bag full of jerseys at the matches, furze bushes had been used as sideline markers in the the 40s and 50s, until Mamie Curran made sideline flags. In 1961 Ardmore won the county final and went on to win county finals in 1965 and in 1977 along with many other titles.

A field was purchased in 1982 and this of course was a most wonderful achievement. It was officially opened, by Mr Buggy, the President of the G.A.A., in 1984, the centenary year of the founding of the Association. In 1987 President Hillery landed there by helicopter when he came to open the enlarged Halla Deuglán. Cardinal Ó Fiaich was also in Ardmore during the same period for the 150th anniversary of the building of the Churches in the parish and he unveiled a plaque to Michael O'Brien, a former member, at the gable-end of the Clubhouse.

51 The entrance to Ardmore GAA Club, 2021.

In the early 90s there was a concentration of interest in the juveniles and that is now bearing fruit, with the under 10s, under 12, under 14 and under 16 teams and a minor one as well, under the watchful eye of John Hennessy, who has represented

Waterford in football at both county and provincial levels. Billy Harty, John Donnell, and Paddy Foley are the other angel guardians.

We are of course very proud of Mary O'Donnell who played regularly with the boy's team and has now played several times for Waterford Ladies Football in Croke Park, though she is only seventeen years old.

Other fairly recent distinctions in G.A.A. circles in Ardmore were:-

> 1997: Paddy Foley was elected Vice-Chairman of Waterford County Bord na nÓg.

> 1997: Michael Supple was voted Young Footballer of the Year in Waterford.

> 1998: Séamus Prendergast was voted Young Hurler of the Year in the County. He is presently a member of the Waterford Senior Hurling Panel.

I am indebted to Paddy Foley for the above which is merely a summary account of G.A.A. affairs in Ardmore up to the present day. Further details can be found in the 1984 issue of the *Ardmore Journal*.

Soccer is not as bound up with the sporting traditions of the locality, as is the G.A.A. but it may be noted here that in 1982 a soccer club was founded in the village and apparently is getting on well. Despite the rules and regulations, there seems to be quite a cross-over between followers of the two sports.

Old Customs and Piseoga

Lighting bonfires on St. John's Night in June is an old custom. John Fitzgerald spoke of looking out his door at Listigue and seeing the lines of fires over at the Ballymacoda side of Youghal bay. Paddy Foley speaks of having the fire at Kielys, Bun an Chnoic and jumping through it as it began to die. The practise of going from door to door on St. Stephen's Day seems to have become extinct in Ardmore but not elsewhere. One which has superseded it is the 'Trick or Treat' visitation by children on Hallow Ee'n. My first encounter with that custom was when Sally and Virginia, Molly Keane's daughters came to the door one Hallow Ee'n and I just didn't know what they were about; I know better now.

The *Cailleach* was an effigy generally of straw, affixed to the outer wall of a dwelling, where there was an eligible young man or woman on Shrove Tuesday night. *Brat Bride* was a piece of ribbon or cloth put hanging from a house on St. Brigid's Eve. It was kept during the year, for giving relief to sores or other ailments.

Easter Water is always sprinkled on fields, especially on boundary fences on May Eve. Most people still place a lighted candle in the window on November night, the Feast of All Souls.

My mother would not allow hawthorn into the house, during May. Alder branches were also taboo. Katherine Lyons recalls a baby brother dying and the women around the fire in hushed tones referring to the presence of alder in the house.

My sister while in Melrose had another unusual experience. She was having wash put up on the front of the house; it just so happened to be May Eve and the wash did not adhere at all to the wall. She never thought of *piseoga*, but one of the men was from Monatrea and said no one in Monatrea would dream of white-washing in May. She didn't take this statement too seriously but did have to get alternative materials some days later. It so happened that the lady who supplied eggs to the house passed in during the operation and this was looked on as a bad omen too.

A grave shouldn't be cut on a Monday, but it is quite alright to cut the sod on a Sunday night. Don't start anything on a Friday.

52 An unidentified couple outside a thatched cottage Ardmore, c1930. The lady is wearing a Kinsale Cloak.

Don't look at the new moon through glass. These are traditional warnings. It is good luck for a black cat to come in the door. On the contrary, a robin coming in betokens ill fortune.

Piseoga

Strange sinister customs prevailed not alone in our area but throughout the country, people had a horror of the 'evil eye'. In the 1940s, Jimmie Burke (who died in 1970 aged 73) was setting potatoes and a women with the reputation of the 'evil eye' came and spoke with him. When he returned to the house, he sat down and told of his encounter and said there would be no potatoes in that section of field, and that's precisely what happened.

Other strange occurrences are recounted locally, such as the following.

One farmer's cows having practically no milk while his neighbour's had plenty was another occurrence. Also, there were accounts of one farmer having a fine crop of corn while his neighbours harvest was a disaster.

There are several stories of women trying unsuccessfully to churn and make butter while butter was at the same time often plastered perhaps to an outhouse wall or a gate pier. Other well-known happening was the planting of eggs in between drills of potatoes and the potatoes as a result did not maturing - Paddy Foley and Jimmy Rooney both experienced this and the burying dead animals or bones in a neighbour's fields and the neighbour's crops being ruined as a result.

Desmond Connery speaks of a man near Villierstown who kept some pigs but one day he found a pigs head impaled across the gate-way; all the pigs died subsequently.

The late Jimmy Burke (previously mentioned) told two other rather scary stories which make interesting recording.

At the top of Geata 'n Bhóthair Aird, i.e. about two and half miles from Ardmore there is a sign post and a road to the right leading to the N25. Just at the intersection, on the North side there is a very small plot of ground occupied at the beginning of the last century by a family of Braonán. Peig the wife died and was buried in the old graveyard in Grange. The following night about midnight, there was a frightful din in the house of delf, chairs etc all moving. The following night a neighbour, probably Mike Broderick, came to keep Tim the widower company and the disturbance began again, whereupon the neighbour addressed the spirit i.e. Peig and asked her why she was troubled. It transpired she was in the wrong grave. This was rectified the next day and the corpse reburied in another grave, a very short distance away. There were no further disturbances in the household at night.

In the same area but some distance downhill where an old boreen crosses, the farmer then in occupation there had trouble with milk, his cows just didn't have any. He began watching and one morning early saw a hare sucking one of the cows in the field and then crossing towards a ruined shed. He went in pursuit with a sprong to pounce on the hare whereupon it spoke "Ó, ná dean, a Phádraig; mise atá ann." (Oh don't do that, Patrick, It is me). It was a neighbour as he suspected.

There are far more spectacular stories than these: I have merely touched on the subject and recounted the more commonplace ones. The present generation will find it hard to credit and will be more inclined to scoff at it but it is only too true. The perpetrators were known and were often frequent visitors to the afflicted households and were regular Churchgoers. The occurrences were serious and most sinister and I cannot understand them at all. The problem of evil is an inscrutable mystery..

Healing And Old Remedies

The gift of healing was a strange one. Bone-setting was one particular way in which it showed itself. The Towlers of Gurteen (near the Seancháí) were known far and wide for this gift. John Towler there was father of Sheila Towler, Ellen Towler (Mrs Hallahan), Mrs Murphy, Glenmore; Johnny Murphy, Summerhill, was son of Mrs Murphy. Mossy Hallihan says he often saw a queue outside Murphys in Glenmore after a match and indeed his own house in Tynalyra, Grange was much frequented by people with broken bones. Sometimes people actually came in the middle of the night. The cure was often simple but more often involved the application of a plaster.

My sister tells the story of her late husband, Eddie Colbert, who had some injury to his ankle which prevented him putting any weight in that foot. The Colberts lived in Ballymacoda and he and his brother went by pony and trap to Youghal, then by hired car to Mrs Murphy of Glenmore. He fully expected the treatment to be painful, but Mrs Murphy merely laid her hand on his ankle, and told him to walk round the table. He reached for his stick, but she said "no" and from that on his ankle was completely cured.

Other families had cures for skin disease, but the story of the 7th son of a 7th son is the strangest of all. Terry McGrath's grandfather (Paddy McGrath, Ballinamertina) was in that category and he had the gift of healing, but a gift which he was most reluctant to practice. Terry says on one occasion, his wife Rose was in really dire straits with frightful toothache, but it took him a long time to yield to her entreaties. When he did and applied his hand to the afflicted part, the pain disappeared.

206

These practices belonged to the Ireland of forty or fifty years ago, though bone-setting is probably still practised here and there.

The following cures and snippets of medical advice are taken from a manuscript of 1855 by Martin Driscoll, Bawnard, Grange (my husband's uncle).

For the Chincough

Take a mouse and flea (?) and dry it in an oven and reduce it to powder and let the party grieved drink it in ale and it will help him. This is also good for them that cannot hold their water.

The Youthful Draught

Make powder of the flowers of Elder gathered on Mid-Summer day being well dried and using a spoonful thereof in a good draught of Borrage water, morning and evening for the space of a month and it will make you seem young.

Periwinkle Venus

The leaves eaten by man and wife together cause love between them.

Somehow I don't think these prescriptions would be acceptable today.

Deuglán Fáilte

The little group, Deuglán Fáilte has had its eighth birthday. It meets in the small room at the front of St. Declan's Hall every Monday evening. The Burke sisters are its guardian angels and oversee and implement all the arrangements including the provision of tea and cakes. The company is usually of about thirteen or fourteen at the most and even though it wasn't originally intended that way, practically all are senior citizens. We spend a very pleasant few hours there each week. Diarmuid Cotter from Dungarvan will play the violin or sing. Maureen Reidy, Ardo, also sings. And her brother Èamon Móinbhial from Cork has a huge repertoire of both English and Irish songs. John Kennedy of Lisarow, a consummate actor, reads selected pieces and he has a most amazing collection of tapes and music rivalling that of the late well-known Mr. T. O'Brien of Clonmel. The St. Declan's Community Association mentioned in the account of the Ardmore Enterprise Co-Op meets in the ICA room on Tuesday evenings.

Travelling People

There were certain personages who paid periodic visits, mostly at Pattern time. Among them were:

God in the Bottle, who succeeded in inserting pieces of wood into a bottle in the form of crucifixion figures; these he sold to several clients.

Ginger Doyle, reputedly a learned man and one time student for the priesthood.

Rua Ward, bard of Armagh and Ulster.

Maggie Lennon, whose speciality was artificial flowers.

Paddy Lawlor, who said he had travelled the world; he used to stay at Duceys and play cards at Burkes.

There were several others who came from time to time and seemingly always got hospitality at Conways of Clarkestown.

Up to about thirty or forty years ago, people waited for the tinkers to come around to buy a quart tin with a handle (very suitable for boiling eggs) or a bucket. Evidently, they were skilful tradesmen and called themselves tinsmiths. Presumably the name tinkers was derived from that.

Over thirty years ago and later the travelling families with whom we became familiar were the Hogans and the O'Connors. The Hogans settled eventually in a house in Tinnock and the children went to school there.

Mrs Hogan was a frequent visitor to Melrose guesthouse - among several other establishments - and my sister always saved a good helping of food for her. She would bring away the containers and return the empties later. On one occasion in particular she asked for some dripping as well "to fry the mackerel your nephew sold to Stephen". My sister was intrigued at the idea of Richard actually selling fish to Stephen (Hogan) but she was reassured by Mrs Hogan that such was the case, and she said they had as much haggling over the mackeral as if they were beasts at a fair.

At that time the laws of strict abstinence prevailed and selling mackerel each Thursday evening in the summer months was an occupation in which teenagers who had access to boats and fishing lines keenly indulged. There was great competition between the different groups in getting to the convents in time. The nuns always looked for the larger fish not realising that the medium-sized ones were more tasty and better bargains. There was a stage when my car was used by my sons on Thursday evenings, to do mackerel sales to the farmers around.

Troubled Times

The War of Independence

The period of the early 20s has always been euphemistically referred to as "the time of the trouble", a really fitting term. In the country in general, as an aftermath of the Easter Rising there was a vast increase of support for Sinn Féin and the Irish Volunteers.

In *The Comeraghs, Refuge of Rebels* by Seán and Síle Murphy, we are told that in January 1918, a Decies Brigade came into existence, Ardmore/Old Parish being one of the four battalions. By 1920 there was a formal staffing arrangement.

The Brigade staff for Ardmore/Old Parish consisted of: -

Jim Mansfield, O.C.
Willie Doyle, O.C.
Paddy Cashel, Adjutant
Declan Slattery, Q.M.
Dick Mooney, Engineer
Jerry Fitzgerald, Dispatch
Tom Mooney, Transport
Declan Troy, Training Officer.

Dick Mooney and Tom Mooney were brothers and Tom was father of Tommie and Christy, Clare and Dick.

In the following paragraphs, Tom gives some of his own recollections.

'Sonny Foley had a grocery shop at the end of the village and his sister Lizzie became the owner after his death. She knew Margaret Pearse and visited her more than once. She accompanied Mick Mansfield (posing as his wife) on a gun running trip to Northern Ireland and came back with a case full of guns. She was the principal organiser of Cumann na mBan in the Ardmore area and her niece Anastasia Keating mother of the Mooneys was one of her earlier recruits. Molly Flynn of Chapel Row was one of the members. Her mother, Mag 'the Chapel Woman' (the Sacristan), on one occasion warned the Curragh people of an impending attack by ringing the church bells.'

'After an attack on British forces in Fermoy in 1918 Liam Lynch, Chief of Staff, was wounded and spent a brief period at Foleys house in Ardmore, it being known to be a 'safe house'. During the Black and Tan period, Sonny Foley, and Paddy Ormonde (as well as several others in their turns) were among the unwilling passengers in Black and Tan lorries, when the Tans took them as hostages and put them in positions where they were readily visible to any intending attacker.'

'Early in the Tan war Tommie Mooney was imprisoned in Ballykinlar. The prisoners were taken by ship from Cork, then to Belfast where the loyal dockers gave them a warm welcome. Later on in the Civil War he was captured in Grange by the Free State Army and imprisoned in Ballybricken in Waterford. Mick Morrissey, a well-known former C.I.E bus conductor shared 'apartments' with him in Ballybricken Gaol where they had apparently constructed a tunnel, which was discovered when a lorry drove over it and it collapsed.'

'Cathal Brugha was a director of Lawlors' Candles and in this capacity paid frequent visits Foley's using his job as a cover for Sinn Féin activities, organising and recruiting. He was elected M.P. for Waterford in the General Election of 1918. The admonition *'Vote No. 1 Brugha'* was tarred on the storm wall for quite some time but this was for a later election period.'

In the upset climate of the times, quite a few lawless acts took place. The inmates of the big houses had fled, and on one occasion a man pursuing his dog found his way into a hide-out in the glen, below the graveyard, where an amount of china and silver from a local big house, had been stored. Jamesy Quain – husband of my aunt, Mrs Quain - was robbed of his salmon, on the way to the Ferry Point. Willie Bulman was attacked and robbed when driving Farrell's Bakery van and bringing bread to Allens who at that stage had a shop in Ballyquin.

The two culprits were arrested by the Sinn Féin police and incarcerated in the Coastguard Station, of which they were then in occupation. Jimmy Rooney remembers seeing the culprits through the windows in the second floor of the central tower.

As British law and order had broken down, I.R.A. courts and police were set up by Paddy Ormonde, Police Officer of the Brigade, working in conjunction with transport officer, Eddie Spratt. In August 1920, the Law Society even recognised the courts according to *The Comeraghs, Refuge of Rebels.*

There were local elections and Sonny (John Francie) Foley became Sinn Fein councillor for the area; Moss Keane was co-opted later on.

In Ardmore, Sinn Féin courts were held at various venues. One of the judges was Tom Foley, Ballylane. The ruins at the top of

Bóthar na Trínse, from where Micheál Ó Foghlú's family had been evicted years before was one venue. The premises were used at a later stage as a band room and when Pierry Foley and a companion went in one night to light the fire they found a strange woman seated there; when they came she got up and went down to the nearby room and just disappeared.

Another venue for the courts was the barn behind the present Youth Hostel. There Jamesy Quain was charged with attacking Jim Drohan and having a row in the boat; he was fined 14/- which he refused to pay.

Jamesy was noted for being outspoken and so got himself into frequent trouble. On more than one occasion, having been previously warned by others 'in the know', he had to leave the house and take his boat and row out to sleep in a cave. He was much harried by other locals who disapproved, for instance, of his continuing friendship with the coastguards, whom he passed every day when going for the cows. That type of behaviour did not come within their terms of reference of patriotism, but Jamesy pursued his independent way. Incidentally, I remember my father saying Jamesy was one of the first subscribers to the National Loan. When Myles Harty of Curragh who had a son in the R.I.C., died, Nick Rooney was apprehended on the strand when returning from the wake, which apparently had been boycotted. Dedication to the national cause was shown in peculiar ways. Because it was the property of the Coastguards, the Boat House, which is on the site of the present Fire Station and public toilet, was burnt down.

The personnel at the Coastguard station had been augmented by twenty-five Marines, who were occasionally sniped at, when up and down from the village. My mother recalled an incident when I was a very small toddler playing outside the door in Tigaluinn, and she ran to take me in because she heard the sound of gunfire. It seemed to emanate from the Rocky Road, from the alcove at the first entrance to Melrose, and was directed towards a Marine coming from the village. Some of the Marines frequented Rooney's pub, so this was boycotted and a notice to this effect placed on the Boat House door, but some intrepid people ignored it. Among them according to Jimmie Rooney, were Tom Doocey - brother of Mrs Conway, Clarkestown and a well-known athlete - Mike Allen, Jack Corbett, and Tom Harty.

The boycott was lifted later, and according to Jimmie "my mother was nearly eaten out of house and home" by visiting Irregulars. He remembers one night, in the kitchen, when word came that the 'Staters' had come and Tommy Quinn went around the kitchen in a frenzy shaking holy water, not realising the holy water was stout.

It must have been at this stage that Jim Pender, Paddy Cashin and Mick Shalloe spent an uncomfortable week in the Putty Hole, in spite of the mattresses purloined from Rock House. The Putty Hole is a rather damp cave to the east of St. Declan's Well. Nick Rooney (Jimmie's father) brought cigarettes and provisions out there during the period. Jimmie himself remembers doing it on more than one occasion. The cave was accessible on foot at low tide by a path which used to lead down from St. Declan's Well. Later on the inmates were taken over by boat by Jim Drohan to Ballyquin.

Apparently the 'Staters' had heard of the refugees in the Putty Hole and they took Johnny Larkin and four or five others as hostages and pushed them into the caves (the caves at the Head were used occasionally too) at the Head, to make first contact with the inmates (who had left). Caves up the glen (at the other side of the graveyard) were used as hide-outs from time to time.

It was previous to this, in August 1920 that the Barracks in Ardmore was attacked. The account in *The Comeraghs, Refuge of Rebels* says "The postman in Ardmore, Patrick Hurton, a volunteer approached the Barracks door with the intention of holding it open for the I.R.A., but they were spotted by a policeman who gave the alarm. The R.I.C. opened fire through the Barracks windows and sent up Verey lights to summon help from the Marines nearby. Other local volunteers kept the Marine Station under fire so that the original attacking group were able to retire. The military arrived from Youghal and took up positions around the Barracks and the Marine Station."

53 Main Street, Ardmore, the R.I.C. Barracks is the fourth house up from the left. Note the water pump with the trough in the foreground, c1920.

My parents lived in Myrtleville at the time, practically opposite the Barracks and my mother was always apprehensive, fearing that perhaps the house might be temporarily taken over, but they suffered no disturbance, even later on, when the Barracks was burned. The only souvenir after the burning was a strong timber mantelpiece, which was found outside their door in the morning. My mother took it in and when they moved to Tigaluinn in 1921, it went with them.

The Piltown Ambush took place in November 1920 and was well-planned. This account is condensed from that of Seán & Síle Murphy. The I.R.A. knew that if Ardmore Barracks was attacked, reinforcements would be quickly on the scene from Youghal, to assist them. The ambush position was selected and a trench dug across the road. The flying column came down from the Knockmealdowns to join the Ardmore battalion. Men were detailed to block the Dungarvan and Cappoquin road. the main body took up their positions at Piltown at 8.30 pm.

54 Police barracks 1920, White Horse Restaurant now occupies this site.

At about 9.45 p.m. column men threw Mills bombs into the Ardmore Barracks and Marine Station. The expected Verey lights were sent up from Ardmore and close to midnight, a lorry of military approached. The column opened fire and after a few minutes the military threw down their arms and surrendered. It was found that two men were dead and according to this account, Paky Whelan said an Act of Contrition into their ears.

The military were given a dray to transport their wounded back to Youghal; twenty-six rifles, two carbines, Mills bombs, revolvers, Verey lights and pistols were captured. The attackers went back by Aglish to the house of Walter Terry.

The episode was commemorated in the following verse by Pat Keating.

At the cross of old Piltown at midnight
We met them with rifle and steel,
The hirelings of Britain who boasted
They'd trample our flag 'neath their heel,
We fought as our fathers before us
We rose at the word of command
To fight for the freedom of Ireland,
In a cause that is holy and grand

Chorus
I give you the brave I.R.A. boys,
The cream of our race and our God
Whose lives they are willing to give, boys
For the sake of their land and their God.

The roar of the guns, it was glorious
The bullets flew 'round us like hail
From the rifles of cowards and of traitors
'Mid the ranks of the sons of the Gael
And every rebel a hero
From Piltown, Old Parish, Ardmore

And down from the slopes of the Comeraghs
With Dungarvan's true sons to the fore.

Pat Keating.

After the Burgery Ambush in Dungarvan in March 1921, the Black and Tans came to Ardmore with intentions of burning the village. They weren't exactly sober and one of them went into Flemings (now Reillys), demanded a bottle of whiskey, said Lloyd George would pay and rolled a Mills bomb on the counter. Jimmie Rooney saw one of them flat on the ground, shooting Mrs Johnny Mulcahy's ducks as they emerged (about twenty of them) in military formation from an outhouse in the vicinity of the church, heading for the river. The Tans didn't forget to collect the dead ducks. Jack Eddy later put a large sign on the gable wall of Ivy Lodge in the centre of the village 'Hens and ducks, beware of the Tans and Buffs'.

An Ardmore man, Jack Eddy (the same Jack Eddy mentioned above) was involved in one of the two spectacular escapes form Spike Island in 1921. Both accounts are recorded in the National Library, Kildare St., Dublin.

> 'The second escape took place on 10th November 1921. Seven volunteer officers Maurice Twomey, William Quirke, Tom Crofts, Henry O'Mahony, Dick Barrett, Paddy Buckley and Jack Eddy, got away under cover of darkness, without any assistance, either from outside or from any member of the garrison, the Cameron Highlanders at that time.
>
> There were over five hundred prisoners on the island then, housed in the two-storey A and B blocks. The escapees had to outwit the count at 4 pm; they had to get through or over eight-foot walls topped with barbed wire and having a

forty-foot moat between. The tunnel leading to the moat was filled with barbed wire. The prisoners over a period put rubbish of every kind into it, and when they were ready to attempt the escape complained to the authorities that the place was a danger to health. The place was cleaned out and the barbed wire removed in the process. The prisoners had to get into the tunnel, before the sentry came on duty, and had to remain in it until after dark.

To get over the wall, they had tied crosspieces to a beam to make a cat ladder. This they took with them, pulling it up to the top of the wall and using it again on the other side. They hid it so successfully that it was not found until the following morning. Up to that time, the method by which they had got out was a complete mystery. They had to evade the sweeping lights and patrolling sentries and when they had done all that, they were still on the island. They had then to search in the darkness for a boat which was not locked and get it away without encountering the patrol boat with its armed crew, which circled the island continuously.

The boat they used was anchored some distance from the shore. Jack Eddy swam out to it, brought it back and picked up the others. When Jack Eddy was cutting the rope by which the boat was anchored, the knife dropped out of his half-frozen hands before he had cut through. He severed the remaining strands with his teeth. The boat had no oars nor rowlocks, but they found oars under the pier and used furze sticks in the one row-lock hole on each side'.

It is intriguing to remember that Jack Eddy was a coastguard's son, his father was from Cornwall.

Patsy Hurton and Henry Conway both joined the British Army. On one occasion, when Patsy Hurton was home on furlough, he decided not to return, but the R.I.C. arrested him. Jimmie Rooney saw him coming over the strand under arrest. Patsy finished his term in the army and later, he became postman in Ardmore and is mentioned in the story of an attack on Ardmore Barracks.

He had joined the I.R.A. and was jailed in Spike Island. When the Truce was declared, he was released, but instead of returning home, he left Cork by train to visit a girl who had worked at Dawsons, (Lacken) and with whom he was friendly. At Thurles station, a Black and Tan lobbed a bomb into the train and he was killed.

He had the most spectacular funeral ever seen in Ardmore, on 18th December 1921. My mother was watching it from the roof of Tigaluinn (it had then a flat roof), as it wound its way up by the sea front on to Coffee Lane, Dawsons Road (now sometimes called the Middle Road), over the New Line and finally to the graveyard. There were of course several bands, so she became very familiar with the air of 'Wrap the Green Flag Round Me'. She tells the story of the funeral of the occupant of Mistletoe Castle, Youghal, which was taking place on the same day as Patsy Hurton's. The mourners had to ask some of those following the first cortège to help carry the coffin into the graveyard, this was certainly a symbol of the changed times. The National Graves Committee commemorates the death of Patsy Hurton, at Easter every three or four years.

55 Easter Commemoration in Ardmore, c1966.

Election Campaigns

During the intervening years we found elections very exciting. I remember the well-loved figure of Micheàl Ó Concubhair, on a platform bowing, almost jumping up and down saying 'Let us give one pull, one strong pull and we'll all pull together and vote for Fianna Fail'. We thought it was great stuff and we loved to imitate him. Miky Ryan, Ballyquin and a Dr White from Waterford spoke on the promenade another day; there were certainly angry feelings with charges flying in all directions, but I must say we youngsters enjoyed it. Mrs Redmond, I recall too, addressing a meeting near the Boathouse; there were great complaints about the price of butter being 'only one and something a pound'.

At a later period, my father tended to drive out his lorry from the Boathouse where it was garaged and the politicians of whatever party said their say from the back of the lorry which Jack Flynn termed 'the steps of Liberty Hall'. A Labour Candidate, J. Guiry informed his listeners that voting for Fianna Fail meant cutting their throats, so Mrs Daly (née Fitzgerald) loudly informed him and those around her that she was going to do precisely that.

We brought a big poster into school one day, featuring Dev's head; 'Our new half-sovereign', the caption said. Mother Ita shook her head and said 'Poor Dev'. Another election time memory is of Betty Flynn (later Reilly) up on the wall boundary of Strand Cottage giving us an election 'speech', at school playtime.

Election proceedings now are very polite and dignified. The residue of bad feeling resulting from all those troubled years has taken a long time to subside. I cannot help recalling the sentiments of the verse about the Pilltown Ambush and contrasting them with the emphasis now on peace and reconciliation.

Austrian Refugees

In 1938 Austria was invaded by the German army and made part of Hitler's empire. Anti-Semitism led to harsh treatment of the Jews. Many fled, and a number of refugees found their way to Ireland. Christmas holidays 1938 were most exciting. Before my arrival home, Ardmore had featured in all the newspapers with the news that Austrian refugees were coming there. Sir John Keane was loaning them Quarry House, his summer residence, so there we were on the front page of the national newspapers, a noteworthy event in a small village in those days.

We soon got to know the group who were quickly integrated into village life. Mary Odell (the last of the Odell landlord family to live in Ardmore and known as Miss Odell to us young people) was an Irish Red Cross representative. She took partial charge and gave English classes to those of the party who needed them. We were greatly amused at 'the thirty thousand thrifty theosophists' whom she used to illustrate the pronunciation of TH. Naturally, we taught them some Irish phrases and we learned German ones. It being Christmas time, there was a round of parties in each other's houses and at Quarry House, and the presence of at least four or five personable young men in the group, gave an added fillip to the dances in St. Declan's Hall.

It was a short but memorable period for us all, Austrians and Irish alike, and people were sorry to see them go in February 1939, when they left for Enniskerry in north Co. Wicklow. I was in college in Dublin and visited them on St. Patrick's Day. One of the refugees, Gustav Beisser, a gifted linguist, came in to Enniskerry to meet my friend and myself off the bus and drove us out by pony and trap to the farmhouse in which they lived in Glencree. There was goulash for lunch and afterwards an iced cake with green shamrocks.

It was lonelier for them there, than in Ardmore. "Nothing ever happens here, except sheep are born or calves run away" one of the young men ruefully remarked. They were visited by members of the Red Cross Committee and greeted them with an Irish salutation learned in Ardmore but were told apologetically they were sorry they knew no German.

On the way out we must have been discussing Hitler and his latest movements in Europe, and I remember Gustav's remark, "Soon he will go to the moon and he will say the moon was always German". That had been his pretext for invading various territories around the borders of Germany. It was a momentous period in world history, and that brief interlude, when we made those good Viennese friends, was the first of its repercussions on our placid life in a small village on the rim of Western Europe.

Being able to include the recollections of two of these Austrians in this article is a great pleasure. They are Fritz Hirsch and Erwin Struntz; the latter had worked with the Kagran group in Vienna helping Jewish people emigrate and form an agricultural community overseas.

Memories Of Fritz Hirsch

'I Still remember vividly arriving in Ardmore on December 13th 1938, with the morning bus from Waterford, where I had arrived early that morning from Fishguard after a rather bad crossing. It was a brilliant and sunny morning - the fields and meadows were green (unbelievable for me coming from winter on the continent where everything was brown and bare). Suddenly the bus stopped and a hunt crossed the road, hounds, horses, and huntsmen. I thought I was in a movie - I had no idea what was going on and there was nobody to explain. On arriving in Ardmore my family and the Strunz family met me at the bus and my life in Ireland began.

For me Ireland was Ardmore of course and although we only stayed there for about two months, it was really one of my saddest days when we had to leave again. This may sound sentimental but it is nevertheless quite true. The kindness and friendliness of you all in Ardmore is not to be believed. You invited us to your houses and made us all feel at home. There were parties and gatherings galore. Singing in the church choir and Christmas carols in the village hall. Perhaps you can remember the dances in the hall? We were supposed to learn about agriculture and some of the Ardmore families took it upon themselves to help us in their kindness. All that helped us to take part in the life of the village and get to know everybody. But of course there was still a time of peace in the world. The war did not start until September 1939. Having come from Austria, which had already been taken over by Germany at that time - the sabres were already rattling in Europe then, the Munich crisis, Sudentenland etc., - Ardmore seemed like heaven. I can still remember the names of most of the families but I would not know where to start to enumerate them.

We all loved Ardmore and I am speaking for all that were there at the time. We often used to speak about it. I am listing the people in our group and what I know of them.

Mr & Mrs Hirsch (Frederick & Maria) and their two grown-up boys Ernest and Fritz. My parents opened the Old Vienna Club in Dublin which enabled Ernest and myself to get to Dublin and study. Ernest became a vet (and Professor at the Dublin Veterinary College) and I a Chemist.

Mr & Mrs Strunz (Erwin & Lisl) and their two small children - Peter aged four years and George about six months old. - Mr Strunz ran the Unicorn Restaurant very successfully in Dublin. His wife Lisl died in 1965 and he is now dead also. Peter Strunz is in Dublin and George is in Canada.

Gustaf Beisser and Ernie Einaugler both joined the British Army. Gustaf died in England in 1970. Kurt Adler studied medicine and went to Canada. Dr. Kurt Stiegwart (lawyer) went to Argentina.

Robert Aberach became a photographer in Dublin and his brother Fritz worked as a waiter in England. They were only here briefly, for a week or less.

We did not all arrive at the same time but we left together in February 1939. This is just a short summary, everybody has his own tale to tell, some returned to Austria after the war as far as I know.'

Memories of Erwin Strunz

'My wife Lisl and our two small sons, Peter four and a half, and George four months old, left Vienna in September 1938 to escape the racial, political, and religious persecution under the Nazi regime. It saved our lives that we had good fortune to meet Hubert Butler, the Kilkenny writer in the International Quaker Centre in Vienna on a project to help Christian Jews, Catholics, and Protestants to emigrate.

Lisl and I had worked for four months in a labour camp under armed S.A. supervision. To be effective in my work I had to identify myself with them, although I was an Aryan. This was regarded as a crime and the order for my arrest went out. Warned of it I was lucky with the help of American Quakers to escape only with hours to spare. Hubert and Peggy Butler invited us to Ireland. We spent three glorious months in Annaghmakerrig, Newbliss, Co. Monaghan, which belongs to the Guthrie family. Tony Guthrie, the Shakespearean producer, and director of the Old Vic in London, was Peggy's brother.

After three months we moved to Ardmore to get some agricultural training which would help us in our further emigration overseas. Sir John Keane offered the use of his summer bungalow. Soon the refugee committee added another eight refugees to our family. They were Marie and

Fritz Hirsch, their grown-up sons Fritz and Ernest, Kurt Adler, Ernest Beisser, Paul Wessley and Ernst Einaugler.

We came to Ardmore just before Xmas 1938. The ancient history of the village, its scenic beauty and even more the overwhelming kindness of its people moved us deeply. To all the romantic beauty came the exotic climate of the Waterford coast. In Vienna we would have been tramping through slush and snow, here I could walk lightly dressed and in shirtsleeves over the strand, breathing a tangy, soft-fresh air, the fields were green and the hedges flowered with veronica. To emphasize this almost subtropical character, there were yucca palms around.

Sunday Church was to me as a middle European no less exotic. Since the church stands close to the strand, it echoed to the cries of seagulls and the solemnity of Mass seemed to be increased by the gently swishing noise of the wavelets rolling over sand and pebbles - the sound of the eternal sea mingling with that of the eternal spirit. As I looked around and over the bent heads of the congregation I felt at home with them, although I hardly knew their language.

The day before Xmas Eve Mr Hurley brought us a huge cod, saying "*take this, we can only be happy if we know that you are happy here at Xmas and have everything you need.*"

This was only the beginning of a shower of presents. That was the attitude of the people of Ardmore. I compared it shamefully with that of my own people, who had robbed us of every penny and were after our lives! I wrote a little Xmas play for the children of Ardmore, which was translated by Mary Odell, who also gave us English lessons, but we picked up a few Irish words too. The songs of the day also increased our vocabulary: 'When Irish Eyes are Smiling', 'I Like to Whistle', 'The Lambeth Walk' and of course the traditional songs 'Danny Boy', 'In Dublin's Fair City' and 'The Bold Fenian Men'.

We made many friends, the Quain family, Guard Cooper and his wife, the lady-owner of the Melrose Hotel, who allowed our boys to play table tennis there. There were so many I can't mention for the lack of space, although they should be thanked also.

We had many visitors like Mr. Frank Fahy, Speaker of the Dáil and Chairman of the Refugee Committee, Arland Ussher, the writer, the editor of the *Cork Examiner* and the reporters of the *Irish Times*, *Independent* and *Irish Press*. People from all around came to visit us. Alas of the fourteen people shown in the photo only four are still alive. A half a century has passed, Baby George in the basket is a successful biochemist in Canada, in charge of a four provinces research laboratory, besides lecturing at the university. His elder brother Peter is a most successful sales manager in a large Irish firm. Ernest Hirsch became a professor at the Dublin Veterinary College and Fritz Hirsch a well-to-do entrepreneur.

Short as the presence of Austrian refugees was, this little episode in the local history of Ardmore deserves to be chronicled as a monument to the kindness of its people. In a world so strongly marked by inhumanity and in Celtic Tiger Ireland where asylum-seekers meet much hostility, it is good to remind ourselves that there exists also much love and generosity. In the Ardmore of 1938/1939, the bible word was made true: 'I was a stranger and you took me in'.' Erwin Strunz has since died.

The Emergency Period

More than fifty Years ago World War II began and the ensuing 'emergency' lasted for six years, with various repercussions continuing for still a few more years. Looking back on it now, it is a glimpse into an altogether different world, of no cars, no petrol, no streetlights, no currants, raisins, oranges or bananas and a strictly limited and rationed supply of bread, butter, tea, sugar and soap. It is almost unimaginable today, but they were the conditions to which we all, absolutely all sections of society had to accustom ourselves in the forties.

Each year, one was issued with a ration book, with a set number of coupons allocated to such things as butter, tea, sugar soap and clothes. If you bought say a summer outfit or a winter one, there was no way you could afford to buy a second one in the year; the coupons just didn't cover it. Of course it was just as important to produce the coupons as the money, when making the purchase. An extremely well-known Irish artist stayed at Tigaluinn during those years and after her holiday wrote back for her vest which she had left behind. It wasn't available, the girl cleaning the room having used it as a convenient duster, so she had to be recompensed 4s/6d for the vest and three coupons.

The shopkeeper had to produce these coupons to replace the stock, so you always came armed with your ration book and those of your family, when buying the domestic supply of bread, sugar, tea, butter and soap. The weekly ration of butter was two ounces; sugar ¾lb; tea was down to ½oz a week at one stage. Jack Flynn who lived in Chapel Row put all his rations into the teapot on Sunday mornings and went without for the rest of the week.

Various alternatives were tried like roasting grated carrots and so on. People keenly missed their tea and the occasions of threshings in particular were agonising for the farmers concerned. It often happened that such and such a shopkeeper had stockpiled before the advent of rationing and tea was available 'under the counter', often at fancy prices, depending on the integrity of the shopkeeper concerned. This happened with other commodities too, such as candles, sweets, biscuits, cigarettes, but most shopkeepers devised their own rationing systems with them and distributed them as fairly as possible to the customers.

One had to be registered for paraffin oil and this was most important in an area like Ardmore, which had no electricity or gas. The bread was brown, as was the flour. Rashers were a luxury rarely encountered. Currants, oranges, bananas never appeared as these had obviously to be imported and valuable shipping space was not generally allocated to unnecessary items.

During my teaching period in Youghal, a small child produced a battered orange one day in the playground and all the children crowded round to see and examine the strange object. It had evidently been washed in on the beach and of course, they had never seen one before.

'No jars, no jam' was a common place slogan in the shops, but the possession of a jar didn't always ensure a pot of jam. These war time jams were referred to by my father as 'and jams', they were never plain strawberry say or blackcurrant, but strawberry and apple or blackcurrant and apple and so on, and we had our suspicions that apple wasn't always the second fruit. An extra ration of sugar was given to beet growers, also to jam makers. Turf cutters were entitled to extra bread rations and we still have a letter of thanks to my father from a man in Araglin. He went there regularly for turf and evidently, the men had had no luck in their application for extra bread. My father filled the form and the bread coupons arrived, so they attributed it to his superior influence with the 'powers that be'. It was probably the result of filling in the form properly.

Fuel was always a problem. Coal wasn't available so the alternatives were timber and turf and the turf was more often than not badly harvested and wet. 'Oh the wet turf' is one of the most anguished memories of the war years. Because of this, trains were often late. A friend of mine was on the platform in Tralee one day, awaiting the arrival of the Limerick train, which was very late. On enquiry, she was told by the porter, "She's shtuck for shtame (steam) in Lishtowel." 'Is your journey really necessary' was another emergency saying. Only doctors, priests, hackney drivers, van and lorry drivers had petrol; there were just no other cars in case of helping possible invaders. There were no signposts on the roads. Bicycles were the normal means of transport, even though tyres were scarce and not easily obtained. One was ready to go practically anywhere on a bicycle.

In spite of transport and other difficulties Lord Longford's and Anew Mac Masters' drama groups made frequent visits to the country towns. We often cycled to Youghal and to Dungarvan to see them. On one occasion, Anew Mac Master hired my father's lorry to transport himself and some of the group and the stage props to Tallow. The load was so high that there was a doubt as to whether or not they could get under the Clock Gate in Youghal, but they made it.

All letters to England were censored and of course there was no communication whatever with the continent. Newspapers had only a few pages and the quality of the actual paper was most inferior. T.V. didn't exist and naturally the BBC war bulletins on the radio were strictly censored; however one got the other side of the story from Lord Haw Haw, an Irishman named Joyce who broadcast in English regularly from Germany, giving of course a completely different account. After the war the British hanged him for his pains

The sea area just to the south of the country was heavily mined and ships were also being torpedoed, so many strange things were washed in on the beach. A raft came in to Ballyquin with blankets, chocolate, and sealed tins of water, packed in Baltimore, U.S.A. Other rafts came too. Great big heavily compressed bales of rubber were often among the flotsam and jetsam, and these were sold to Dunlops in Cork of course. There was plenty of timber to be retrieved.

The mines themselves came floating in too, but thankfully caused no damage, apart from a few broken windows, when these were blown up by some of the military personnel stationed in Youghal, who were sent out on those occasions. The report of the blown up mine could be heard miles away. One particular mine was being washed in one day and was heading for the bend of the storm-wall at the end of the village. Many onlookers blithely watched its course; I myself was on the roof of Tigaluinn observing it, but instead of hitting the wall with terrible consequences, it landed harmlessly on the beginning of the strand. Our safe deliverance was attributed to St. Declan.

There was a ring of 83 lookout posts right around the coast, each one linked by telephone. These were manned day and night and we frequently dropped into our local one on Ram Head and sat at the fire and chatted and surveyed the logbook. These were accounts of planes and convoys of boats and floating mines and of various explosions. Éire 20 was delineated clearly on the cliff top by large white stones now completely covered by grass and heather.

232

And then, at last, the war was over, and things gradually got back to normal. There were still shortages; babies were being wheeled around in prams with wooden wheels, no rubber as yet. I got married in November 1945 and had a conventional wedding cake. Two friends married in August of the same year and had none; currants and raisins were still in short supply.

English people began to come over to enjoy good Irish food after their wartime privations. One day in Dublin, a visitor asked me "Could you tell me the origin of......." And I prepared myself for a dissertation on some historical monument, but he finished his question "the peat walls in your Phoenix Park." The government of the day had stockpiled turf along the roads there.

It all seems so incredible now in 1999. Another 'emergency' is unimaginable. Indeed, it is unimaginable, as well we know, next time it wouldn't be merely an emergency; it would be the end. May the Lord preserve us from it.

The Coast Watching Service

56 Look Out Post no 20, Ram Head near Ardmore, 2021.

The Coastwatching service was set up by the Irish Government in 1939. Eighty-three Look-out Posts (L.O.P.s) were established at coastal sites around the country and manned by local recruits during the 'Emergency' years of World War II (1939-1945). Their function was to observe and report. In effect, the L.O.P.s were glorified telephone kiosks with bay windows facing seawards and tiny fireplaces. Each L.O.P. was provided with a logbook, telephone, telescope and binoculars, fixed compass card, Admiralty charts, silhouettes of ships and air craft, visual signals apparatus and a bicycle. The above information is taken from several articles by Comdt. Quinn in *An Cosantóir*, (April 1983 and January 1988).

The Logbooks of all the L.O.P.s are preserved in the Military archives at Cathal Brugha Barracks in Dublin. Comdts. Owen

Quinn, Peter Young and Sergeant White were most helpful, while I was researching this article there.

L.O.P. no 20 was on Ram Head near Ardmore. Its undistinguished remains remind me of fireside chats there in the course of Sunday evening walks, being allowed look through the binoculars at perhaps a passing convoy, or talking of the mines, or discussing the aircraft which sped here and there, through the skies on their unknown journeys.

57 Look Out Post no 20, Ram Head near Ardmore, 2021.

The first available logbook for Ram Head begins on 2 January 1941 and they continue on to 15 June 1945. A point worth noting is the excellent standard of language and spelling in these reports done by men who had had no access to second-level education. The logbooks deal with mines, passing ships, convoys, air traffic, gunfire, explosives, and barrage balloons. Life was exciting out at sea and in the air overhead, but the coastwatchers could only surmise the causes and effects of all these comings and goings.

Some days were quiet enough, punctuated by the changing of the watch, the lines being tested and found in order, reporting the weather conditions and visibility.

Each L.O.P. had an eight-man team. They worked eight-hour shifts, around the clock and seven days a week. Dressed as soldiers they were paid a basic subsistence allowance of half a crown per day (12.5p) in addition to two shillings (10p) Army pay.

The Ram Head personnel consisted of: Jimmy Troy of the Cliff, Tom Monsell, Jerry McCarthy and Tom Foley of the village, Willie Whelan of Ballyquin, Pat Troy of Curragh, and Ned Foley of Duffcarrick. Tommie Mooney was corporal. Willie Whelan resigned in 1944 and Tommie Hallahan replaced him.

Jimmie Troy, who had emigrated to England, paid a visit to Ardmore in the summer of 1989 and called to Willie Whelan to discuss old times. He died shortly after returning to England and his remains were laid to rest, under the shadow of the Round Tower, exactly fifty years after his entry into the Coastal Service.

The first months of service were spent under canvas in the castle field, near Ram Head, until the outpost was built out on the peak of 'The Head'. The letters Eire 20 were white washed into the ground beside it, the coastwatchers all around the coast having been ordered to cut out these signs in order to delineate our neutral territory. Dick Mooney who was a schoolboy at the time, and whose father Tommie was corporal, remembers the castle being sand bagged in order to provide extra shelter.

Willie Whelan the only surviving member of the outpost personnel says,

'The war started on Sunday and Jimmie Troy and Tom Monsell were the first two to go on duty. On Sunday night I started with Tommy Mooney; he was a corporal. We went on, at 12pm on Monday night. We had no real orders at the time, only to walk along the coast and watch it. We walked all the cliffs along by Ardo to Whiting Bay Strand and back again by Terry's and the Round Tower and the New Line. We sat down in the glen below McKennas (propably Gleann Phiarais) to have a smoke in the shelter. This almighty crash came over our heads. 'There's something wrong. Jump up', said Tommy. What was there but a jennet belonging to Deug Connell. She stood up on a stone fence and the fence went from under her and crashed down behind us. It gave us a bit of a fright. We thought we were being attacked.

We were based at the Ram. We had no cover, no shelter or nothing but the four walls of the castle for about a month or six weeks, until we got one of those big army tents.'

It was a big draughty, but one day, the military lorry came along and the blocks were laid and the hut put together in one day.'

The men got one month's training in the Curragh, at the beginning and there was a fortnight's annual training at Haulbowline.

Jimmie Troy also spoke of a period, learning signals at Collins Barracks in Cork, and he told also of being brought in an open lorry on a wet day from Ardmore to Dublin. They left Ardmore at 3p.m. picked up men at Helvick, Dunabrattin, Brownstown and Hook Head and arrived in Dublin at 5am, cold, wet, hungry and exhausted. Jimmy got pneumonia and spent some time in St. Bricin's Hospital in Dublin. He was sent home eventually by train to Dungarvan, where he had to spend the night, as there was no bus to Ardmore on Good Friday.

He survived these hardships to serve his full time at Ram Head. So did Tom Foley who as asthmatic; when he joined up, the neighbours shook their heads and forecast a short period of service for him, but in point of fact, he never missed a day's duty. The fresh air and sea breeze seemed to have a decidedly beneficial effect. There was no telephone first. Willie says "The Guards used be cursing us. We had orders at the time to report everything we'd see." A Guard at that time used sleep in the barracks every night. Jerry McCarthy was only wild to go down. "I'll go I'll go" he'd say. He got a great 'kick' from interrupting garda slumbers.

The post was equipped with a compass, which was attached to a tripod outside and there were Zeiss binoculars. Willie says "I saw my mother filling the kettle from the bucket of water she had brought from the well in Moss Kean's". Willie's house was in Ballyquin, away at the other side of Ardmore Bay.

Dick Mooney talks of them joking. "Begor, the lads over in Knockadoon are smoking Woodbines today. There must be cigarettes in Ballymacoda." The whereabouts of cigarettes in the war years was a fact to be noted; they were an under-the-counter commodity. The binoculars of course would have had 'magical' qualities, to distinguish the cigarettes, across eight miles of sea.

Ram Head was an admirable situation for an outpost, facing north-east towards Ardmore Bay, Mine Head and a long sweep of Waterford coast. To the other side were Knockadoon and Capel Island at the entrance to Youghal Harbour and the Cork coast away to the west with the lights of Ballycotton lighthouse flashing in the night. It was a wonderful place to be on summer days, but could be often terrifying on winter nights. Willie Whelan speaks of Tom Monsell and himself holding grimly on to one another, going along the cliff path, when a fierce south-westerly gale threatened to blow them right over.

They had frequent visitors in summer, including the many nuns holidaying in Ardmore. Neidín (Ned Foley) referred irreverently to them as 'bunches of magpies'.

Life could of course be quite monotonous, punctuated perhaps by some fishing in the Licneán below, or going over to Fr O'Donnell's Well for water. Ned Foley had a pet crow, called General Joubert (presumably after Piet Joubert, commander of the Transvaal forces in the Boer War) which followed him over to the LOP, first lured by breadcrumbs which later became unnecessary. Tom Foley and Willie cooked a pollack (caught by Neidín in the Licnean) one night, only to discover they had no salt. Willie tells the rest of the story.

> "You're lucky," said Tom. "Monsell isn't in bed yet. Run down and ask him for a grain of salt" (run down involved crossing over two fields, negotiating a long boreen and then cycling down the village). "Tom knew the reception I'd get" said Willie. "No fear he'd come himself. Tom Monsell was in bed, and I knocked him up. He wasn't too civil at all. I didn't tell him what I wanted till he was at the door. 'We've the pollack boiled above now Tom and we've no salt, so I came down for a grain', Willie said very seriously. May the divil blast you. If I knew what you wanted.............'. But he gave me the salt"

Neidín devised a grid-iron with a long handle for grilling mackerel over the anthracite fire. "You'd eat your fingers after them."

Coal was supplied by military lorry. "Sometimes, the supplies were unpredictable and we'd be stealing from one another in the meantime."

The outposts were under constant surveillance by the military authorities. "Fellows in command used come at all hours of the night. They used do one outpost after another first and we'd give each other the tip, but they got wise to that." The Guards were liable to come too. Willie recalls:

> 'Sergeant Gallagher came one night about 2am. There was an unmerciful shower of hailstone about an hour before. "Had you any shelter from it", said Willie. "Where I was, was under the stand at the creamery, where Tom Fleming gives out the skimmed milk". The creamery was four miles away at the other side of the parish. He sat down at the fire for about an hour and had a smoke. He was a great policeman, always on the beat, a fair-minded man.'

The nearest look-out posts were Helvick Head towards the east and Knockadoon to the west, and when after about twelve months the telephones were installed, they were in frequent communication with each other. Let it be said the messages did not always deal strictly with matters of national import. I remember Tom Monsell coming in and calling to my father, "Martin, I had a ring from the Knockers", which meant that the Knockadoon people had sent a message, that consignments of periwinkles were ready to be collected.

Thady Shea of Knockadoon often entertained the Ram Head men on the telephone, with tunes on the melodeon; these were pre-transistor days. Willie Whelan made an appointment to meet him at Killeagh on May Sunday for the annual fun at Glenbower Wood, but was at a loss as to how to identify him, so Thady told him "the tallest fellow in Tattan's pub, that will be me" and so it was.

Santa Claus used Ram Head as a branch office, one Christmas. Paddy Foley during his school days in Ardmore, remembered being invited in to the post office by Michael Moloney, the Post Master, who put him through on the telephone to Santa Claus. He and his classmates were thrilled at the idea of speaking to him and giving him their orders, personally for Christmas night. It was some years afterwards, before they discovered Santa Claus had been on duty at Ram Head.

However, life wasn't always as light-hearted as that. An important part of the watchers duties was to observe and report the course of any strange object in the water, and there were plenty of them, especially in the years 1940, 41 an d41 when about 100 mines came ashore between Ring and Ballycotton.

The Allies had laid a minefield in the Celtic Sea. According to International Law, neutral ships were given passage. 'During the war years, the British Admiralty had an office in North Wall house, staffed by three men who were kept informed of any Royal Navy mine-laying activity, the object being to lessen the danger to Irish merchant ships'. (*The B&I Line* by Hazel Smith.)

The first mine to be recorded in the Ram Head logbook was on 24th January 1941.

On 27th January 1941, it was recorded that five mines were ashore between Whiting Bay and Ballyquin.

On 30th April 1941 a message came from Cork to inform gardai, if any more mines were coming ashore in Ardmore, to get the inhabitants to evacuate.

These extreme measures were not resorted to, even though the people of the locality became quite familiar with mines during the war years. On some occasions they were rendered harmless by military from Youghal; this must have been a hazardous operation. On other occasions, they were blown up by them, and this often caused broken windows in the district.

On 8th June 1941 the post was informed by local gardai, that a mine had been washed ashore at Caliso Bay. A message was received from Youghal to notify the Corporal and get him to send men to guard same until the military arrived. Comdt. Shaw was the recognised authority on mines and their disposal. Willie directed him and accompanied him to Caliso Bay one night for that purpose.

On 17th December 1941 the post was informed by Cpl. Mooney that mine reported yesterday was ashore at Curragh Strand.

These are just random samples of the innumerable log entries about mines. Familiarity fortunately did not breed contempt. People had read of the chilling incident near Annagray in Co. Donegal on May 10th, 1943, when 18 people died after a mine had exploded on the strand. There was a similar tragedy nearer home. On May 2nd, 1945, three Ring men were killed when a mine got entangled in the trawl of their boat, the *Naomh Garbhan*.

A great deal of air activity was noted right from the beginning. Planes, flying boats, monoplanes were noted, most of them English but some German. There were constant log entries dealing with passing aircraft. For instance:

On 21st June 1941, 'two aircraft came from the south, attacked two British traders and dropped two bombs, which fell wide, then went west. At 17.00 hours on 9th July 1941, heard noise of aircraft about 7 miles south of post, came from west. When south of post, noise stopped instantly as if something went wrong. Nationality unknown. At 23.00 hours, heard noise of aircraft south of post seems to be going west. Heard noise of explosions in same direction. Nationality of plane unknown.'

In 1943, there was an enormous amount of aerial activity both British and American. A great deal was in conjunction with naval craft. This activity was stepped up in 1944, when for instance, on 14th January 1944, ten aircraft were recorded between 07.50 and 13.30, all except one, going east. In the spring of that year, there seemed to be a regular stream of U.S. aircraft, about an hour or two apart. The numbers recorded varied from nine daily to twenty-four on 17th February 1944.

On 11th June 1944 between 07.26 and 21.07, thirty planes passed, going both east and west, most U.S. but some British. During the night, from midnight on, there had been noise of heavy gunfire about three miles south of post and noise of aircraft, and at 1.00am flashes of four morse lamps, about 400 yards between each flash.

June and July entries of 1944 dealt repeatedly with noise of heavy gunfire, explosions and flashes as if from gunfire. These were all calculated to be almost twenty to thirty miles south of post.

Incidents like these were being reported from 1941 on; bombing and explosions of mines. For instance on 24th March 1942, there had been noise first of fourteen explosions, then of nine, thought to be heavy gunfire.

In spite of all this there was heavy traffic at sea through those years and their passing appears in the records. The east and west passing of the *Lady Belle* of Dungarvan is recorded several times in 1942 and 1943 as is the *Kathleen and May* and various vessels of Irish shipping - the *Irish Pine*, *Irish Ash* and *Irish Poplar*.

Trawlers and coal boats also passed Ram Head at intervals, as did the Irish patrol boats, the *Muirchú* and *Fort Rannoch*.

58 Near the Second World War Lookout Post is a watch tower dating from the early 19th century. It was constructed to give early warning of an invasion by the French.

Convoys were constantly on the move. Willie says "What used to be very exciting was seeing the convoys going. They used have those barrage balloons to ward off the planes, twenty or thirty of them going together. The *Innisfallen* used pass regularly. Monday, Wednesday and Friday, she'd go down. We could see the men on the deck plain and she used sound the siren and give us a bleep."

On 15th August 1941, eight destroyers were sighted, 'fifteen miles south of post, with two planes circling'. The list goes on and on. These are just samples of the entries. On 1st April 1943, a convoy is noted 'twelve miles south of post, twenty-seven merchant ships, five destroyers with one aircraft circling'.

On 31st October 1943 at 14.15, 'fourteen landing barges passed escorted by one-armed trawler and at 15.56, 'three landing barges towed by two patrol boats, going east'. 27th July 1943, 'noises of heavy gunfire, eight naval aircraft, also plane'. 7th September 1944, 17.08 hours, 'convoy of four disabled merchant ships being towed by two tugboats escorted by three destroyers and two cruisers, one plane hovering overhead'. 17.25 on the same day, 'one merchant ship carrying two planes on her decks, fore and aft, going to meet convoy'. 30th September 1944, 'hospital ship four miles south of post, going west, one troopship, fourteen miles south of post, going west, looks like *Queen Mary'*.

On 13th October 1944, a message from Mallow that 'six Russian launches under British escort are making for Bantry Bay. They are meeting with trouble in the Atlantic and some may have broken loose or may be damaged. If seen, report to Mallow'.

Entries like these continue right into 1945, but the end of the era came rather abruptly.

The following laconic announcements appear in the logbook:

12th June 1945, received following message from Captain O'Riordan, Ram Head. LOP is closing down tomorrow.

13th June 1945, 'Lieut. Busteed is calling for all equipment in LOP which must be labelled Ram Head. Duty is to be continued as usual until Lieut. Busteed arrives. Windows are to be fastened up, doors locked, and key given to the owners of land. Travelling vouchers will arrive tomorrow and all personnel will proceed to Collins Barracks on Monday 16th June 1945'.

And thus, a brief but exciting and important period came to an abrupt end.

The 50th anniversary of the outbreak of World War II was commemorated on 10th September 1989 in Clonmel. There was a parade of about 5000 veterans representing all the services, from opposite Hearne's Hotel to the Barracks, where speeches were made. Willie Whelan met a confrère from Helvick that day and also from Ballycotton, but there was no representative from Knockadoon, though Thady Shea still survives.

Events and Changes

Ardmore Water Scheme

There has been a profound change in the general standards of living, since the early decades of this century. The introduction of the Water Scheme in 1937 brought about one of those fundamental improvements. Up to this, there was no conception of the idea of running water in a house. We still have a copy of a plan of a proposed house at the Cross, in Ardmore, in 1920. This plot of land was at that time considerably bigger than the present one at the top of the street and extended far more to the east. My parents were fairly newly married and this was probably the house of their dreams, but there is no bathroom; an outside i.e. dry toilet is indicated as also is an ash-pit and a sewer pipe. Later, another property became available and they did not proceed with this plan.

Dry toilets and ash-pits were the order of the day for years to come. There was a sewer down the Village Street, which emerged at the bend of the storm-wall. My father laid a sewer and a sewerage pipe later from the back of Tigaluinn down behind the houses in Coffee Lane to the storm wall; an existent pipe already led from behind Brisen. We were aware of other sewers like this coming from the Convent (Stella Marie) and from the houses along the Cliff.

Drinking water was brought home from various wells; and in the village from the 'fountain' in the Village Street, now not functional; The village pump stood on its own site in Sleepy Lane on the steps, which are now the back entrance to my garden.

Bringing water home was a constant chore. We in Tigaluinn had a large water can on wheels; it contained seven or eight buckets of water and was left in position at the other side of the road opposite the house and one went out for a bucket of water for the house as necessary. I have vivid recollections of this operation, also of being sent around the corner to see if there were many people at the pump, before going down. Patsy Walsh who worked at Pollocks (Maycroft) was constantly up and down with a similar mechanism, and so was Will Mockler on behalf of the nuns at Stella Maris.

59 Main Street, Ardmore, 1926.

The campaign for piped water went on for years. There wasn't an enthusiastic response to sign the petition to inaugurate the scheme. There was also the question of the source of the supply and it was eventually decided that it be taken and piped from Lios Coilte. This has been augmented by a supply from Monea.

The scheme was finished in 1937, but very few people availed of it at first, the rent varying between £3 and £5 per year, was

248

thought to be exorbitant. This was increased very much over the years, but now there is no water rate at all to pay. At first, the pipes extended out the Grove (Youghal Road) only as far as the parish priests house, but of course, it was much extended in later years, as people began to realise what a wonderful boon running water was.

People of this generation would not or could envisage houses without running water and indoor toilet facilities, and when we go on holidays, we expect rooms en-suite, but as the old saying goes, "far from them were we reared".

Electricity & Muintir na Tíre

In 1947, a branch of Muintir na Tíre was founded in Ardmore with sections representing farmers, business people, professionals, labourers and last but not least, a ladies' section. At its very first meeting, Rural Electrification was on the agenda, and letters were written to the E.S.B. Fr. John Walsh had initiated it, but resigned in 1948. Michael Moloney, the first secretary retired at the end of the first year and John Cashman succeeded him. the long arduous campaign went on for many years under the auspices of Muintir na Tíre.

The Parish Council members of 1954 were:

Hon. President - Rev. Fr. W. Cahill P.P.
Chairman - Francis D. Nugent
Treasurer - James Prendergast
Hon. Secretary - John Cashman

The other members were: Ref. Fr. Phelan C.C., James Quain, Richard Lincoln, Declan O'Connell, Maurice Colbert, John Larkin, James McGrath (Tower View), Edmond Lenane, Mrs Johanna Cullen, Mrs Helen Fitzgerald, Mrs B. O'Brien.

Members of the organisation had to do the very difficult job of canvassing through the countryside, but at last, it was successful and it was announced that preliminary work would start shortly. The Area Office was set up in Coláiste Deuglán, then vacant. Some lorries were distributing poles, coils of wire and other equipment. Householders began preparing and electrical contractors got busy, but there were still a reluctant few who had refused to accept.

60 Switching on the electric lights, 1954. Front row; Mr Cronin (ESB), Fr. Cahill,P.P., Mr. Enright (ESB), John Mansfield. Back row; Jim Quain, Mr Reddy (ESB), John Cashman.

Finally, 'the switch on' was announced for 24th May 1954 and crowds flocked into the village and speeches were made on a platform near the Boat House. About 10pm, Fr. Cahill flicked the switch, the church was illuminated, so was the Round Tower and there was loud cheering as lights appeared all around, from the village over to Curragh, Ballyquin and Lisarow. People wended their way to the church for Benediction and later on to Halla Deuglán for the dance. All were in jubilant mood. It is difficult to imagine now, the excitement of the occasion and what a wonderful, extraordinary event it was in the life of Ardmore. Rural Electrification and Muintir na Tíre are terms which go hand in hand in Ardmore. It is easy to forget now what an enormous milestone it was in our lives and it was Muintir na Tíre made it possible.

The last account of the Rural Electrification campaign has been condensed from an account by John Cashman in *The Ardmore Journal* of 1992.

A point worthy of comment as regards the introduction of new improvements was the suspicion and reluctance with which they were met. Both the piped water and the electricity programmes were reluctantly received and the canvassers found it very difficult to get people to sign up for either scheme. At first the piped water extended only as far as the Parish Priests house. The E.S.B. scheme wasn't enthusiastically received initially, but that was nearly twenty years later and the housekeepers, i.e. the ladies were exerting domestic pressure. The joys and wonders of it soon made themselves apparent. One old man in the village said wonderingly "Little did I think I'd live for the day I'd see the kettle boiling out of a hole in the wall."

One central village household installed a single light. This was a house always used as a rendezvous for the lads, even though the presiding genius was a lady, who pointing to her fireplace on occasion said, "that wall was the dividing line between Cork and Waterford", as so many of the wives who lived at the top of the village were from the neighbouring county. Anyhow she was gone before the coming of the E.S.B. and her son installed one electric light in the house and bought a kettle, but after the arrival of the first E.S.B. bill he had the electricity disconnected and reverted to his former domestic arrangements.

Previous to this in the 30s Gaeltacht grants became available for glasshouses. We were then classed as a Gaeltacht area and my father tried to persuade the Curragh people to avail of the grant but to no avail. Later on, he installed a glasshouse himself, self-paid, independent of any grant and he teased the others, telling them he had got a grant for it.

Muintir na Tíre is the national organisation founded by the late Rev. John M. Hayes of Bansha, Co. Tipperary, which has branches throughout the country. In the late 1930s, they began to have Rural Weeks at various centres in Ireland. These were conventions with a family atmosphere, attended by delegates from all the branches and by people well known in public life.

Rural Weeks were held in Ardmore, centred in Coláiste Deuglán, both in 1937 and 1938. 'Fireside chats' were held nightly, as well as various daily lectures by people prominent in different aspects of Irish life. Maud Gonne Mac Bride was one of those who spoke; De Valera and Dr. Ryan then Minister for Agriculture stayed at Coláiste Deuglán. Dev walked down to daily mass in the local church and en route visited William Harris from Bruree, Co. Limerick, his own native place. He even took to the floor at one of the céilithe in the Grianán, having been asked to dance in Rogha na mBan (Ladies Choice).

At the 1938 Rural Week, there was an International Day and it was strange to see the Union Jack among those flying from the College. There was an Italian Count there who spoke of the monastery of Bobbio, the Italian foundation of St. Columbanus being on his lands.

Well known newspaper correspondents, like Gertrude Gaffney for the *Irish Independent* and Aodh de Blacam for the *Irish Press* gave first-hand accounts of the day-to-day events in their respective newspapers. Ardmore figured very much in the news for both of these Rural Weeks.

Muintir na Tíre interested itself in various aspects of life in the parish, apart from the rural electrification campaign. One memento is the concrete stiles placed here and there out on the cliffs, to prevent cattle from straying, but they have no function nowadays. There just is no bovine presence on the cliffs, and bracken and briars are taking over from grass. The field at the left-hand side, on the way down to St. Declan's Well was grass-grown in our youth, also the fields beyond, both above and below the path. Musgraves did have cows when they owned Rock House in the 30s and 40s; Johnnie Brien from the village worked for them and was always up and down on his donkey, so Johnnie's donkey must have been partially responsible for the preservation of the grass. There was a little plot out beyond Faill na Sleannaire, which was the last plot that people remember being tilled.

Transport

Long journeys were not undertaken readily at the beginning of the last century. There were no public systems of transport available in Ardmore i.e. no buses or trains. One simply walked, went on horse-back, by donkey and cart or by pony and trap or by jarvey car. Children always walked to school, many of them having journeys of three miles. On bad evenings their fathers (i.e. those fathers who possessed such means of transport) came to collect them by pony and trap.

On Sundays during mass, some farmers stabled their horses in what was then known as Harris' Stables, right in the centre of the village and now occupied by new housing. Most people left them in front of the church.

The hearses bringing coffins to the church were of course horse-drawn, with the horses caparisoned in black, the black earpieces in particular looking decidedly odd and macabre.

61 A jaunting or jarvey car in Ardmore, c1920.

According to Jimmie Rooney, born in 1909, the jarvey car owners in the village were Johnny McGrath, Dysert; Tommy Quinn, Main St; Patsy McCarthy at the end of the village where McCarthy's still have premises. Dick Power and Ahearns of the Hotel had carriages; and he says Billy Kenneally of Youghal and Mary Ellen Begley of Ardo went to the church in a carriage, the last pair who went to their wedding in such a conveyance.

Travelling Salespeople

In pre motorcar days most country people were delighted to avail of the services of people with horse-drawn vans who came at regular intervals and supplied them with groceries, which they had probably but not necessarily ordered from the previous week.

Troys of Curragh and Batty Healy of Rodeen (near Power's Cross) were the better-known local ones, also Miky Allen of Ballyquin.

254

Pasleys came too from Youghal, as did Dan McGrath: 'Market Square, Youghal', the notice on the outside of the van declared, but Dan was a native of Ballinamertina (one of the seven sons referred to in the section on Healing, but not the 7th son).

Mrs Burke of Chapel Row used to buy eggs, then set out on a donkey and cart to go to the railway station in Waterford from where the eggs were exported to England. She would have been travelling all-night and then set out for home again. Jimmie Rooney has recorded this account of these almost incredible feats of endurance.

He also tells of Jim Keevers (John's father) who had the first rubber-tyred trap in Ardmore. It cost the colossal price of £50 and would have been the equivalent of a BMW nowadays. There were two large brass lamp standards into which a candle was inserted. One day, Bob Drohan met him at the Marine on the way home from Dungarvan Fair, Bob having been there with a horse and dray with creel. They had a race home and Bob won.

Hackney Cars

The very first private motor car in Ardmore was owned by Fred Keane, cousin of Sir John Keane of Cappoquin (of whom more anon). This would have been in the second decade of the century and he occasionally drove in it to Cappoquin. It invariably broke down. According to Jimmie Rooney, a telephone message used come to the Allens in the Post Office on Parsons Hill, instructing Mike Troy to go out with his mare to tow the car home. The village youngsters would go too and thoroughly enjoyed escorting the equipage back.

Hackney cars began to make their appearance about the early thirties. In 1923/24 Mike Leahy in Whiting Bay had one of the first. Then there was Jim Quain who drove Fr. Galvin P.P. to mass on wet mornings or brought him on sick calls or the Stations.

Jim Prendergast who lived in what is now McGrath's house in what has become known as Sleepy Lane, did some hackney driving too, as did Tom Foley who kept his car in the out-house on the site of what is now Ian and Caroline O'Sullivan's house. There was also Johnny Galvin who lived with his aunt and uncle, Mike and Mrs Troy in Chapel Row. Jimmie Rooney came on the scene later in 1938.

The Ferry Boat

62 Ferry boat with passengers and crew at Ferry Point looking across towards Youghal, 1876.

A popular way of getting to Youghal was walking or going by donkey and cart or pony and trap to the Ferry Point, leaving the animal at Hydes of the Ferry Point and going across in the ferry boat, which crossed the harbour every half hour, costing ½d each way (C.1900).

From Ardmore, the route went to Whiting Bay, crossed the bridge there and proceeded along the road to Ballysallagh and Monatrea. The road and bridge are now gone due to coastal erosion. I remember crossing it, in the forties, in my father's lorry and he and his helper had to get out and shovel away the gravel, to make a passage.

Until the late 60s when the ferry service ceased to exist, it remained a popular way of going to and from Youghal. One cycled there and the fare was 2d per passage and 2d for the bike. The most of the Monatrea children in those days, used the ferry for availing of secondary school education in Youghal. The Youghal people used it freely on Sundays for going on picnics to Monatrea, or visiting the popular Monatrea Hotel.

Public Bus Service

By the late twenties Mrs Keane, grand aunt of Denis & Terry McGrath, ran a bus service for a time called 'The President'. The driver and conductor were named Bradshaw and Flannery.

The service of the Southern General Bus Company between Cork and Ardmore (and Waterford) commenced operation on 26th November 1928. It was owned by a Francis Duffy of Dublin, but was based in Cork and was acquired by the Irish Omnibus Company on 11th October 1929.

The Irish Omnibus Company, the I.O.C. had been founded in Dublin in 1926 and in 1927 became an agent of the Great Southern Railways. In 1934 the G.S.R. absorbed the I.O.C. as its own Omnibus Department and in turn became part of C.I.E. in

1945 (C.I.E. Córas Iompair Éireann). In 1987 Bus Éireann was set up as a subsidiary of C.I.E. to operate bus services outside Dublin.

63 The Cork - Waterford bus on the Waterford side of Youghal Bridge, 1945. Luggage is being transferred to the roof rack.

It is interesting to note on the timetable, for the summer of 1929 that the bus journey, Ardmore to Cork took 1 hour, 55 minutes.

The fare from Waterford to Cork was 6/6 single (66p).

The fare from Cork to Youghal, 2/6 (26p) single 4/- return (40p).

All this information was kindly supplied by Mr Cyril McIntyre, Manager, Media & Public Relations, Bus Éireann.

Bicycles

During the war years one felt very independent with a bicycle. One could bring a bicycle by bus or train in the forties. I have happy memories of cycling trips in Donegal, Sligo, Connemara and Kerry, all done with the preliminary help of bus or train and all on signpost-less roads. Owing to the shortage of coal, trains ran only on certain days, and were often unpredictable. Ciss Quain has memories of during the war sitting out on the grass at the side of the railway line with the other passengers in the middle of the countryside.

We cycled to Youghal and Dungarvan when Lord Longford or Anew Mac Master brought their theatrical companies there. This happened perhaps once or twice a year. In spite of the gruelling cycle home around the Sweep on perhaps a bad night, we loved it, but it was years afterwards before we realised, what a privilege it was, for ourselves, the ordinary people of town and country, through the length and breadth of Ireland, to experience the dramatic performances of these artistes. It is remarkable also, to remember the hardships and vicissitudes they endured in doing so.

During the war, petrol was strictly rationed and supplied only to doctors, private hackney cars, and lorries. The war was over before people began to buy cars. It happened very slowly at first and we all spoke wonderingly and enviously of so-and-so having bought a car. No comment is necessary as regards the present proliferation of cars. We all take them for granted now, and never stop to think of what a vulnerable situation it is, say in the case of an oil crisis and the petrol pumps go dry.

Youghal Bridge

64 An Austin car crossing Youghal Bridge, c1955. The delicate nature of the bridge meant that barriers were erected on it to limit the speed of vehicles.

In the realms of transport, the condition of Youghal Bridge was a vivid war-time memory. The bridge was structurally unsound but could not be repaired or rebuilt owing to war conditions and the absence of materials, so about 30 barricades were put into position right across, and traffic had to zig zag over. No buses were allowed across. Passengers on the Cork/Waterford route vacated the bus at one end of the bridge and walked across to the waiting bus at the other side. A hackney car came from Youghal to transport luggage, and technically speaking, one could stand on ones' rights and insist on being driven across, but realistically this arrangement was not feasible. The bridge was a long one and the walk across on a bad winters day could be most unpleasant.

A man was on duty in a little hut at either side of the bridge, to oversee the weighing of lorries before being allowed to cross. Any excess weight had to be unloaded; the lorry went over, unloaded at the opposite side and returned for the rest of the load, a rather cumbersome and time-consuming procedure. I remember on one occasion, returning from Cork with my father in a loaded lorry, and instead of taking the turn for the bridge and home, he went up to Cappoquin to cross the river, a rather exasperating experience at the end of a long day, but preferable to the unloading and reloading.

Even cycling across could be a hazard. On a fair day, I remember quickening pace to get on to the bridge before a large flock of cattle. This I succeeded in doing, only to discover that still another flock was in front, so I was now between two lots and cattle tended to get restive and frightened and to jump the barriers.

Another war-time memory was encountering a long line of military jeeps and armoured cars, returning from the big manoeuvres on the Blackwater in I think 1944, and being subjected to various snippets of military advice and wisecracks as I wended my embarrassed way in and out between the tar barrels.

The barricades remained for some years after the war, while the expenses and the site of a new bridge were being disputed about. In pre-driving test days, one's ability to negotiate and deal with oncoming traffic on Youghal Bridge was the acid test of driving ability.

The new bridge was at last opened in 1963 some distance up-river from the old one. There had been long delays on account of the controversies on the allocation of the costs between the two counties (no EU funds then) and also on its location. One school of thought wanted the crossing at the Ferry Point but eventually, we got the present one at Rhincrew.

Martin Hurley's Lorry

I suppose one could say my father's lorry (a 3-ton, later a 5-ton truck) featured to a certain extent in the transport system here at one stage. In the thirties he paid regular visits to Ring, buying lobsters and salmon, and quite a few of the ladies of the locality generally availed of the accommodation in the back of the lorry for a trip to Dungarvan.

He often went to hurling or football matches in places like Clashmore or Pilltown and always left with a number of passengers. Jimmie Rooney says they went to a match in Villierstown one Sunday and that 75 people emerged from the lorry there!

My sister and I remember one trip to Pilltown with a relatively small compliment of passengers; the match didn't take place on account of bad weather, but we went down to the old mill (the actual mill, not the pub called after it) and went upstairs and had a great evening's entertainment of music and sets, upstairs in the mill. It is now a complete ruin.

Then there was the memorable occasion of the Eucharistic Congress in Dublin in 1932, when a group of at least 20 people left Ardmore for Dublin in Martin Hurley's Bedford truck about 3 am, on a June morning.

Travel Abroad

The most remarkable transport phenomenon of this century is air travel. It is difficult to imagine that the first flight by the Wright brothers in a heavier than air machine was in North Carolina in 1903. A Waterford man, Colonel James Fitzmaurice, after a period with the British force, joined the infant Irish Air Service in 1922. In 1928, with two German colleagues, he accomplished the first East to West crossing of the Atlantic against the prevailing winds.

In the mid '60s, Ardmore I.C.A. went on an I.C.A. outing to Cobh. Part of it was on a trip in the tender out to the liner and a tour of the liner. Liners were always some distance out in the harbour and were serviced by tender from the quay in Cobh. There liners went on to Southampton and Le Havre. A French exchange student to our household in the early 1960s came by liner to Cobh. I remember meeting two visitors from Germany there too.

My mother Johanna Hurley went on a pilgrimage to Lourdes in 1937. It involved travelling to Dublin by train, going by boat from Dun Laoghaire to Holyhead; by train to London where the pilgrimage stayed the night; by train to Dover; by boat to Calais and then by train to Paris, where there was also an overnight stay before undertaking the long train journey to Lourdes. Now the pilgrims go to Cork and arrive in Lourdes a few short hours later.

When my brother, James Hurley SJ, first went to Hong Kong in 1952 it was by P&O boat from Southampton and the voyage took 4 weeks. When he returned to Ireland in 1955, it was by Italian boat to Naples and when he and his group went back to Hong Kong in 1960, it was also by Italian boat. In 1961, the Jesuit community first used air transport between Hong Kong and Ireland. Now more or less at the drop of a hat, people fly to the ends of the earth and take it quite for granted.

During the war period, we were completely cut off from the rest of the world. There was limited and strictly monitored transport (some of it by air from Baldonnel) between England and Ireland but one did not ever, ever entertain the possibility of going to Europe. One might as easily have thought of going to the moon.

The Eucharistic Congress

The Eucharistic Congress was an exciting event not alone for Dublin but for the whole country, but it is difficult to envisage a similar outburst on nationwide enthusiasm nowadays.

The 31st International Eucharistic Congress was held in Dublin, in June 1932, an achievement of which our infant State might well be proud. It was a mere ten years since the turmoil of the Civil War and now with absolute precision and due pomp and ceremony, we hosted this immense (about a million people) gathering of dignitaries and pilgrims from all parts of the globe. We were also celebrating the 15th centenary of the coming of St. Patrick to Ireland.

At that period, there was no question of the Pope himself travelling abroad and Cardinal Lauri was appointed to Papal Legate. The difference between his coming and the coming of the Pope in 1979 was striking. Pope John Paul left Rome and arrived in Ireland a few hours later. Cardinal Lauri with his suite left Rome on June 16th, arriving in Paris on 17th, where they were received by Cardinal Verdier of Paris. Two days later, they left Paris for Folkestone, London, Chester and Holyhead, being greeted on the way by crowds of the faithful. At Holyhead, he embarked on the special steamer, the *Cambria* which arrived in Dunlaoire at 3.00pm on June 20th and was escorted into the harbour by a squadron of aeroplanes. The Cardinal and his suite were met by a crowd of about 50,000 which of course included all the dignitaries of church and state and addresses of welcome were read in Irish and English. A feature of the Congress was the number of important addresses and lectures given in Irish.

The Garda Síochána Band played; mounted trumpeters sounded a fanfare; a squadron of cavalry saluted with drawn swords and the party set out on the triumphant journey into Dublin. Before and behind the car rode an escort of brilliantly uniformed hussars. At Merrion on the city boundary, two ornamental pylons had been erected and here Alderman Alfie Byrne, the Lord Mayor who had arrived in the centuries' old mayoral gilded coach, formally received the Legate. Again there were addresses in English, Irish and Latin before proceeding in to the Pro Cathedral, the way being lined by tumultuous crowds. Nothing quite like it had previously been seen in this country.

There followed a week of celebrations with special men's masses, women's masses, and children's masses in the Phoenix Park. The special choir of 2,500 children at the children's mass on Saturday 25th was directed by Dr. Vincent O'Brien. The sectional services and masses were for French, Polish, Dutch, Lithuanian, Italian, Oriental, Canadian, Spanish, Scottish, Australian, American, Argentinian, Austrian, Belgian, German, Portuguese, Hungarian, Uruguayan, and Yugoslavian groups. Thirteen liners, serving as hotels for their passengers were anchored in Dublin Bay. Of the ten cardinals who assisted at the mass in the Phoenix Park on Sunday 26th, five bore distinctly Irish names and five were of Irish birth. Among the bishops was one named O'Rourke from Danzig, whose ancestors were Irish and whose mother tongue was Slav.

The solemn High Mass on Sunday 26th June in the Phoenix Park was the climax of all the proceedings. It was to begin at 1pm but eight hours before, people had reached their places. The great open space had been divided into sections, according to countries, dioceses, parishes' etc., and stewards, Gardai and Boy Scouts were in attendance. Restaurant tents, first aid depots, information bureaux had been erected and a water supply connecting with that of the city had been laid down. The choir of more than 2000 was directed by Dr. Vincent O'Brien. At the offertory, Count John

Mac Cormack who wore the distinctive robes of a Knight of Malta sang the Panis Angelicus.

Another deeply moving moment was when the ancient Bell of St. Patrick was rung at the Sanctus. "There was heard a sound that must be almost unique in human history. Faint as the sound of a far-off bell..... it was the bell of St. Patrick" (G.K. Chesterton).

Just before the end of Mass, the voice of the Holy Father was heard in a greeting from the Vatican.

There were pilgrims from Ardmore present too, at this momentous event. They travelled however, not in any special liner or train, but in a Bedford truck owned by Martin Hurley and they sat on three hard seats, in the back. A bus journey to Dublin nowadays on upholstered seats and over excellent modern roads would be regarded as tiring. The mind boggles at the prospect of sitting up straight for at least 4/5 hours on hard seats without a back, but this is what they did.

They left Ardmore from outside the Boat House, about 3am that Sunday morning. Jim Quain a fast but skilful driver, was the chauffeur and Mrs Deasy and Ciss Quain were in the cab with him. As to the route, they only remember Leighlinbridge, as there, there was a temporary breakdown and the other lorries with passengers whom they had passed now drove by and waved jeeringly. But off they went again. Two Americans were on board and at one stage one of them lost his straw hat. It was blown off and they didn't stop to retrieve it and he kept lamenting his ten-dollar hat. Tom Walsh speaks of the swaying of the lorry when it rounded curves at speed. Incidentally, it is fairly certain that the lorry had no insurance for carrying passengers, but then people of those days were not insurance conscious.

Our pilgrims are maddeningly vague about such details as eating or toilet facilities, but agree they had a most satisfactory meal at the Barn Café in Lucan in the evening. As regards the ceremonies themselves, Ciss Quain remembers the singing of John Mac Cormack: Jimmy Rooney, the American Indian priest in full regalia. Kathleen O'Brien was chatting with the boys from a Tullamore lorry, who on the return journey were involved in an accident with fatal casualties. A camera was stolen from Mary Ellen Flynn and a silver fox fur from Mrs Deasy, so evidently the pickpockets had a good day out. Mrs Deasy was in medical difficulties at one stage, she had given birth to a baby not long before, but a nurse was got and all ended well.

They were in O'Connell St., later on and met Sheila O'Brien (later Mrs O'Byrne of Kinsalebeg now deceased). She had come by train from Dungarvan and her memories were of being very frightened in the huge crowds at Kingsbridge, now Heuston Station. She was a girl of 16 at the time. Ciss Quain and Kathleen O'Brien were 17 and John Fitzgerald, a youngster of 13.

And so after a long day they set off for home, Johnny Moloney calling out "Next stop, Geata na bhFranncach" (i.e. Crossford Bridge). They travelled through the night, arriving in Ardmore about mass time in the morning, very tired and very dirty. Various versions of their adventures must have been going the rounds in Ardmore for some time after.

Those who travelled were: Jim Quain Tom Walsh, Michael Ducey, Ciss Quain, John Fitzgerald, Kathleen O'Brien (Rooney), Mrs Deasy, Jerry Crowley, Mary Ellen Flynn, Willie Curran, Whiting Bay (returned from the U.S) Johnnie Neill, Curragh (returned from the U.S.) Johnnie Moloney, Richie Troy, Micky Troy, May Lynch, and Jimmie Rooney.

Most of the information on the Congress is based on *The Book of the Congress 1932* by Rev. Canon Boylan.

The 1955 Historical Exhibition

An Historical Exhibition was held at the College, Ardmore in Pattern Week 1955. It was organised by the local guild of the Irish Countrywomen's Association. The exhibition was a great success and an account of it was published in *Ár Leabhar Féin*, Our Book, the I.C.A.'s official Year Book (1956). This article is based mainly on that account.

It all began away back in January of 1955, with the appearance of the newly published *Romantic Slievenamon in History, Folklore and Song, a Tipperary Anthology* edited by James Maher, 1954. We followed Mr Maher in and out through the centuries with Finn, Diarmuid and Gráinne, with Lady Iveagh and the Butlers of Kilcash, with Kickham at Knocknagow, with the Fenian men of Slievenamon and with the flying columns of this century. It was enthralling, but then we began to think of all the lore of Árd Mhór Deagláin that was being forgotten and ignored. "Ah well, what could busy housewives like us do anyway," we said; but all the same we could not shake off the persistent nagging idea. An t'Athair Ó Muirthille, S.J. was written to for advice, and back came a long, enthusiastic letter, suggesting a historical exhibition as the best way for stimulating interest in local history. Included were directions for running one, ranging from insurance to such details as cellophane and sellotape, and also enclosed was a catalogue of the Archaeological and Historical Exhibition held at Tullamore, during An Tóstal, 1954. At the next committee meeting, we gasped as we read of Bronze Age javelin heads and crannóg boats and ancient woodcarvings. We had never heard of any stray axe heads or javelin heads around Ardmore; indeed, the question was, was anything at all available?

Feeling very doubtful about the whole project ourselves, we introduced the subject at the next Guild meeting. It was received rather uncertainly, but at least it was not rejected and we did hear of five or six possible exhibits. Then came the Annual General Meeting of the I.C.A. in Dublin at the end of March, and a few of us found ourselves between meetings, pouring our troubles into the ears of Mr Sean O'Súilleabháin of the Folklore Commission. We had a sympathetic hearing too at the premises of Fógra Fáilte on Pembroke Road, and then there was Mr Lucas of the National Museum who, with his advice and invaluable pamphlet on the Folk Culture Department of the Museum, gave us the definite direction we needed and put us, so to speak, on the right road at last. Shortly afterwards, we opened our campaign in explanatory letters to the local papers. There could be no turning back now.

The next few months we kept pestering all our acquaintances and had the whole parish turning out their lofts and outhouses for such things as settle beds and roasting spits and butter prints and hooded cloaks. Pattern week in late July, was arranged as the ideal time for the exhibition, in spite of the forbidding fact that four or five of our small Guild would be quite unable to help us, this being their busy summer season. There were sessions with Mr Fergus MacMurcadha, our County Librarian, who was most kind and helpful in choosing books for us. The Old I.R.A. (3rd Battalion, West Waterford Brigade) sponsored a complete section of exhibits relating to the '98 period and the War of Independence.

Exhibits came from far and near, one of the butter prints from Belgooly near Kinsale; the hand-woven sheets loaned by the late Bridgie Kenneally of Lissarow and the baby's shoes of 1807 from Mrs Quain; a copper plated strainer for poteen making from Ballyglavin; the 200 year old chalice from the Curran family Ballylangadon; *An Bíobla Naomhtha* by Bishop Bedell from the late Justin Condon, Youghal; the account of the first Feis in

Munster held in Ardmore in 1899 from the late Thomas Mulcahy B.E. who with Abbot O'Faolain of Mount Melleray had worked hard in its preparation.

From Rock House came a plank with the name *Jeune Austerlitz* - a ketch lost in Ardmore Bay in 1895. The late Tommie Lincoln, Cappoquin loaned a very interesting set of exhibits from the War of Independence period; one of these was the photograph of Terence McSwiney, with Fr. Bonaventure O. Cap, who came to see the exhibition.

One whole section was loaned by the late Comdt. Pax Whelan 3rd Bat. Old I.R.A., West Waterford Brigade, and he and his son Donal (then a student) came to Ardmore and personally arranged all the items. We were most appreciative of his interest and enthusiasm. This section was a very important and striking part of the exhibition, which caused a great stir of interest in Ardmore and its environs during that memorable week.

How shall we tell of the anxious weeks preceding the exhibition - the problems of transport, of tickets, of trestles, of preparing a catalogue of items many of which had not yet appeared in spite of the most urgent exhortations. There are the moments of deep despair when it seems as if the venture is to end in disgrace; the exasperating moments when the rolls of sellotape all disappear as if by magic; the scissors vanish, the bundles of captions have evidently taken wings, and then the wonderful moments when at last out of chaos has come order. The five-foot tall photograph of the Round Tower (loaned by Fógra Fáilte) looked magnificent opposite the doorway; the array of pewter is most attractive, the old hand-woven sheets and towels have been arranged to our satisfaction, the books, photographs, and maps are all in order, and the ladies (figures borrowed from the drapers) in their hooded cloaks smiled down, quite unperturbed by the array of pikes and guns so near them.

The event was held in the new building, built in 1935 as an adjunct to Coláiste Deauglán to provide accommodation for its summer students.

Seamus Pender, Professor of History at University College Cork and no stranger to Coláiste Deuglán, officially opened the Exhibition and also gave a very interesting opening talk. Mr Michael Mulcahy B.E. of the Military History Society of Ireland gave a most comprehensive lecture on Ardmore and its Monuments matching the historical interest aroused by the whole ethos of the week. Mr Maher, having been told of the frenzy of activities for which he had been largely responsible, came from Mullinahone to see what it was all about. Father Bonaventure also attended and discovered that he was among the exhibits, and sure enough there was his photograph with Terence MacSwiney.

The *Dungarvan Leader* had a notice saying 'The Historical Exhibition under the auspices of Ardmore I.C.A. Guild at St. Declan's College, which opens on Pattern Sunday at 3 p.m. will continue during the following week', and then on August 6th 1955, we read 'A sidelight of the Ireland of the past and a sketch of the ancient See of Ardmore were given in the unique Local History Exhibition, the first of its kind to be held in Ireland, which was under the auspices of the Ardmore I.C.A. Guild who are indeed to be highly complimented on their very successful enterprise. Amongst the speakers taking part were Professor Séan Pender and Mr M. Mulcahy B.E.'

The exhibition organised by the Guild was also a financial success. That, of course, was rather important and it certainly indicated a lively interest in local history. We were scheduled to close on the fourth day, but by popular request extended it over the following weekend as well.

The closing paragraph of the article in *Ár Leabhar Féin* might be quoted here. "We hope that we have helped to foster and strengthen the natural pride we ought all to have in our native place. It is not altogether that we think it superior to all other places, but it is here our roots are, here we were born and reared and our people before us for long generations back, and please God, our people after us, in the generations to come!"

The Ardmore Irish Countrywomen's Association

65 The old Ardmore National School photographed in 1951. The building was demolished in the mid-1950s.

The I.C.A. Guild was founded in the old schoolhouse in Ardmore, on a cold January night in 1953. Mrs. Rooney had initiated the project and Anne Roche, the organiser came to explain to a mildly curious not over enthusiastic audience, what it was all about.

272

From the very beginning, the Ardmore and Grange Guild was deeply involved in inter-Guild and county federation activities. At federation level, our members have held the following posts: two Presidents, two Vice-Presidents, Secretary, International Officer, Timire, two Arts Promoters, ACOT Representative, Crafts Promoter, and Teachta. One of our members, Margaret Leahy, is at present, Chairperson of the National Executive, a highly prestigious office.

At our inaugural meeting in January 1953, we realised and noted the importance of having a comfortable meeting place. At that time, F. Nugent and J. O'Brien owned Monea House, more commonly known as 'The College', it having functioned as an Irish College from the early 1940s. They were approached with a request for accommodation, and the rejoinder was, that we could have it free for three months, as that was as long as we'd last. We're still going strong forty-six years later.

We occupied the large room on the right-hand side of the hallway, enjoying our Adams fireplace and Georgian grandeur for four years. There were just oil lamps. Rural electrification came to Ardmore in 1954, but the College wasn't wired. The owners' plans changed and in January 1958, we got a notice to quit. For most of the next fifteen years, a small room at Ivy Lodge, was our home. The Parish Priest Fr. Power was approached with a proposal to build a new premises in the field behind the Hall. He agreed, provided the site remained parochial property, in case the I.C.A. ceased to exist.

Fund-raising was now going on, in earnest, and included jumble sales, whist drives, raffles, sales of work, and dances. In the meantime, Jim Quain had drawn up a plan for the premises and planning permission was granted in April 1973. In November 1973, John Keane and Gerard were on the site with a bulldozer and marked it out, and the building at last began. During the winter of 1974, the foundations were laid and required many loads of stones, so again, husbands and some of the I.C.A. members were requisitioned to bring them in, at various times and meitheal of I.C.A. came together on appointed evenings to throw these stones into the foundations. Mrs. O'Brien came across with tea and currant cake and we really enjoyed those sessions. Jim Quain took over the long, tedious job of building up the walls, Saturday by Saturday. We ought never forget the deep debt we owe him.

The opening of the I.C.A. room in January 1976 was a memorable occasion. Mass was celebrated by Fr. O'Gorman and all who were involved in the building were invited, as well as the Federation President and members of neighbouring Guilds. Our first proper Guild Meeting in the room was in 9th March, 1976, but the work was by no means completed. October 1976 found us discussing insurance and connecting with the water mains.

The next gala occasion was the celebration of our Silver Jubilee in our own premises, in 1978. Our room is regularly used by other organisations, for example for kindergarten classes a few times a week, for the weekly outing of the senior citizens of St. Declan's Community Centre, for which the Ardmore Enterprise Co-Op in conjunction with the Board of Health have helped to refurbish.

No account of I.C.A. activities is possible without special mention of Anne Roche who not only helped to bring us into being in 1953, but guided our first faltering steps and continued to be our special mentor and friend down through the years. It was she who introduced us to debating. In 1954, we became County champions and got our name on the shield for the Eleanor Gibbon competition for the first time. On two other occasions, our name figured on the shield, for portraying five fascinating women.

We got involved in drama and in the 1950s the I.C.A. play was an important date in the Ardmore calendar. Other activities followed, set dancing, fashion competitions, flower arranging and cookery. Teresa O'Connor became National Seafood Cook of the year in 1984. More recent successes were in the 1987 Guild of the Year competition, involving among many other things, a monthly record of the various Guild activities, and besides winning at county level, our entry was among the top eight in the country. We were co-first in the county in the 1993 A.I.B. competition.

The Historical Exhibition in 1955 was the most noteworthy of all our activities in the early years. It took place in the new building of what was the Irish College at Ardmore in Pattern Week.

From 1955 to 1962, the Children's Sports, including a sand castle competition on the strand, was an annual event, as was the Christmas party presided over by Santa Claus. This later became a children's Céilí. Our records are peppered with accounts of whist drives and socials in our own premises or in the hall, in aid of ourselves of for some parochial cause. The socials in the mid-fifties and later, were really socials in the full sense of the word. The music was supplied by Michael Mansfield's local band (The Sea Breeze). All age groups came and there was a festive party air, as people danced and sang. Afterwards tea and cakes were handed round. The Pattern was also celebrated by a Céilí and bunting was put out.

Since 1956, the Guild has been deeply involved in Water Safety activities, including organising and fund-raising. Courses in Swimming and Lifesaving take place twice each summer in Ardmore, and we are represented on the County Committee.

In January 1993, the Guild celebrated its 40th anniversary and invited ex-members to attend the celebrations. There was a gala night of speech making, song and reminiscing. Anne Roche who initiated us into the I.C.A. away back in 1953 was an honoured guest and a wonderful night was had by all. We have competed with distinction in among other things, Federation Day in Dungarvan, involving baking, crafts, flower arranging and drama. Since the 1990s we have had ambitious summer programmes at Pattern time.

We have still got four founder members, all of whom have held office at various times. It may be disconcerting to note that many of our more recent members were not born on that January night in 1953, when Ardmore and Grange I.C.A. guild came into being, but it is a healthy and heartening sign for the future and we can face the years ahead with confidence and assurance.

Founder Members still alive are: - Eileen Colbert, Kathleen Keane, Siobhán Lincoln and Ciss Quain.

Past Presidents: -

Chrissie Rooney 1953 - 1954
Ciss Quain 1955 - 1956
Siobhán Lincoln 1957 - 1958
Mary Troy 1959 - 1960
Helen Curran 1961 - 1962
Shiela O'Byrne 1963 - 1964
Ciss Quain 1965
Marie Quain 1966
Eileen Colbert 1967 - 1968
Kathleen O'Connell 1969 - 1971
Angela Keane 1972 - 1973
Bridget O'Brien 1974 - 1975
Anne Hallahan 1976 - 1978
Margaret Leahy 1979 - 1981

Patricia Cockburn 1982 - 1984
Nora Connery 1985 - 1986
Teresa O'Connor 1987 - 1988
Bernie Keane 1988 - 1990
Mary Colbert 1991 - 1993
Liz Dolan 1994 - 1996
Margaret Cronin 1997 - 1998
Eileen O'Callaghan 1999 - 2000

Buckleys of Ardmore and Melbourne

Vincent Buckley is a most distinguished Australian poet of Irish background who taught in the University of Melbourne for many years. He and his wife and two girls came to Ardmore for a period of some months and the two girls attended the local school from January to March 1987. At the request of Victor Mullins Principal/teacher at the school, he composed a poem about Ardmore which Victor put to music and the children often sing it. He composed another poem, *Ardmore Bay*. The family returned to Australia and he died in 1988. After his death a number of Irish poets, including Seamus Heaney came together in Dublin and read poems to his memory. An article by Sean Dunne, commemorating Vincent Buckley's memory is in the *Ardmore Journal* 1991, as well as fuller reference to the Buckley stay in Ardmore.

Ardmore Bay

This morning in the tiding the waves were green with spray
And the land seemed moving outward from the sea.
Though I must leave it soon, to go twelve thousand miles away,
Ardmore will never see the last of me.

The angles of the light
And the blackbirds in their coursing
They fall away together
To the wide strand of Ardmore.

The people in their kindness, in the delicate deep town,
They're living out the dignity of Here:
The sea they'll walk in Summer, the land they'll keep
their own.
This is the Ireland no one has to fear

The angles of the light
And the small birds in their coursing
They lift away together
From the headlands of Ardmore.

The seagulls come down grunting on the tailspin
of the gale.
They are speaking Munster Irish to our heart.
The past that gives us courage will keep
our country whole
And the future lift away the bitter part.

The angles of the Light
And the blackbirds in their coursing
They fall away together
To the wide strands of Ardmore.

34th Waterford Scout Unit of Ardmore & Grange

The Scout Unit of Ardmore and Grange began in September 1991
with eight boys and four leaders, James Moloney, Pat O'Shea,
Michael O'Brien, and John Mansfield. From this small beginning it
has blossomed into a unit to which most of the young people of

278

the parish belong. The Boy Cubs began with eight boys and two leaders in 1992. Girls entered the unit as scouts in September 1992 with twelve girls and three leaders. Beavers began in the November of that year joined by Girl Cubs in November 1993 and Venturers began in spring of 1994. By this time over one hundred and twenty children were involved in six sections under the guidance of eighteen leaders.

Among other things, they have contributed to the winning of the National Tidy Towns Award of 1992 by doing daily litter patrols. They produced a fortnightly newsletter for the community, *Out and About*.

They have taken part in the St. Patrick's Day Parade in Dungarvan winning the best Youth Float. The Scouts have taken part in two successful summer camps, a Jamboree on the Air and regional events including the winning of the O'Farrell Shield. Their first pantomime in 1993 proved a roaring success; *Sinbad* Meets the Vampire in December 1996 was just as successful.

The fortnightly newspaper *Out and About* was a wonderfully lively and witty resume of parish affairs; from birthdays to marriages and deaths, G.A.A. and soccer news, Macra na Feirme, advertisements, pictures of various people in the parish, cookery recipes; the list is endless. Issue 65 in June 1996 was the last one, I count myself most fortunate in having almost all of them. One of my treasured memories is of the Scouts at the graveyard on July 1995, having gone to Cashel and spent three days returning to Ardmore along St. Declan's Road, for its official opening by Minister Allen on 16th July 1995.

The Scouts have been extremely fortunate to have had people of the calibre of James Moloney, Michael O'Brien, Brigid Shelley, Jane Moloney, Margaret Meehan and so very many others as guardian angels. Circumstances have compelled the retirement of James Moloney after six years of dedicated service and this was a great blow to the organisation.

In late 1999, about fifty children are in the Irish Girl Guides, which comprises Ladybirds (ages 5-7) under the direction of Brigid Shelly and Anne Mooney; Brownies (ages 8-10) under the direction of Jane Moloney, Anita Supple and Anne Troy; Guides (aged 10½-16) under the direction of Martha Tierney and Margaret Meehan. And so the good work goes on.

Ardmore Twinning Association

Chairman - Pat McGrath
Secretary - Eileen Fitzgerald
Ass. Secretary - Sandra McGrath
Treasurer - Elizabeth Dolan
P.R.O. - Caroline O'Sullivan
Educational Officer - Ruth Lynch

The association has about 80 members to date.

The inaugural meeting was held on 22nd April 1996. Richard Lincoln chaired this and future events were discussed re twinning with Abbotskerwell in Devon and later with Le Pré d'Auge Les Menceaux in Normandy.

It all began when a Devon tourist visited Ardmore and came to the conclusion that Ardmore was an ideal twinning partner for Abbotskerswell.

In February 1996, a small group from Ardmore visited Devon. In April the inaugural was held. In May, some members travelled via Devon to France. At the end of September 1996, a group of Devonians visited Ardmore with their chairman, Tom Banks and at the end of October, we welcomed some French people with their chairperson, Murielle Hauvel. We are very lucky to have Ruth Lynch as interpreter.

In order to get E.U. funding, the Association was registered and a copy of the constitution sent to the European Commission.

We were very grateful to the Ardmore Enterprise Co-Op who donated £600 to our funds. Various fund-raising activities took place, for e.g. a Christmas Party, Valentine Party, Concert, Tabletop Quiz, American Tea-Party, and Fashion Show, as it was necessary to raise a good lot of money to cover the cost of signing the Charter.

During 1996-97, French classes were held under the guidance of Mary Cashman. Ruth Lynch also touched up our meagre knowledge of French before our visit there.

A group of French teenagers visited Ardmore in July 1997 and some 5th and 6th class children travelled to France at the end of May 1998. A group of Adults travelled to Abbotskerswell in May 1997 and to France in May 1998 for the second part of the Charter signing.

Autumn 1997 was a very important and busy time in the history of the Ardmore Twinning Association. The signing of the Charter took place during the October weekend, when the three groups met and enjoyed the craic, bia agus ól. The main function was held in Halla Deuglán, which was tastefully decorated. Food and wine were served, and local musicians played into the early hours. Speakers included Lar Hart, Chairman of Waterford Co. Council, County Manager, Donal Connolly and Canon O'Connor P.P. Ardmore.

All three groups met again in Abbotskerswell in mid May 1999 for the third phase of the charter signing. An immense fund of goodwill and a spirit of camaraderie has been engendered between rural communities in three countries, a basis for real international friendship.

See article by Michael Mulcahy, 'St. Declan's Road' in 1988 issue of the *Ardmore Journal*.

The Rediscovery of St Declan's Way

The rediscovery of St Declan's Way, the Rian Bo Phadraig, St Declan's route from Cashel to Ardmore, was prompted by the perusal of an article on it by the late Canon Power in the Journal of the RSAI (Royal Society of Antiquaries of Ireland) for 1905.

In the mid-80s Michael Mulcahy BE and myself, armed with maps from Jim Shine BE, Waterford Co Council, began a tour to re-discover the whole Rian or at least the nearest section to Ardmore which is called Bóthar na Riolog, Saint Declan's Road. It took us some few years, as the tours had to be done during Michael's holiday periods but we were very pleased when we eventually succeeded in tracing the Rian as far as Lismore.

After that my son, Richard, proceeded to investigate the rest of the Rian between Lismore and Cashel and did Herculean work not alone on this section but also on the revitalizing of the sections between Grange and Cnoc na Sceach crossroads, not far from Ballinameela. The Rian is now way-marked as far as Cashel and a professional guide-book has been published.

Part of the work involved consultation not alone with the Waterford and Tipperary County Councils but also with land-owners along the route, not all of whom were enthusiastically cooperative.

In July 1995 Richard and his daughter, Sarah, went to Cashel with a group of local Scouts and their leader, James Moloney. They spent three days returning home on the Rian, arriving in Ardmore for its official opening by Minister Bernard Allen at Ardmore graveyard. A plaque on the wall commemorates the event. I must admit that I am very proud of this achievement. (Cf. Article on St Declan's Road by Michael Mulcahy in the 1988 issue of the *Ardmore Journal*).

Epilogue

And so we have crossed the Rubicon as it were and we are in the new millennium. We hear so much discussion on it that we are inclined to forget what it really means. It celebrates the two thousandth anniversary of the coming of Christ and therefore the advent of Christianity. A mere four hundred or so years later, the news of Christ's coming had spread across thousands of miles of land and sea and had reached our little island. In Ardmore we pride ourselves on having been the first on this island to hear the amazing new message of Christianity, brought to us by St. Declan whose name is ever fresh here in the Deise.

The last century had been ushered in by midnight mass at the local church, the Parish priest being Fr Walsh, more commonly known as 'Geallaim-se' as he prefaced so many of his sentences of his sermons by the remark "Geallaim-se dhaoibh-se a bhráithre" (I promise you brethern). Besides the celebration of Mass this century and millennium were ushered in by an astonishing concert in a packed church, a torch light procession to the Beannachán and Cathedral and a wonderful display of fireworks.

The village has changed enormously in the course of the years. There was a change of language from Irish to English, changed ways of thinking, of living conditions. I have tried to put before you a picture of life in Ardmore through the century by describing various aspects of it, how the village grew and continues to grow, the various houses and who lived in them, the more important buildings, the organisations and their functions in the parish transport and communications, interesting happenings such as the Eucharistic Congress, the Austrian Refugees, the war period in general.

Young people will perhaps find it difficult to visualise the different ways of life described in these pages. Older people will perhaps look back with nostalgia while at the same time they realise the enormous changes for the better that have taken place. Still these changes that have made life so much better have to be paid for in terms of pollution of the planet and we wonder what kind of a world are we leaving our children. However, let us step forward bravely together; some of us will be dropping out of the march soon enough and in the word of the traditional Irish blessing we say to all the people of our beloved of Ardmore:

"Slán is beannacht, is go n-éirí on bóthar libh".

"Blessings on you and may the road rise to meet you."

66 Monument to St. Declan erected in Ardmore to mark the Millenium.

Siobhán Lincoln

Siobhan Lincoln lived her whole life, of 91 years, until her death in 2011, in Ardmore, Co Waterford. She was the local teacher, and was deeply interested in folklore, history, and the Gaelic tradition of the area.

She published four books in her lifetime and contributed regularly to many publications. She also wrote poetry, and articles, principally in the Irish language for publications like *An*

Linn Bhui, Iris Ghaeltacht na nDeise, the *Ardmore Journal* and *Decies* (Journal of the Waterford Archaeological and Historical Society).

Her first book, made its appearance in 1979, entitled, *A Walk around Ardmore*. She felt the need to tell people about the beautiful and historical place that Ardmore was, and is. She followed this with a publication about St Declan, *Declan of Ardmore* (1995). Her granddaughter, Katie, illustrated this popular book. This is a shortened version of fables, stories and folklore about St Declan. Its format makes it an easily read book.

Next off the press, was a book on St Declan's Way called, *Along Saint Declan's Way*, an ancient roadway from Cashel to Ardmore, rediscovered by Siobhán.

Her final book was entitled, *Ardmore, Memory and Story*. This was a book commemorating the millennium, in the year 2000. It recounts the Ardmore she knew as a girl growing up there.

The BBC journalist, neighbour and friend, Fergal Keane, in a foreword to one of her books, says of Siobhán, "I can only describe her as a formidable character, a woman of learning and wit. I know of few grandmothers who would happily set off for China with her teenage granddaughters and meet every challenge along the route with relish". And about her book, *Ardmore Memory and Story*, he says; "It is said that every village in Ireland has a historian: I can't vouch for that but know that Ardmore is blessed to have a woman like Siobhán, who is so passionate in the cause of saving memory for the coming generations."

She was a fearless campaigner for the things she valued in life; like her beloved Ardmore, the Irish language, the environment and the celebration of St Declan. The files of local newspapers, government departments, and the local council have volumes of her letters advocating actions concerning these things, of passionate interest to her. Her legacy are the research and publications she left to us. And the practical organisations she help found in the area, such as the local branch of the ICA (Irish Country Women's Association), Tidy Towns Association and the local Water Safety Organisation.

Image Credits

Waterford County Museum Collection: 1, 3, 4, 6, 7, 8, 9, 10, 11, 13, 14, 15, 16, 18, 19, 20, 22, 23, 27, 28, 29, 30, 31, 34, 35, 36, 40, 41, 42, 43, 44

Willie Whelan: 2,

Eddie Dee: 5, 12, 21, 24, 25, 26, 32, 33, 37, 38, 39, 45

Horgan Family: 17

About Waterford County Museum

Waterford County Museum is a volunteer run museum dedicated to preserving the history of County Waterford, Ireland. Based in the town of Dungarvan, the museum is open to the public throughout the year, admission is free of charge. The museum operates a very active volunteer community archaeology group. A number of lectures, educational events and exhibitions are run by us during the year. We also publish books and e-books relating to County Waterford history. You can keep up to date with museum news and happenings at:

Email: history@waterfordmuseum.ie

Web: www.waterfordmuseum.ie

Twitter: @waterfordmuseum

Facebook: @waterfordcountymuseum

Other Books in the Series

This book is part of a series of Waterford history books that the museum is republishing as Ebooks or making available to print on demand on the Amazon web site. For a complete list of our books search for "Waterford County Museum" on Amazon. Other books in the series include:

The Comeraghs, Gunfire and Civil War
by Seán and Síle Murphy

The story of the War of Independence and Civil War in Dungarvan and West Waterford in the words of the veterans. This important work was originally published in 1980 as *The Comeraghs, Refuge of Rebels*. In 2003 a revised and expanded version was published under the title *The Comeraghs, Gunfire and Civil War*. The 2020 edition has been further updated with additional content including notes from the original interviews and 31 photographs. The book's importance derives from it being compiled using the first-hand accounts of the Co. Waterford veterans who participated in the struggle for Irish independence. The republication of this seminal history of the Déise Brigade IRA from 1914 to 1924 is a collaboration between the authors, Seán and Síle Murphy, Waterford County Museum and the Commemorations Committee of Waterford Council.

Ardmore: Memory and Story
by Siobhán Lincoln

The history, traditions and stories of an Irish village told with a 'blend of history, tradition and humour'. Siobhán Lincoln records the social history of Ardmore village, tales of school days, dances, fishing, work, language and tradition. This book will be of interest to anyone who wants a picture of life in rural Ireland from the late 19th century to the dawning of the Millennium.

Desperate Haven: The Poor Law, Famine, & Aftermath in Dungarvan Union
by William Fraher, Bernadette Sheridan, Seosaimh O'Loinsigh, & William Whelan

Originally published in 1996, this book is the definitive study to date of the Great Famine (or Irish Potato Famine) and its effects in the towns and villages of West Waterford, Ireland. This long out of print and much sought-after volume was the product of more than 5 years of research by Dungarvan Museum Society (now Waterford County Museum). It provides a fascinating insight into the lives of the poor in mid-19th century Ireland, the response of the authorities to the unfolding tragedy and the conditions which saw many Irish people create new lives for themselves in America, England, Canada, Australia and elsewhere. Tracing the development of the Dungarvan Poor Law Union from its establishment in 1839 to its abolition in 1920, the workhouse figures prominently in the story. The chapters covering the Famine period are based on the minute books of the Dungarvan Board of Guardians, the Famine Relief Papers in the National Archive, and contemporary newspapers. The book examines in detail the lives of the workhouse inmates, with sections on diet, education, work, the workhouse farm, religion, the treatment of women and children. There are also chapters on the effect of the Famine on the fishing industry, and on emigration from West Waterford during and after the Famine. At the height of the Famine 4,000 men, women and children from all over West Waterford were housed within the workhouse and auxiliary workhouses of Dungarvan. Thousands more were dependent on soup kitchens and 'outdoor relief' to prevent themselves starving.

For specialist historians and genealogists, it is hoped that the book will be of assistance in prompting further research. For the general reader, and particularly for those whose origins are in the locality, it is hoped that it will provide insights into a tragedy which even yet marks the area after the passage of over a century and a half.

A History of Dungarvan in 33 Illustrations: The Grattan Square Heritage Plaque Project
by William Whelan & Rachael Power

A handy introduction to major events, people and industries from Dungarvan's past. This 'Greatest Hits' of Dungarvan history had an unusual genesis. It started life as a project to lay commemorative plaques in Grattan Square, Dungarvan. The story behind each plaque was originally told in a series of articles written for the local newspapers. These articles by Willie Whelan, have now been compiled into this book. We have included the original illustration for each plaque drawn by Rachael Power.

Illustrated History of Dungarvan
by Edmond Keohan

Originally published in 1924, this first Dungarvan history book set the standard for future local historians. It is an important eyewitness account of the town's Victorian, Edwardian & revolutionary periods. Keohan used all his journalistic skill to provide an entertaining and very readable eyewitness account of the Dungarvan from over a hundred years ago. This new much expanded edition published by Waterford County Museum includes an author biography by William Fraher, photos from Keohan's photographic career, a tourist guide to Dungarvan from 1917 and a history of Abbeyside Castle published in 1916.

This volume also contains annotations to the original work by Cian Flaherty and William Whelan. These annotations provide definitions for terms no longer in common use and notes occasions when Keohan may have been incorrect in his historical suppositions. This is no fault of the author as he was working with the material available at that time.

The real strengths of the book are the chapters covering the 19th and early 20th centuries when Keohan provides us with an eyewitness account of events that shaped the town and country to this day.

Printed in Poland
by Amazon Fulfillment
Poland Sp. z o.o., Wrocław
16 September 2022